13   03

$ 2.00

Marita Missing in Mexico

©1996 Mari Vawn Bailey
All rights reserved
Printed in the United States

No portion of this book may be reproduced in any form
without written permission from the publisher,
Aspen Books, 6211 South 380 West,
Murray, UT 84107

Publisher's Cataloging in Publication
(Prepared by Quality Books, Inc.)

Bailey, Mari Vawn.
Marita : missing in Mexico / Mari Vawn Bailey.
p. cm.

1. Missing children--Mexico--Case studies. 2. Kidnapping, Parental.
I. Title

HV6762.U5B35 1996   362.82'97'0973
                          QBI95-20522

10 9 8 7 6 5 4 3 2 1

Labyrinth of Solitude by Octavio Paz ©1961.
Used by permission. Grove/Atlantic, Inc.

Cover design: Kristine M. Roberts
Cover photo: Michael Roberts

Marita Missing in Mexico

Mari Vawn Bailey

ASPEN BOOKS

Dedication

I dedicate this book to my Lord and Savior Jesus Christ. I offer it to him for his purposes. Without his power to guide, save, and open up the way, the realities mentioned in the book would not have been possible.

I also dedicate this work to my steadfast and noble parents, Manson H. Bailey Jr. and Betty Jean Bailey, whose support and love enabled me to go to Mexico and to stay there long enough to recover my daughter. They are the salt of the earth, true Montanans "all heart from the belt up."

Of course, this book is for my dear daughter, Andrea Marita, that she will always know of the love we all have for her.

Acknowledgments

Over the last ten years or so, many people have read this account as I prepared it for publication. There have been so many kind friends, colleagues, and family members involved, that I cannot begin to name them all, but I offer them my deepest appreciation for their questions, comments, suggestions, and encouragement.

I truly thank all those who helped make this book a reality, including those who were a part of our lives in 1976-77 and added their part to make things happen, whether or not they were mentioned in the book. However, I want to specifically thank four women who have contributed the most toward the editing of this version—Marcha Fox, Lavina Fielding Anderson, Darla Isackson, and Jennifer Utley.

My thanks also goes to my husband and children who gave me the gifts of time and patience while I wrote and edited this book.

I am grateful to the Spirit for waking me up at 5:00 A.M. on January 15, 1983, telling me to go look at my journals from Mexico. When I stared down at the pages written seven years before and wondered "Why?" I was told, "Now is the time to write a book about this." It was not my idea to write this book, and only the Lord knows why he wants it to go forth. I do not know why the right time for it to be published is twenty years after Marita was kidnapped, but I know that he wants it for others to read now, starting in 1996.

Preface

MARITA: MISSING IN MEXICO is a true story. All the places are actual and, with a few exceptions, so are the names.

This account of my fourteen-month separation from Marita is based on the four journals I wrote during that ordeal. Because that life episode had been so painful and confusing, I left those four books packed away for seven years. On the occasions I did open the journals looking for some specific information, I could not read for long because I would become physically ill just from remembering. I wanted to close the door on many of those events and not look back.

But the passage of time has finally brought welcomed healing, enabling me to discuss my experience with some measure of objectivity and serenity—and without bitterness. I resolved that others in similar situations struggling to fight abuse and injustices should have the benefit of my experiences. Ann Richards said, "We women assume that if our cause is just, everyone will do what we want them to do. But it's not that way. You have to find the solution with the kind of approach that will make people get on your side."

This resolve has been strengthened by the realization in recent years that there is power and meaning in sharing the lessons of adversity. Women today know that painful realities of life do not disappear when we ignore them. And so I add my voice to the voices of others who are willing to risk the pain of self-disclosure in order to spare others far greater pain. Even Marita's father agreed that this story might help others learn from our mistakes, but he hoped no one would recognize him now. I have respected his request and used pseudonyms for his name and the names of people in his family.

"The palest ink is better than the best memory," a quote I heard years ago, undergirds my belief in the power of writing our experiences while they are fresh from our hearts and minds. I began writing in diaries and journals when I was ten years old, and I had filled over forty volumes before I was forty. Now as a maturing woman I especially treasure my journals because they hold the essence of myself and my unique journeys.

Indeed they have been life-saving tools on more levels than one. The act of writing in my journals was as crucial in recovering my daughter as hiring lawyers was. Although journals are not commonly thought of as essential for working through a crisis or for recovering a missing child, they filled several functions for me. Some entries give more than just what happened on a given day; they reflect thoughts that fed the process and contributed to the total shaping of efforts to get Marita back. Therefore, I have included quotes from my journal that have greatly influenced the internal journey of my mind, soul, and will. These pages not only describe my trip to Mexico and back, but they record my inner journey and eventual triumph over naivete and subservience. They record my path of progress in overcoming scripts that did not work to creating scripts and actions that were valid and useful. The reader will also find quotes from great literature which enabled me to transcend my current situation and gave me insights and strength to continue my quest. Repeating aloud or rereading some quotes, thoughts, scriptures, or promises from my journals brought me power to visualize and to strengthen my resolve. Because I have worked as an English teacher, instructional designer, and writer, words have always been the tools of my profession. In 1976 and 1977 especially, words were a companion and comfort to me, tools that saved my sanity and our lives.

Because so many facts were recorded daily in my journals, I stood with an extra measure of confidence in speaking the truth at crucial moments in the Mexican courts. I studied those journals before confrontations with Antonio or the judge. If I thought I needed to bring events or spoken words to the attention of others, I could quickly review my record of them and report them accurately to strengthen my position. Without a record of the often overwhelming trail of details and events in this case of a missing child, I could easily have lost my way and given up too soon. Because I needed to talk but could not trust many people around me, I used the journals as a sounding board. Once the words were on paper, my mind was freed up and I could think more clearly. Often, while I was in the act of recording elements of an issue in my journal, new and viable perspectives and solutions appeared. Also writing the facts down helped clarify the decisions I had to make.

Those four journals were my reality check. They were my friends, especially when I felt totally alone and my family and friends were 2000-3000 miles away. Ever since the ordeal, people have often commented, "I don't know what I would have done if that had happened to me. Weren't you afraid? Didn't you feel alone? How did you keep going?" Of course, there were several sources of power that made it possible to accomplish my mission, but I could not have done it without my journals.

How fragile life is! There are no guarantees that even after working hard and making good choices we will get the results we expect. Events happen beyond our control, and we are faced with choosing how we will respond to the new situations. So many life-changing consequences are hidden in our daily lives by small details we hardly notice until we look back. As for those momentous decisions I made on days when I knew the outcome would forever shape the rest of my life—well, I have few regrets about my choices. I like the woman I am now. I live in peace, health, and happiness. I am excited about the possibilities the future will bring and what will be written of my life as I am further refined and developed.

But in January of 1976 I had neither those insights nor that strength and peace. Only the process of time and healing allowed me to write those words fifteen years later. In 1976 I began a new journal, keeping in mind that my daughter Marita would read it later. I wanted her to know my side of the story of what had happened to disrupt her young life. It would be through my words to her on journal pages that she would know of my love for her and what I did to bring her home to me. I never intended other eyes to read the journal pages, except possibly lawyers or judges. Because many conversations might have been useful in court as evidence, I wrote them down carefully in the journals the same day they happened. However, on other days I only had time to write summaries and impressions of what happened.

As a young woman I was afraid to speak in public and hesitated to become a teacher for fear of standing in front of a class. I overcame those fears, but even in 1976 when the ordeal began, I was still shy and often too passive for my own good. My voice was soft and did not project the mental strength I felt. The past ten years have forced me to leave behind those weaknesses and parts of myself that are no longer useful. The writing of this account has helped our family to heal, and the pain previously connected to these memories has been transformed by greater understanding and forgiveness so that all of that pain has passed from my life. Now I can read the words from those four journals in awe as though my trials happened to someone else.

I share this story now with no feeling of either vindication or vindictiveness. What it represents is my conviction that the Lord does love us as he allows us to feel the sting of the refiner's fire. He allows adverse circumstances to enter our lives which are hidden opportunities for personal growth as we respond to situations we do not understand. Life has meaning and exquisite beauty, and once we have paid the price to possess life's magnificent hidden gifts, we will. He has all power and he waits for us as we learn to draw from that power. He knows the value of each soul. My soul. Your soul. Marita's soul. We are still far from Home. And He is still waiting to get us back.

Mari Vawn Bailey,
December 1994,
Gaithersburg, Maryland

Chapter One

Saturday, January 3, 1976, Utah

WEARY OF THE STRUGGLE that had followed me from Mexico City to Montana to Utah, I wondered if this were finally the time and place to end our marriage. I hoped it was. I spent all afternoon in the Provo Temple praying for help. I had to make a decision. I meditated in the chapel for almost an hour, and again in the celestial room. As I sat in the quiet room, peaceful memories of our courtship and of kneeling at an altar in the Arizona Temple in 1972 were shattered by stronger scenes of suffering and the raw reality I faced in 1976. Since I knew so few people who had been divorced, I did not know what to expect once I started the divorce process. Adultery was the main acceptable reason for divorce among the Saints, and I did not know if abuse and incompatibility were valid grounds for a temple cancellation of my marriage vows to Antonio.

I reviewed details to present to the Lord in prayer to justify my release from an intolerable marriage. In all my growing up years, I had never imagined that my life would be any different than the "happy Mormon family" picture presented in talks and lessons to the young women of the Church. I had expected that if I lived a righteous life and did what I had been taught, I would have a good life and a good marriage like my parents' marriage. Reviewing the past few years, I still could not comprehend why something so hellacious as this abusive marriage had happened to someone like me.

I was born to devout Mormon parents, the first child in a family of four, and had grown up in Glasgow, Montana. My life had gone according to schedule. I seemed to be on the right path that would lead me not only to the fulfillment of the American dream but to eternal happiness as well. In my early twenties, I felt sophisticated indeed with my degree from Brigham Young University, going off to the Colegio Américano in Torreón to fulfill my dream of teaching in Mexico. Four years later, while I was teaching English as a Second Language at the Church's Benémerito de las Américas prep school in Mexico City, I fell in love with Antonio Cruz.

I had no intention of marrying him at first. In fact, the night I met him at an alumni dance at Benemérito, I couldn't stand him. He was a show-off—pushy and immature. Antonio offered me a ride home when I discovered my roommate had left the dance early and I was stranded without a way back to Tlaltelolco. No one else was going in that direction, so I accepted. I discouraged his attempts to kiss me in the elevator. At my apartment door, he asked if I would go with him and others to a dance in his hometown. I agreed and went to Puebla and met his family.

Months passed with nothing in my journal about Antonio until the first week in April when I noted that "my love had finally come" and I would be getting married. Although many Mexican men I had dated were shorter than I was, Antonio was exactly my height, about five feet five. Antonio was handsome with thick black hair, moustache, straight nose, and soft brown eyes, but I was more attracted to his creative mind and surprises. I decided I wouldn't be bored married to him.

His father, Daniel Cruz Lopez (Mexicans go by the father's sir name, but the full name ends with the mother's maiden name) was the district president for twenty-two branches of the Church in his hometown. Antonio had been baptized at eight and raised in a recently converted Mormon family. When I first met his family, they all seemed so familiar to me, and I liked them more than I had expected to. I liked them more than I liked Antonio, and when they invited me to spend Easter vacation with their extended family at Tecolutla Beach in Veracruz, I accepted. I had never been to Tecolutla, and I enjoyed traveling in Mexico. Why not go? We left after dark—cousins, aunts, and uncles—traveling in a caravan which wound through steep valleys in the foggy night. Few times in my life had brought me so close to the edge of so many precipices on roads unprotected by guardrails, a condition common to Mexican mountain roads.

As I feared for my life on certain hairpin turns, I was comforted by the Holy Ghost to know that I would arrive safely. More importantly, the Spirit reminded me that I been praying for years to find someone to marry and I should not ask any longer. I was in the car with him. That news surprised me because I had never considered marrying anyone like Antonio. However, the impression came so strongly that I knew it was not my own thinking, and I paid attention to it.

The next afternoon while we explored the beach and bought treats from Indian vendors, Antonio's mother teased us, saying, *"¡Cuidado con el agua del coco!"* [Beware drinking coconut milk!] while we were eating a coconut and drinking its milk. Some Mexicans had the tradition that you fall in love with the one you share coconut milk with.

I had begun wondering what it might be like to love Antonio enough to marry him. He certainly was amorous during our trip—that day especially. But that was expected of Mexican men during the pursuit stage. I had been engaged before, and since Antonio did not fit the image of the kind of man I had hoped to marry, I had gone to the beach with him as a whim. That was all. I only intended to be there as a friend and have fun on my Easter vacation.

People falling in love are often blind to many realities at first. Looking back, I wished it could have been something as simple as sipping coconut milk together that transformed my vision of Antonio as someone who might be more than just a fun person to date. Events beyond my expectations touched my soul on that trip and changed the course of the rest of my days on earth.

With the moonlight reflected on the ocean waves before us as we walked along the sand towards the tent where his brother sat, Antonio stopped and made a proposal of sorts.

"You can either marry me or my brother. Take your pick."

I looked at his brother sitting there in the semi-darkness. He was closer to my age and already working as a teacher, like me. He was okay, but I didn't want to marry him. I didn't know if I wanted to marry Antonio either. He had not graduated from college yet and he was six years younger than I was. He was not the kind of man I had prepared all my life to marry and not someone most people would expect a *profesora* to marry. But I remembered the impression from the Spirit the night before: to pay attention to him at this time in my life. I didn't say anything right then. We continued walking along the shoreline.

An hour or so later, we returned to the area where the family had set up their tents on the beach and approached the parked cars. Antonio asked me again if I would marry him. While I leaned against an opened car door, eternity opened up to my mind and the veil became very thin. I could feel myself standing in the premortal life agreeing to give Antonio a chance on earth. I knew we had agreed then to meet later and get married. The impact of that ancient promise impressed itself permanently upon my soul, and I could never deny that experience on the beach at Tecolutla.

Although I did not discuss it at the time with Antonio or say yes to his proposal for another month or so, the impressions received that night made all the difference in my dedication to find out more about him and not dismiss his proposal as an illogical, crazy whim. After that paradigm shift, my memories of falling in love during that Easter vacation remain the brightest of all. As the weeks passed I felt happy and more excited about life. I hoped for the best for us.

As we dated and talked more seriously of marriage, Antonio's father told him a few times that I was a young lady of value and he was not good enough for me. He asked us to wait a few years for Antonio to mature. Most Mexican couples had courtships that lasted for five years while they amassed land, furniture, and all they would need to make it on their own. I knew it would be better to wait and I was willing to do it. Antonio refused.

On the day we announced our engagement to his family, we were sitting around the kitchen table in Puebla telling our story of falling in love. His mother, nicknamed Mama Rosita, was famous for her wit, endless supply of jokes and stories, smiles, and gracious hospitality. She listened to us and said to Antonio, *"Sacaste la Gran Loteria."* [You have just won the National Lottery's grandest prize of all.] She made him raise his arm to the square and make a promise to be an upright, hardworking man and take good care of me. He swore to it. I also promised in front of them all that I would love him always and be a good wife.

A few months later, his parents had another serious talk with him to point out that we were building our dreams of a future based on little more than "pure plan." His mother reminded him that nothing was sure and who could say that he had enough ambition or capacity to finish studying for his career. His father had more concerns. What if Antonio never came through? What would Mari Vawn do? Go home to Montana? Separate or divorce? Or stay by him and suffer? What would she do? Severely shaken, Antonio turned to me more humbled than I had ever seen him. He had his doubts as well, and he asked me what I would do if he failed.

Since I did not feel as upset, I told him, "It all depends on you." I let him know it was my intention to stay by him but that he would have to rely on the Lord for help and answers to find the way. I asked him to pray about it and find out for himself if we should marry so soon or if he should marry me at all. I began fasting and praying for him to be guided in our plans. I hoped he would be strong enough.

After all, he claimed he wanted, as I did, a marriage ceremony in the temple where we would be sealed for eternity and enjoy living together forever with our hoped-for children. We shared a vision of lifting his people, unleashing their potential, building a Zion society in Mexico! We wanted to be a part of preparing a mighty people ready to meet their Lord in fulfillment of prophecy for the House of Israel in the crucial years before the Millennium is ushered in. Of course, I dealt with the normal fears everyone has just before a marriage. But so many important details fell into place as we prepared, and I felt encouraged on many levels to go through with the marriage.

The dream fell apart quickly under the reality that whatever power women had in Antonio's culture was informal, carved out between the pillars of subservience. We had not been married one hour when his nature towards me drastically changed. He started yelling and ordering me around as soon as we walked outside the courthouse from getting our marriage license at the civil ceremony. It was the last thing I had expected on our wedding day. I didn't understand, but he had an audience there in the street. Maybe it was just to show others that he was indeed the boss now. He seemed so angry. Was he already sorry he had taken on so much responsibility at his young age? Did he resent giving up certain "freedoms?"

Even our honeymoon was not abuse-free and I was deeply shocked at the first incident of physical abuse the week after we were married. I assumed Antonio would have known better as the honorable priesthood holder he said he was. Proud of winning a *gringa* but suspicious and insecure about any *gringa* ways, Antonio had walked out the doors of the Mesa Temple after our marriage sealing to begin a cycle of wooing and patronizing, of flattery and humiliation, lies, bullying, slapping, shaking and coercion. He poured out torrents of verbal abuse that confused and depressed me.

I painfully learned that Latter-day Saint ways had not erased the *macho* man and *mujer abnegada*, the self-abnegating woman. Perhaps machos use of force gave them a feeling of power and control which covered up their real inadequacies for the moment. The women were expected to obey, always submissive to their lord-and-master husbands. This was their lot in life. But since Antonio and I were both active members of the LDS church, I had mistakenly assumed that application of gospel principles and practices would somehow be enough to save me from being treated as other Mexican women. I had never seen his father treat his mother abusively, so I had not expected it from Antonio. As a free-spirited individualist from Montana, I thought it would be different for me because I had been raised in another culture and we would have enough love, gospel help, and personal ability to be equal to the challenges of our marriage.

As abuse became the reality of my daily life, not much I had learned at church, college, or at home growing up seemed to work for me. I felt betrayed by the Lord because so many times I had been told that it was right to marry Antonio. At the same time, I blamed myself for not waiting longer as his father had asked.

Only a few months after our wedding, I could no longer find reasons to feel glad I had married Antonio or see how he could possibly be a good match for me. Yet to leave was not an option I would consider at first. How could I? I had just made eternal commitments in the temple and I resolved to do my best to find a way to be happy. I naively hoped that the verbal and physical abuse I had already suffered were isolated incidents and would not be repeated. I stayed with Antonio because I wanted the Lord's support and didn't know if the abuse justified disrupting our new union. The same kinds of abuse were probably happening to other women in the Church there in Mexico, and I had not heard of any of them divorcing their husbands. Maybe more time would bring new insights, so I could resolve the internal and external conflicts as the other women must have done in order to stay married.

Little by little I learned that Antonio was selective in the commandments that he decided to keep and also selective as to when he would keep them. He wanted me to be worthy to go to the temple and be an active Latter-day Saint, yet his actions were incongruent. For example, he wanted to go shopping on Sunday whenever it pleased him, and he hemmed up my skirts to show off my legs to other men. I unhemmed the skirts and put them back down to a proper length. After the hemlines had been changed several times, I left the high-water skirts in the closet. Intellectually dishonest, but compelling with creative ideas and grand promises, Antonio had a long way to go to meet the LDS standards I had been raised with as a fifth-generation Mormon. Still I hoped more time living together would change him.

Marita was born on April 25, 1973, nine months after our marriage. I had not planned on a baby immediately, but it was part of the pattern—that was what Mexican men and Mexican women did. And so much the better if the first child was a boy, they thought. But I wanted my baby and was thankful I had a gentle, happy girl who was in good health.

For a few moments right after she was born, I didn't hear her cry, and I was worried. She was born a few weeks early, and I thought something was wrong with her. But then she sneezed. The doctor laid her on a table near me. She waved her arms around while she kicked peacefully, but she did not make a sound. As I gazed at her, a transcendent peace joined an indescribable force of fire and light moving from the top of my head in a wave down throughout all my body until it reached my feet. I felt certain that angels were attending us and that the room was filled with them.

As I lay there, I was given to understand that Marita was one of the ancient ones, a great princess in Israel. I felt then that her soul was older than mine, and I felt humbled to know that I was her mother. She didn't seem like a tiny five-pound baby lying there, but a special sister and friend finally sent to be with me.

For years I had wanted a Mexican baby because they are so gorgeous, and when my own Mexican baby was placed in my arms for the first time, my heart was content. Unlike most Mexican babies, she had no dark hair and her skin seemed fairer. I thought she looked like me, but Antonio thought she looked more like her Cruz cousins.

Even as a small baby, Marita enjoyed having people around her. I took her with me to work at Benemérito every day and left her across the street with a house mother and sixteen high school girls who played with her in that cottage until I picked her up at 9:00 P.M. after my last class. Eventually we found a live-in maid and Marita stayed at home with her while I taught. By then, all that mattered to me was Marita's company and my job since my disillusionment with marriage to Antonio had left me numb inside to anything else.

It was Marita that gave me the will to struggle. I became seriously depressed the second year of my marriage and developed psychosomatic illnesses stemming from it. It would have been easy to die. In some ways, I wanted to, many times. But there was Marita, the joy of my life. As she grew from a baby to a toddler, my love for her grew. Her quick laugh and fast fingers brought many surprises, and I cared for her all I could when I was not grading papers and preparing lessons. She played with her dolls and toys and our maid. In spite of the illnesses and my desire to leave Mexico and Antonio, I loved her too much to let anything happen to me and leave her there alone with Antonio. I held on until we returned to the United States in 1974. I enrolled in graduate school at BYU, and there, in my own culture, it had become clearer that Antonio and I had no real marriage.

We had gone to several counselors, and throughout 1975 I had wavered between leaving Antonio and staying. Counseling forced me to examine my life and work on our problems. This gave me hope at times that we might be able to salvage our marriage. Some things improved as we learned together, yet I still had to tolerate more than was healthy for either of us.

It was hard to ignore the name-calling, especially in public, for he did and said what he wanted in spite of me and in spite of the teachings of our Church. By age two Marita probably thought my name was *gringa fea* since she heard it more than MariVawn. I just hoped she didn't understand it meant more than "ugly American." The rejections, the digs, the threats, and put-downs continued when I didn't do as my husband ordered. Month after month I stayed with him because of my temple covenants. Nothing else was holding me there.

As our marriage deteriorated, Antonio told me he was reading pornographic magazines at work. Sometimes he brought pornographic pictures home and taped them to our bedroom wall, hoping to motivate me in some way—to what, I was not sure exactly. I tore them down. Each one only made me angrier and more disgusted with him. He liked to think of himself as a gangster, calling himself *mafioso*, acting on the edge of the law if expediency required it, driving recklessly, swaggering, dragging me around the house by my arm while I cried and struggled. But more than anything he tried to be a striking example of the traditional macho man.

I learned to fear being alone in the house with him. Sometimes I'd run out of the house crying. He never went to look for me, but when we lived in Mexico City I knew I wasn't safe alone in the streets all night, so eventually, I'd have to go back home, hoping he would be in better control of himself. Time had not changed him much, and it did not seem to matter if we lived in Mexico or the United States. The years had not brought him a sufficient level of maturity to ease my feeling that too much was too far out of control in our marriage. Antonio kept things stirred up, and I yearned for a "normal" marriage that others seemed to have. The more Antonio tried to force me into the *abnegada* mold, the more I loathed him.

After four years of dealing with his unpredictability, I had a hard time seeing any of the talented, affectionate, or ambitious person I thought I had married. I wished I had been given a few more glimpses from pre-earth life to understand why I said I would marry him. My best friend felt it was because Antonio could have begged Father to give him a chance to walk through mortality with me. My friend said she could imagine Antonio telling Father, "I just know that if thou wilt let me marry MariVawn that I can make it back Home. Please let me marry her."

Considering how my life had gone so far, I was nearly as sure that I also had a particular visit with the Lord before I left Home. Part of it probably included this line of conversation, "Would it be possible for thee to arrange it so I won't have a boring life on earth?" And since we were writing up the script and things I promised to do on earth, he knew it would be an easy request to grant. I think he smiled and said, "Of course, my dear, I promise you will never suffer from having a boring life."

How little I knew then that mortality would become a spook alley once I got married. Exhaustion from constantly being on guard haunted me. I learned to use reverse psychology to prepare situations so that Antonio's reactions would lead him to do what a more responsible person would have done in the first place. Far too often, I felt like his babysitter.

None of this was a surprise to others who knew us well. My

mother never said, "I told you so," but I knew she also suffered because I had married Antonio. At least I felt safer living in Utah if I needed to leave the house and talk to someone until I felt better.

I had counseled many times with our bishop, Steven Morrill. It helped to talk to him. He was not only an older, wiser person, but had his stewardship over me as my bishop and an ordained servant of the Lord. I received much inspired counsel that I would not otherwise have thought of. Bishop Morrill was my friend, too, and sometimes he would say, "Right now, this is not the bishop talking. The Church policies and procedures aside, you should also consider such and such . . ." And he would give me more ideas to analyze or things to try.

I knew I was responsible for my own decision to leave or to stay. Occasionally I had sought priesthood blessings from home teachers or my bishop because I believed the priesthood received inspiration from the Lord as they prayed and spoke in the Lord's behalf. It had always been a natural thing for me to ask for a blessing when I was groping for direction, when I needed information, counsel, or comfort, or when I wanted a major decision confirmed by the Lord. I tried to have faith that things would get better as indicated in earlier priesthood blessings I had received during my struggles to stay married. I had clung to the words of a blessing given in the spring of 1975 by our marriage counselor after a counseling session with Antonio.

From it I learned that the Lord was pleased with my efforts, that the Lord had taken me to Mexico, where I fell in love with Antonio and married him—all of which the Lord had wanted me to do. I was told that the comprehension of what all this meant would not be apparent to me for a long time, but it was crucial to us both, and as the years passed, I would begin to understand more the greatness of it and comprehend the need for it. We both had important missions to fulfill.

After the counselor had removed his hands from my head and the blessing was over, I could not move or walk for some time, the power of the Spirit had engulfed me so strongly. I had to be helped out to the car. The man who pronounced the blessing told us that those words were not his but were given through the Spirit, and we needed to take heed. The surge of power he had felt as he received the words to say was more than he had expected. As the months passed after the blessing, I did not doubt the words I had heard. But I was beginning to realize that *both* Antonio and I needed a common desire for a more uplifting relationship with more tenderness and love in our lives, or we would not stay married or receive the promised blessings.

Not long after that blessing, we stopped going to the counselor. Yet, a few months later, the pain, confusion, and struggles again overwhelmed me and I found myself counseling with the bishop more and more. My bishop had been divorced himself before he had joined the Church, so his experience had given him a sense of the need for our divorce. However, he admitted that there were so few divorces in the Church then (in the '70s) that he did not have much experience in counseling us what was best to do in the eyes of the Church. He knew that as a bishop, his instructions were "to keep the family together." However, both the bishop and I knew in November of 1975 when he gave me a priesthood blessing that a change would come soon.

In the blessing, I was told that I would know in a short period of time whether or not I would have to endure any more of Antonio's weaknesses and unwillingness to follow the Lord. The last battle of proving his worthiness to remain married to me was approaching, and I had to allow him one more time to use his free agency to show if he would measure up. Instructed that I should forgive him as outlined in the Doctrine and Covenants section 98, I was told that the Lord would send special personages to protect me and I could call upon the Lord himself to fight my battles for me when "the fourth time" of trespasses came against me. I had only to call upon him, for he was pleased with my efforts and he did not want any more cruelty inflicted upon me. He asked me to be a companion and helpmeet to Antonio until the Lord said, "Enough." Because I was a faithful daughter, if I divorced him after this testing time, no blessings would be withheld from me.

After the blessing, Bishop Morrill verbalized his impression of the blessing and our situation: if Antonio really did not change this time, then the Lord required no more of me and I should get a separation and a divorce. He asked me to consider the celestial perspective also. How would I feel if I met Antonio in the celestial kingdom (if he had made it without me), if I had divorced him because of my impatience? But mostly, the bishop reminded me I must be wise and careful during this critical time to consider my own covenants and my own relationship with the Father and be sure my own life was in order. The bishop felt that Antonio and I could do great things together if Antonio would prove himself worthy. I left his office feeling comforted that some closure would come soon but still wondering when "Enough" is "Enough."

Two months later brought the end of 1975 and a gloomy New Year's Eve party where Antonio ordered me to "Go to hell!" I was too afraid to go home after the party, and I knew I could not delay making a decision about divorce any longer. I spent the night with my friend Linda, two doors down. I went home to be with Marita on New Year's Day and then went to the temple the next day for guidance. So, as I knelt at the altar as a proxy for sealing others in eternal marriage, all I could think about was wanting to be unsealed myself. I could not imagine being married and sealed to Antonio for all of 1976, not to mention whatever "forever" could mean. I decided to return to the temple the next day with the decision that I must divorce Antonio soon and pray to find out if the Lord would confirm and accept my decision.

Unmistakably, finally, after years and months of pondering and prayer and pain, I knew I did not have to ask any more. By the time I stood in the lockers changing into my street clothes on Saturday afternoon of January 3, I had received enough sweet assurance to go forward with my plans for a happier life without Antonio. New ideas filled my mind of things to do immediately to get my divorce started.

Before I left the temple, I used the pay phone near the entrance to call Bishop Morrill with my newfound peace in the decision to divorce. I was so excited and relieved that I could hardly say the words fast enough. He was not surprised and said, "That's what I expected you to tell me. I've already advised the elders quorum president not to try to save your marriage. It's been dead a long time. Now that you have decided to go through with it, I think you should tell Antonio tonight."

By the end of our visit, he had advised me to take my neighbors Linda and Ron as witnesses and also for protection for the confrontation. Linda had been my roommate at BYU and had remained my best friend for almost ten years. She was petite with perceptive blue eyes, long blond hair, and a pleasant round face. Ron was a complement to Linda in every way, same coloring, same spiritual strengths. The cheerfulness in Ron and Linda's home just one house away from ours had been a haven and a comfort to me many times when my home had become unbearable.

They willingly came over Saturday night after Marita was in bed, and they sat near me in the plain little living room. The room was just big enough to hold a small sofa.

Antonio came in and sat down near the table, on a chair directly across from me. I stared at him as he sat resolute, so *conchudo*, so sure he would get his way and not caring much how his actions affected anyone else. This was not a social call, and Antonio knew it, so I cut the chit chat and made the Big Announcement. It was no surprise. He had been pressuring me lately to decide about getting a divorce.

Without hesitation, his eyes narrowed slightly as he asserted, "That's fine if you want a divorce. You can leave. You can do what you want. But I keep Marita."

My throat tightened. He meant it. He had held the same threat over my head every time I had discussed leaving him. I loved Marita too much to leave her, so I had stayed with Antonio. That night, I chose my words carefully, trying to convince him that I be the one to care for Marita until the courts awarded custody.

He held firmly to his demand. Neither one of us cared about the furniture, the car, or the house. We *did* care about Marita. We both wanted the best for her in our own way. We were both terrified of losing the one we loved the most in the world—our daughter. We talked, but he refused to leave. None of my words seemed to matter.

I begged him, "I'm her mother! Little girls need their mothers so they can grow up right. You have to work eight hours a day and go to your classes. I can be with her almost all day long! I only teach a few hours a week. My other classes won't take long. I can be here with her while I grade the compositions. Let her stay here with me."

And when he declared, "No way!" I'd continue. "She is used to being in her own home. She needs to stay here while we figure out what to do. Why should we disrupt her life any sooner than necessary? You could go stay with your friends in Provo a few days until we come to an agreement."

"No. I think you should leave. YOU are the homewrecker. YOU are the one who is asking for a divorce. You left after the New Year's Eve party. You can just leave again. I don't want you here anymore."

Then my friends spoke up. Linda's and Ron's persuasive reasoning might have convinced anyone else, but Antonio didn't respond to their efforts. I knew he wanted the divorce, so I wasn't prepared for his stubborn resistance. Looking back, I don't know why I thought it would be different this time, unless it was because I was so much more sure of myself and so determined.

Wary of his explosive temper and physical strength, none of us wanted to provoke him. I called the police, but they refused to come since no one had been hurt physically. I called the bishop, and he came immediately since he lived only one block away. Linda and Ron made room for him on the couch.

Bishop Morrill restated many of the same facts and concerns we had already examined. Antonio only became more defensive, stubborn, and irrational. After some time, he wasn't even listening. He just repeated his demands and the words, "I keep Marita."

Still we held firm.

Antonio's loud voice and occasional shouting woke Marita. She wanted to come out of the bedroom, but Antonio wouldn't let her at first. Then when he opened the door, she wanted to come to me. For fifteen minutes, she tried to wiggle free from his arms and run to me, but he forced her to sit on his lap.

I stared across the room at my two-year-old toddler with honey brown skin, sparkling brown eyes, baby-sparse dark hair, tiny gold loops in her ears. I prayed she could be with me somehow.

At last he let her go, and she ran across the room to me. I held her tightly as I smoldered inside. Anger and fear and caution all took their turns within me. So far we had avoided violence. During this impasse I was torn between using my usual methods of dealing with Antonio and casting wisdom aside and running out of the house with Marita.

My mind raced ahead to the probable consequences of the flight approach. Antonio would have reached the door as soon as I. We would each clutch a part of her and wrest her from each other until one of us gained control. He was stronger, and I imagined he'd take her away and I'd never see her again. I also considered the possible emotional and physical damage to her if we literally fought over her.

I was being forced into the *abnegada* role one more time. He expected me to give in to his demands. In good conscience I couldn't do it. Finally there was very little to say or do. The proverbial "Mexican stand-off" was a grim reality. I couldn't talk to a lawyer until offices opened on Monday. We both had equal rights to care for Marita until the courts assigned temporary custody. I was angry at my ignorance of how to protect her and myself. I wished the bishop had had more experience. I had done what he suggested in bringing my friends for the announcement, and we were stuck. None of us knew any better how to proceed or how to put Marita on safer ground. We had not anticipated how irrational Antonio would become. "Looking at our options" was not a phrase or process I was used to in the mid-1970s, and we could think of no more acceptable options that night.

Bishop Morrill shook his gray head and made one last attempt. "Antonio, we have been here for hours talking about what to do. We all agree on the divorce. We are all concerned about Marita and what is to become of her. You insist that you will stay here in the house with her. You say you will continue your job and attend your classes at BYU. Is this your true intent?"

Antonio looked the bishop straight in the eye and promised: "Yes, Bishop. I will stay here with her until the courts decide who gets the house and who gets Marita. I'm registered for classes that start Monday. I'll find a way to care for her, keep my job, and attend school. But MariVawn needs to be punished. I don't want her around."

Bishop Morrill sighed. "It's probably just as well that she doesn't stay here tonight. It's morally wrong for her to live with you now that you are planning a divorce. Besides, after all the times you have mistreated her, she's afraid of you. Why does she need to be punished, Antonio?"

"She just does! She needs to suffer for what she is doing! I don't want to talk about it anymore," Antonio shouted. He sprang to his feet and grabbed Marita away from me.

We all stood up. Bishop Morrill asked, "Will you promise to come to priesthood meeting tomorrow morning?"

He agreed.

I felt weary, frightened, and backed into an emotional corner. What could I do? Trusting Antonio's promise to the bishop, I decided to leave for the night and go somewhere he would not expect—to Linda's mother's home. Remembering that Antonio always mellowed within hours of a scene, I counted on the patterns of the past holding true and hoped the morning would bring a more rational, repentant Antonio and another chance to get Marita.

Grabbing a few boxes and my old brown Samsonite suitcase, I started packing a few clothes and the files I needed on Monday to start teaching classes for the new semester. The pile on the bed was small: my pajamas, underwear, a dress, a skirt and blouse, curlers and makeup, shoes, and boots. The boxes held my journal, scriptures, typing paper, lesson plans, and some textbooks. In the kitchen I picked up some soup, cereal, and the typewriter.

Ron helped carry some boxes to my car. Antonio, still holding sleepy Marita tightly, stood at the doorway as I made the last trip with my supplies, and I said to him, "I'll call you in the morning. We can make arrangements then."

I set my typewriter on the floor behind the driver's seat and slumped into the car behind the steering wheel. As I turned the key in the ignition, a song on the radio blared out, *When you hit the road, baby, there ain't no turnin' back, ain't no turnin' back.* Startled by the profound truth of that statement, I started to sob. Was it too late to turn back? How could I go back into that house and somehow get Marita out of there when hours of effort had not been enough? No. I had tried my best and there was no turning back from the day's decisions and events. I silenced the radio and backed out of the driveway. As I turned down the street, I knew I could not look back but only forward.

Alone in an attic bedroom many blocks away from my daughter, I recorded the details of the previous hours on the last few pages remaining of the 1975 spiral notebook—never suspecting that those events had irrevocably changed our lives forever. None of my thoughts or fears in the night could have prepared me for the shock of emptiness I found the next morning.

Sunday, January 4, 1976

The sun was shining on the early Sunday morning streets as I returned to my home. As I turned the corner onto 50 East and approached our pumpkin-colored house, I wondered if I had made the best choices the night before, but reminded myself that no divorce is ever without complications. After all the confrontations, I wondered how Antonio would act in the daylight. It had only been a few hours since I had left him in the doorway, gripping our sleepy, confused baby girl. I kept swallowing past a lump of fear in my throat as I anticipated seeing him again in a few minutes.

I pulled into the driveway. All the lights in the house were on. I could hear music echo off the winter-seized yard. I shivered as I left the car and approached the front door. If the music was deafening on the front porch, what could it be doing to my daughter inside?

I unlocked the front door and stepped into the small living room. The stereo was blasting with the control arm lifted so the same record would play over and over. The beat pounded at my ears, and I felt adrenaline rising as I leaped across the room to silence the racket. I stood in the silence with my heart pounding and my mind racing.

My eyes opened wide to survey the damage, then narrowed to block out the upheaval. Beside the old portable stereo lay several shoe boxes and dresser drawers, their contents dumped and scattered on the carpet. Documents and contracts. Unpaid bills. Photographs, my favorite jewelry, and several piles of my underwear. Someone had been searching our home! Yet someone had wanted the neighbors to think people were in the house, as usual. Was I alone? Where were my daughter and my husband? They should have been there, getting ready for church. If I could only squeeze out the answers as easily as I had shut off the music.

I forced myself to stand up, to search beyond the living room. I ran into the hallway. Our bedroom was undisturbed. Marita's room held only her empty crib, the bright blue handmade Mexican chair, the little dresses inside the open closet, dolls and diapers on the dresser. That was all. No daughter smiled back at me.

I searched the bathroom, the kitchen, the garage, the backyard, hoping against hope. Snow had drifted in piles behind our house, but there were no footprints but my own as I trudged to check each section of our property. Then I stopped. Over and over my mind screamed out, past the empty yard, past the empty house and to the Wasatch Mountains that ringed Utah Valley.

"Marita, Marita, Marita . . . Oh, where are you?"

No answer. In the bleakness of a wintery grey January sky, the adrenaline stopped pushing me to react. I stood still long moments until I could force myself back to the empty house.

I got down on my knees in the living room to examine the mess. Half in denial, I considered what had probably happened in the last few hours. The scraps of papers and documents on the floor were the most valuable ones we owned. No thief would have known where to find them. I shook my head as I threw papers and old letters out of my way. Which documents were missing? It soon became evident which ones Antonio had been looking for: Marita's birth certificate, American identity card, and Mexican passport. A few months earlier I had hidden them at Linda's house down the street, anticipating that he might try to hide them himself. I pounded the floor with a triumphant fist as I realized that he did not have the papers he wanted. But he had my daughter.

Nothing seemed to be missing except her blue winter coat and her shoes. Would Antonio bring her back soon? She would need fresh diapers, breakfast.

Mechanically I began to pick things up. If only I had been more experienced, better prepared. It was too late. I sat on the living room floor staring for some time at the ransacked house. I did not want to think what this all meant. Slowly, deliberately, I gathered up piles of papers and scattered clothes. Tears dripped on the last of the papers as I bundled them into a drawer.

Chapter Two

Same day, later on

Outside, fresh snow was falling. From my empty house I drove to the chapel three blocks away and saw Antonio's car parked by the curb. Perhaps he had kept his promise after all.

People milled through the foyer and crowded into the hallway leading to the chapel. No Antonio. No Marita. But the bishop walked toward me. He gave his usual cheery greeting, "Hello, hello, Sister Cruz. How is everything?"

"Not so good. Did Antonio attend priesthood this morning?"

"Why, yes he did . . . but only for a little while. He brought Marita with him. They left before I had a chance to talk to him."

"But his car is still outside." I frowned and let the next words out slowly. "I wonder where they are now and who picked them up? Antonio turned our house into a total mess looking for Marita's passport. I'm worried, Bishop. What if he's left for good?"

"Maybe he needs time to think things over. Maybe he's visiting friends in Provo."

I drove down the hill that separated Orem from Provo and went to see Juan, Antonio's best friend on earth. Blond-haired and blue-eyed, Juan looked American but was born and bred Mexican. His wife, Veronica, was also blond and fair. We had moved into their vacated house in Colonia Lindavista and lived there until we bought our own a year later in Aqueducto de Guadalupe. Juan had taught at the same *preparatoria* school in Mexico City where I had taught English. We were together again in 1976, attending Brigham Young University.

Turning off University Avenue, I parked near the once-white house and knocked on the splintered screen door. No one answered. I made numerous trips during the day, alternating between checking out our own home and Juan's. I spent long, cold hours sitting in the car watching, hoping someone would come. I made a lot of phone calls. I prayed a lot.

I used up my old journal documenting the previous night's events. The old year, our old life together, my old journal—all finished at the same time. I opened a new journal and wrote to Marita about what I had done trying to find her all day. I knew she was gone, probably on her way to Mexico. This new journal was for her, the Marita of the future, who would someday read it and comprehend what had happened to her that frightening, confusing night and day in 1976.

Dear Marita,

The house is quiet now. I hear only the pops and purrs of the gas heater and the whir of the old refrigerator. No voices. Nothing is the same as it was yesterday. After today, I know this year will not be the same as any other year. On New Year's Eve, just days ago, I promised myself that 1976 would be a new beginning, a new kind of year in my life, a year of change, of progress . . .

Was it only twenty-four hours ago that you sat on our bed watching me pack a suitcase, load up the books and files I would need to teach with, and put on my old black coat? You wanted to come with me, but your father told you that I was going to work. It wasn't true, but I didn't have anything better to say to you myself. There were no words a two-year-old could understand about our impasse.

I didn't really say good-bye to you, for I thought I would see you today. I didn't tell you where I was going because I didn't want Antonio to know. Trying to act normal, lest the tears and sadness I held inside would spill out and upset you, I only gave you a big hug and kiss and left you.

When I got into the car and heard a voice on the radio sing, "When you hit the road, baby, there ain't no turnin' back," I began sobbing because that was exactly what I was doing at that precise moment. I was leaving Antonio because it was impossible to live with him any longer. Unfortunately, I also had to leave you for a while because he wouldn't let you go with me. There is no turning back now.

I can only strongly guess what happened after I left the house. Somehow, Antonio understood the American divorce routine. If he stayed around for the divorce, the courts would give you and the house to me and would ask him to pay us money. He probably reasoned that he would have nothing in the end, so he decided to take you to Mexico.

What saddens my heart the most is to think that it is very possible for you to forget me, to forget my face, my voice, my love for you—the longer you stay in Mexico.

Now it is late at night. I am weary with worry, filled with fear, and numb from the stress of the day. Linda made me a bed of blankets on her couch. I'm sleeping here because Antonio could come back and hurt me. I'm afraid to go home. Good night, Marita, wherever you are.

Monday, January 5, 1976

By the end of the day I had little to show for my labors, little information gained from all the phone calls—and little hope that I would see my daughter again soon.

My neighbor, Joann Embry, was a legal secretary for a law office in Provo. By the time I arrived at the office that morning, Joann had forms prepared for me to fill out. Her boss, Konrad Becker, had agreed to handle my case. He wrote down pertinent details of the past weekend's events as I related reason after reason I was filing for divorce.

Then he told me something I didn't want to hear: "We will do what we can to help you. You will have a paper called an *order to show cause* which also includes a restraining order and temporary custody of Marita. Antonio is not to take her from the jurisdiction of the court. In fact, he is ordered to return her to you. He is not to harm you or use your home. However, if he has already taken her from the state of Utah, then it will be much more difficult and more time consuming to track him down and bring legal processes to bear on him."

"And what if he *has* returned to Mexico with her? He isn't a United States citizen, and she is a dual citizen. Are these legal papers enforceable in Mexico?"

Mr. Taggart lowered his eyes to the stack of papers on his desk and shook his head. "I'm afraid not. Extradition laws deal with criminals charged with specific crimes. What your husband has done is morally wrong, but until these papers become official by being served on him, you both have legal rights concerning your daughter. He has not yet broken the law."

By 11:00 A.M. the sheriff and I had papers ready to serve on Antonio. We went to the Volkswagen repair shop where Antonio worked, but his boss informed us that Antonio had quit his job and picked up his pay early Sunday morning.

We went back to Juan's. He assured us that although he didn't know where Antonio was right then, he had eaten breakfast with Antonio and Marita at the Y Center that morning. I wanted to believe that my baby was nearby, but the logical part of my mind asked, "Why would Antonio stay around any longer if he quit his job and had money to travel with? Why would they eat at the Y Center? Why not at Juan's house?" I listened at the door, hoping to catch some of Marita's light laughter or her sweet voice saying, "Mama." I only heard Juan say "good-bye."

The sheriff left the papers with me and drove away. I went home, called my supervisor, and asked him to teach my English 111 class so I would have more time to search for Marita. I called the police, the Salt Lake Airport, the bus station, the bishop, my parents . . . my search seemed to lead nowhere.

Discouraged and oppressed, I turned from the kitchen table where I sat by the phone and caught a glimpse of myself in the hallway mirror. I hardly recognized myself. A tear-streaked, freckled face stared out at me from under a mess of uncurled light brown hair. My copper-colored glasses had slipped down on my nose, and bags puffed up under my bloodshot eyes.

I attended my evening class in Ed. Psych, hoping for a break from the mental treadmill. But I was too exhausted to get cleaned up. I hoped for a meaty lecture to take my mind off my situation, but the instructor said, "And now we are going to have each of you introduce yourself. Please tell the group if you are married, and let us know something about your children."

In a class of only seven graduate students, it didn't take long before the man next to me finished by saying, ". . . and when my sabbatical is over, I will return to the school where I am principal."

Taking a deep breath, I began, "My name is Mari Vawn Cruz. My graduate major is Linguistics. I filed for divorce this morning. My husband took my two-year-old daughter away from me. I've looked for them for two days, and I can't find them anywhere. I'm afraid he has taken her to Mexico. I guess I'm only kind-of married."

I stopped. Nothing more would come out. The strained and surprised faces in the room indicated I had said plenty already. I stared at my desktop during the lecture that followed, taking in very little.

When class let out at 7:00 P.M., wet, heavy snow was falling, and my hair was soon plastered to my head. By the time I had scooped and brushed the snow from my car, my clothes were soaked through. I drove on slippery roads for a few blocks until I reached Juan's house where Veronica nervously invited me in.

"Veronica," I begged, "how would you feel if you came home one day and little Juanito was missing? I'm so worried. They left with the clothes on their backs. Marita isn't fully potty-trained and she needs some of her things. If you know where Antonio has taken her, please tell me."

"I'm sorry. I don't know anything," she mumbled.

"Well, why did Juan say that he ate breakfast with him this morning at the Y Center? Don't you usually fix breakfast here?"

Evasively, she said, "They made special arrangements."

"Have *you* seen them today?"

"No," she said firmly, with conviction.

"Veronica," I screamed, "I have a right to know where she is! I'm her mother! You must know something! Please tell me!"

Juan came out of the kitchen and spoke to me in *English*. He had always spoken to me in Spanish before. By the time I left, I knew they were lying. The stiff, cautious body language, the defiant look in his eyes, and the tone of his Juan's voice made me all the more suspicious.

As I drove away, I reminded myself that a lot of Mexicans feel it a point of honor to help a friend, no matter what it takes, lying included. I remembered my students in Mexico who, during exams, gave answers to their friends and were shocked when I ripped up their tests. They lived by different standards of honesty. They didn't feel guilty experimenting with different ways to cheat. I recalled several stories of LDS bishops in Mexico who had "borrowed" the tithing for awhile, intending to replace it when times got better. Of course, they knew better and they were later disciplined by their leaders, but somehow the old ways of culture got in the way of their newer beliefs. Was Juan any different just because he was living in the U.S., in the thick of Mormon culture?

I knew Juan had told the same story to Bishop Morrill, and something had to be done to find out the truth. I called Bishop Morrill when I got home, and he agreed to talk to Juan again. Then I called to ask advice of my former mission president, President Arturo R. Martinez, who lived in Salt Lake. He didn't have any additional ideas I hadn't tried. Next I called my folks because I knew my mother would be sick with worry. She could do nothing but pray and wait for news. I felt helpless enough. How must she feel so far away in Montana?

Tuesday, January 6, 1976

At suppertime, Bishop Morrill came with the bad news while I was at Linda's house. My lawyer had subpoenaed Juan, requiring him to tell the truth. Once Juan understood the jeopardy to his student status and job at BYU if he were taken to court for lying, he changed his story: He and Veronica had driven Antonio and Marita to Las Vegas on Sunday. Once there, Antonio bought airplane tickets to El Paso.

I moaned and slumped down on the tan Naugahyde bench by Linda's back door. As numbness spread through me, I felt heartsick, desperate.

I had hidden Marita's documents, hoping Antonio wouldn't try to enter Mexico without them, but I had not considered his influential cousin across the border in Ciudad Juarez who could easily fix up documents for Marita with the officials there. I knew that in Mexico many things are possible with enough money passed to someone in the right place.

Bishop Morrill spoke with regret, "I'm sorry now that we didn't try harder to take Marita with us Saturday night."

Jerkily, I spoke, "She's gone! She's gone! We underestimated him, and she's gone!"

I felt like vomiting, but I couldn't. Hindsight! We knew better after it was too late. I regretted the conflict, the scene, the choices, the decisions. Yet I would have to go on from there. I asked, "Did you find out anything else?"

"Antonio had called a lawyer in Orem, who called your lawyer today. He had given Antonio the standard results of a divorce in Utah: the woman is awarded custody and the house while the man makes monthly payments."

I glanced at the bishop. "I can see how well that news went over with Antonio. Knowing he would lose so much under our legal system, he probably reasoned he would have little in the end if he stayed here. Why not take Marita? He said that's all he really wanted."

The bishop left soon after that. I cried, but it was actually easier knowing for sure. Linda showed concern for my situation, but she didn't allow me to wallow in self-pity. Instead, she offered hope, and we talked of action I could still take for Marita. I stayed for supper. After three days of not being able to swallow a bite, I forced myself to eat.

I began sleeping at home once more. For protection while I was alone in my own house, I had the windows nailed shut and the locks changed on our doors. I didn't know when Antonio might come back and try to hurt me. I decided to take down the Christmas tree, teach my class, and begin doing whatever it took to bring Marita back home.

Chapter Three

Saturday, January 10, 1976

I CALLED ANTONIO'S FATHER, in Puebla, Mexico. Although my in-laws had misgivings about our marriage to begin with, they had supported us and accepted us, hoping for the best. I had felt close to Antonio's family from the first day I met them, and I appreciated their loving concern because my own family was three thousand miles away. Mama Rosita had even taken time off from her work at the family business to come help me for a week when Marita was born. I wondered how they felt about me now.

Antonio's father had recently accepted a stake calling in the Church and he was regarded by all as an honorable man. I hoped he would speak the truth. When I called, he confirmed that Antonio and Marita were indeed at the border but said that perhaps Antonio would return this weekend to Utah to negotiate with me.

I hoped against hope that somehow he would repent and return. I stayed home and waited for him all day long, just in case. I graded my students' diagnostic essays, and I was delighted to find some good writers in the group already. But even that pile of papers eventually came to an end. Hour after hour I waited. Alone with my thoughts, I reviewed the past events, hoping to find new insights. *Why?* after *Why?* marched through my mind. *Why hadn't I divorced him right after Marita was born?* I had tried to, twice.

In early 1974 my Relief Society visiting teachers, the home teachers, and the bishop in Acueducto de Guadalupe, told me they would guide me through the legal tangle and help me leave Mexico if I would divorce Antonio. They knew I needed to. I knew I needed to. Yet when I prayed about it, I never received the answer I wanted. Instead, the impression was, *Give him another chance. Stay with him.*

With this answer, my body had given in even more to the depressed state of my mind and spirit, and I finished the school year crippled by depression and burnout. I was still teaching English to young adults at the Benemérito de las Américas prep school in Mexico City then. On my last day on campus, I turned in behavioral objectives on every lesson plan for the coming school year, the manuscript I had written for a new English syllabus to be printed, and the camera-ready pages for the next literary magazine. I had graded the last *extraordinario* final test and picked up my summer paycheck. I assumed I would be back for the next school year.

That night I packed enough diapers and clothes to last a month or so because I was taking Marita to Montana for my vacation. Although my visiting teachers thought I was a fool for not packing all my valuable belongings to leave Antonio and Mexico forever, I packed only the essentials because I intended to make our marriage work. Antonio planned to meet us in Montana when his finals were over.

We left June 19, 1974, flying from the Mexico City airport to the Salt Lake airport. My throat tightened as I walked down the concourse in Utah surrounded by my own people! Just seeing the familiar gene pool of light hair, eyes, and skin, I felt welcomed to home and safety. Before long I wept in gratitude to be in the United States again.

After changing planes, we flew toward Great Falls, Montana. The closer we got, the more emotional I became. Montana! My own dear land and big sky! My eyes were hungry to sweep up the views of familiar mountains, buttes, and prairies. At last, about 4:00 P.M. we landed. My mother and sister Kim were waiting for us. I hugged them, kissed them, and cried again.

We stayed at my uncle's in Great Falls that night. A lightning storm and heavy rain followed us along the Hi-line across eastern Montana to Glasgow the next day. My dad and my sister Tana greeted us when we arrived home. On the dining room table were two roses, one for Kim, the other for me. My father's handwriting on the card read, "WELCOME HOME!" The rose is my favorite flower, and giving its beauty is a tradition in our family to welcome someone home after a long absence. It felt good to be home. I felt safe, loved and very relieved.

Those were healing weeks—fitting into my family again and seeing that Marita also had a place, roaming around "Bailey's Back-Achers" as my father calls our farm-ranch. I enjoyed feeling the forces that shaped my roots, loving again things so foreign to Mexico City's clamoring streets. The meadowlark singing nearby, my father's alfalfa fields rolling up to another color-filled Montana sunset, our small LDS chapel, the endless big open sky, the wind shaking the leaves in the cottonwoods, the wild roses down by the slough—all these things brought back my childhood.

Encircled by it, I realized that part of me had never left Valley County and its imprint had continued to be a part of me. Whatever I had become since I left the valley in 1965 to attend BYU hadn't changed me in any basic way but only added to the core. I believed my father's words—that Montanans are strong, persevering people who endure the incredible hardships dealt them by severe winters, isolation, hordes of mosquitoes, drought, and yearly floods. I had experienced all these, often. I was proud to be a Montanan and knew I was strong enough to survive my troubles with Antonio, too.

Or was I? As the days passed, I found myself just sitting in my father's rocking chair, staring. I had started out making lists of items that were difficult or impossible to buy in Mexico. By July 3, I realized that planning to return made me feel steadily worse. Some days I couldn't read even one sentence and understand the idea because my thoughts were so disconnected. This situation scared me.

Facing the cause and the effect for the first time, I could admit how much in my life had been wounded, destroyed, and cast aside during the years of my marriage. I wasn't my usual self anymore. For the first time, I asked myself if I could change the way I felt by changing the decisions and thoughts I had harbored. For example, I had always told myself I had to stick it out with Antonio forever because of our temple marriage covenants, yet I felt continually wretched when I was with him. How *could* I stay with him if nothing drastic happened to change us? Would I feel depressed forever? I couldn't imagine spending eternity with him. This life either.

New ideas came to mind. What if . . . what if I didn't have to go back to Mexico? What if I weren't married to Antonio any more? What about ending all that abuse? Wouldn't it feel good to live freely, without fear? To laugh again? To hope again?

By the end of that afternoon, I had decided *not* to return to Mexico. The results were astounding! My mind cleared, my body relaxed, and my spirit reached for hope! I wrote a letter to Antonio and asked him to release me. I informed him I was leaving for Utah on July 17 to look for a job and a place to live. I made it clear I wouldn't return to Mexico or to him because I feared for my sanity and life if I did.

As I thought about mailing the letter, I looked at my wedding band. Inside he had had it engraved with the words *Una promesa de amor eterno* [A promise of eternal love]. Later on, after we had been married a while, he laughed, saying, "Well, it was only a promise!" I could no longer take him seriously or hold him to his promise and the covenants we had made. I had trusted him, and he had betrayed my trust and love too many times. There was nothing left in me to make me keep trying anymore. Still I didn't mail the letter to him.

That same afternoon, for the first time in the two weeks I had been home, my mother asked about my marriage. My parents were always careful not to pry, but I knew they worried about me. While we were both working in the kitchen, my mother observed, "You've been sick ever since you've been home. Don't you think it's possible that you won't get much better as long as you are married to Antonio?"

I finished my glass of water and put it down by the kitchen sink before I turned around and answered her. "You're right, mother . . . I won't get much better as long as I stay in this marriage. I couldn't feel right about divorcing Antonio in Mexico this spring, but maybe I will do it now that I am in the States." My mother stepped closer to me and wrapped her arm around my waist.

I made an appointment to see a doctor on July 5, the day after Independence Day—two days after my own independence day. He was horrified to discover that the doctors in Mexico had prescribed a strong drug that I had been taking for three months. Dr. Hall shook his head and explained, "You don't need this! No wonder you feel confused. I'll give you a lighter tranquilizer instead. But you know, there isn't any medicine in the world that will help you with what is really wrong, is there?"

He was right, but I didn't answer. Dr. Hall probed gently into the reasons for my confusion and depression before he gave me advice that served as a catalyst for action. "I'm worried about you. I can see that you are miserable, and I wonder what you are going to do with your life now. You went to Mexico, a land of paradise and dreams. You have been gone for many years now. Did you find what you were looking for?"

A smile appeared as I recalled how most of my young adult dreams had become a reality. "Oh yes! I felt at home in Mexico. I felt loved, and I was happy teaching the people there. I learned so much from them too, and things were okay until I got married," I admitted.

"There's no Bali Hai in life," he continued. "Even though you found professional fulfillment by living and working in Mexico, there is often no worse feeling of failure than when your family life is falling apart. You've read *Hamlet*. What was his main problem?"

"Perhaps it was staying away from Denmark too long. His family was carrying on in such destructive ways that he couldn't save much that mattered to him."

The doctor added, "Much of Hamlet's problem lay in Hamlet himself. Remember the *to be or not to be* speech? Making the decision took him so long that everything was ruined before he did anything. Mari Vawn, by recognizing that you are in Hamlet's situation, you'll be taking the first step. Act! Even if it's the wrong thing to do, you will find out soon enough, and you can try something else. Eventually you'll find out what *will* work."

"What do you mean, specifically?"

Dr. Hall leaned back against the desk and spoke out reflectively, "We are all human. We don't do things perfectly, always. We all have problems, and no one has all the answers. But when we don't find solutions over a long time of trying—well, that creates stress, conflict, and suffering. If it causes tears, it's pain. It's a hurt, just as real as a broken arm. But the emotional hurt is a harder pain to cure. You may have some physical symptoms I can give you a prescription for, but until you deal with what is really bothering you, it won't make a lot of difference how much medicine you take. Mari Vawn, you are only going to get worse until you *do* make a decision and act on it." He waited until I looked at him again before he asked bluntly, "Do you want to stay in this marriage? Or can you get out?"

I told him clearly what I had not yet been able to tell my parents: "I need to get out. I feel trapped and abused. I've lost the person I used to be. I've already made the decision to divorce Antonio. In fact, I've written a letter to him, but I needed a boost to actually mail it."

I sent the letter. I talked with my parents, and they supported my decision. They would keep Marita with them until I got settled in Utah. Before I left to look for a job in Utah, I visited our lawyer for advice. He was specific: "Never step into Mexico again. If you do, you will have very little legal protection because the Mexican legal system is different from our own. Your husband can create a host of undesirable legal problems for you if he wants to. Their system is based on the Napoleonic Code, so they consider a person guilty as charged until proven innocent. You could disappear under a pile of trumped-up, false charges. There may be no way in the world to prove your innocence. You must do what you can to get a divorce in this country."

"How can I protect Marita?"

"Keep her in this country. Since she is a dual citizen right now, why don't you fill out the requirements for her to obtain her American Certificate of Citizenship?"

On July 17th I packed up my belongings and took a bus to Great Falls where I called my mother from my uncle's home near the airport. Antonio had just called her. He said to tell me that he still loved me and would be in Utah on Sunday! My mother was worried. Would I change my mind? No. I would be firm. I was emphatic, yet I felt a terror at having to see Antonio again.

I was staying with friends in Provo who had also known Antonio, and my mother had given him their address. Tension compounded each hour until my friends and I returned from church that Sunday, and I had to face Antonio again. I was braced for shouting, threats, insults—afraid of being slapped or shaken. But he was visibly happy to see me, tender, even humble. He didn't try to touch me, but begged sincerely, "Mari Vawn, I know you don't want to see me. I know you feel that I have destroyed you. I know I have hurt you, but please, give me a chance to talk to you."

I agreed to walk around the block with him while he poured out his story. I felt stiff and fearful, careful to keep a distance between us. He told me how my letter had confused and upset him. He insisted, "I don't want to divorce you! I *never* expected that news from you! After I read your letter, I didn't know what to do. But I had to go ahead and take one more final exam that day. Right after the test, I went home to talk to my parents, and then I left Mexico. I had to come in person. I have to ask you, please forgive me! Please come back!"

I did not answer.

His voice changed. Quietly he said, "I didn't want to tell you here in the street like this, but I had a vision the night I received your letter."

As he talked to me, my skepticism dissolved. He had been given insight into our marriage that I had despaired of his ever understanding. His own soberness and sincerity spoke to me, my heart softened, and I felt compelled to believe him. I knew that many Mexicans had such great faith that visions, ministering angels, and powerful spiritual experiences were heard of more often than among my own people. But more than anything I believed his words because his description of the vision graphically portrayed what I had experienced while married to him. Even though I had lost my trust and love for him, I knew I would have to consider reconciliation.

That week, he wrote his account of the vision down for me on the back of some calendar pages bearing photographs of gorgeous roses, and I translated it from Spanish in my journal. It helped make sense of our lives when little else did.

THE VISION OF THE ROSE

I write of a revelation that changed three lives. When I knelt to pray in my bedroom, I called to my Heavenly Father a lot . . . many times. I raised my voice so that he would hear the words of my mouth.

"Please," I begged him, and I asked him why he taught us in the gospel that we should pray and that our Heavenly Father listens to our prayers, when I didn't receive any answer nor could I see or feel that anyone was listening to me.

After a very long time of trying, I received a sensation near me—a pleasant feeling of power, at the same time majestic and awesome.

Then, my mind began to see a beautiful garden full of roses. There were many roses. God was especially interested in one of them. He watched her grow. He took care that she had no bad influences, nothing evil near her. He gave only the best to this rose. It grew and became stronger until it came to be the most beautiful of all the roses. It was an enormous red rose.

Then God walked closer to her, he knelt down and gently cut her from her stem. He took her in his hands and walked over to where I was. He turned the rose over to me. He didn't say a thing—absolutely nothing. He gave her to me and went away. This personage was dressed in a white tunic. I didn't do much to receive the rose—all I did was to stretch out my hand, and I received the rose.

Once I had her in my hands I couldn't understand the magnitude of what having this rose meant. As I didn't know how to take care of her, I began to play with her. My hand shook her from one side to the other, and I didn't care about the damage I caused her. Finally when I noticed, now she was the beautiful rose no longer, nor was she as large as when I had received her. Now she had fewer petals. There were only a few protecting the bud, but these outer petals were bruised and hurt. The rose was dying. Scenes flashed through my mind when she had suffered while at my side.

To see all this, I was greatly impressed, so much that I felt I shouldn't live any longer. I begged God to destroy me, that I shouldn't be allowed to live.

But then I felt I would be sinning against the Holy Ghost to ask something like that, so cowardly. So, then, I asked for forgiveness. I repented of all my sins—for so many sins against my rose and against myself. Then I told God, "I love her. Please don't take her away from me." I begged him many times.

During all this time I received a spiritual strengthening, and I still felt the presence of God listening to my words and dictating to my mind these revelations.

Then I asked him why he had given this rose to me—Why? Why? "Why did you give her to me, Father? You know my mind, and you knew that later on I was going to hurt her. So why did you give her to me?"

And God said, "Because you are special to me, and I wanted to give you this rose because you need her to bring about the missions and plans I have for you in the future."

"Oh, Father," I said, "please forgive me. I didn't mean to destroy her. I love her so much. Please, don't permit us to separate. Tell her to forgive me and listen to me."

Then I saw the bedroom where my rose was lying. God and I went there. She was sleeping. I asked her to forgive me, but she refused to listen. She did notice I had repented, however, and she finally smiled after hearing me for a long time.

My Heavenly Father was there all the while, and when I was asking forgiveness of my rose, I told my Father, "Tell her to forgive me, Father."

And he told her, "You should give him another opportunity because he has repented." It was then she smiled, turning her head. She looked me in the eyes and smiled. Then was when I felt that she had forgiven me. I made many promises to God to never again sin against my own body that is a temple, nor against her. I promised him from that moment onward I would never waste my free time. I would use it for my progress and for the progress of my wife and family . . . so that we'd be prepared when he called us to work on the important calling that he has reserved for us.

I asked him a question. "How do you want or believe that I can best take care of my rose so that she can receive the sun and water that she received when she was in your garden? How will I do it if I am only a wild weed? I grew up alone. I don't know what she is used to when you took care of her in your garden."

God said, "Come to my garden. Take care of her here. Learn how she's used to being treated and take care of her. Give her all your love. Besides, although you are a wild weed, you can give a lot of love. Your heart is big. Don't think you are just a weed because I, God, am thinking about you a lot for my work on the earth. But remember you'll only have pardon for what you have done if you begin to make up for the mistakes you made with your rose. You have to help her find happiness and well-being. Give back all the beauty your rose had when I gave her to you the first time. If you can manage that, heaven will have forgiven you."

I finished my prayer and I felt as if I were falling from a very high place. I felt the influence leave that had surrounded me during the whole revelation. It was my spirit that was going down to where my body was. Upon opening my eyes, I had a tremendous force in my body; I was receiving a confirmation of the Holy Ghost that all these words and visions I had received were indeed through the will of God that I had received them.

Antonio Bulmano Cruz Maya
July 24, 1974

After Antonio had told me of his vision that Sunday, I stood stunned until he broke the silence.

"Did you realize that God and I visited you in Montana and you smiled?"

"No. I only remember having a dream last week that I was on my way to the celestial kingdom, and I wanted to get in, but the angels stopped me at the gates by saying, 'You can't come into the kingdom until you forgive Antonio.' I walked away from the gates very sad."

"Mari Vawn, I promise you that you'll never have to work again. You can stay home with Marita, rest, and get your health back. I'll come to the United States and we will live wherever you want to. This way, you can live in your 'garden' again and not die. Please think about these things and forgive me. Let's be a family again."

It was nearly dusk. We had walked around the block many times by then. Sadly, I stood on the sidewalk, staring down the street a long while, not saying anything. Then, I saw two men with familiar faces walking toward us. Jorge and Servando Rojas were in Provo for summer school, but Servando had lived a few houses down the street from us in Mexico City, and Jorge had just interviewed me the month before for my temple recommend. He knew of the struggles we were having.

Since Jorge Rojas was a member of our stake presidency in Mexico City, he asked Antonio to talk things over with him privately at their apartment. I stayed on the living room couch and relived the "divorce-or-not-to divorce" issues I had struggled with so many other times. I had thought my decision was final on July 3rd. I had told my mother I would not change my mind. Yet, only two weeks had passed, and the agony had returned with all the new information given to me the past hour. I was divided against myself, and I felt miserable, torn in so many directions, with conflicts of emotion, reason, and will.

But I was also impressed with Antonio's new humility and sincerity, his obvious concern for me. There were no scenes, no abuse, only hours of tender pleading. I also knew that I was still too burned out to work full time and care for Marita alone. Living in the United States would offer me some legal protection and separate Antonio from his machismo culture. Living in Utah would allow us to be closer to family and friends, and Antonio could learn more about the Church. He could serve in the Church with people who had stronger testimonies of how living the gospel had truly blessed their lives. He could see how other Christian men treated their wives. I hoped he would adopt more of the Church teachings in his own life. There was no temple in Mexico when we were there, but I could attend the temple often in Utah and receive strength and inspiration from each visit. Also, my repugnance at the idea of breaking a temple sealing by divorce was strong. Still, if I did take Antonio back, I did not know how I would do it, and I did not know what was best for us.

When it was my turn to talk to President Rojas alone, he told me he had heard Antonio's vision and he thought I should give my husband another chance. After a long discussion, my resolve to get a divorce toppled in the face of new possibilities and in light of the vision. By the end of that Sunday night, I agreed to give our marriage another try even though I felt no love for Antonio anymore. Looking back on that night, I was amazed at my mother's self-control when I explained why I had changed my mind about a divorce. She still had fears for us and tears I never heard, but she quietly accepted the new plan and welcomed me back to Montana until Antonio could return to Utah to be with us.

A few days after that, he left for Mexico to sell our new home and furniture and to haul our other belongings to Utah. I returned to Montana to take care of Marita and to regain my health. I spent the next few months refinishing my grandma's old furniture, and as I scraped, rubbed, and painted, I gradually built up a strength I knew I would need for another round of new beginnings and "chances." Antonio arrived in Utah by October, and we put a down payment on a house in Orem and moved in during December 1974. He had found a job the first day he looked for one, and we felt blessed that most details of our move had gone smoothly.

Chapter Four

Sunday, January 11, 1976 4:00 P.M.

Are you as sad without me, Marita, as I am without you? Did you go to church today? I felt so alone—this first Sunday without you. I couldn't sing. I didn't talk to people. I ached too much, especially after the phone call this morning from your grandfather in Puebla with the news that Antonio had brought you into Mexico. Hour by hour you are traveling farther from me.

Waiting for you both to return yesterday from the border reminded me of the dread and terror I had felt in July of 1974 as I waited for him to arrive. Yet, I have matured and feel stronger now than the Mari Vawn who waited back then. I had hoped he would return this weekend, repentant and willing to work things out, as he did in 1974. After the phone call this morning, I know he will never return with you. I'll have to find a different way to get you back, and I'll do whatever it takes.

I'm waiting to go to the bishop's office to discuss what we can do and also get a priesthood blessing tonight. Always in the past it was a natural thing for me to ask for a blessing when I was groping. I know I'm not smart enough to figure out the best thing to do in the situation I'm in now, and the bishop hasn't dealt with one like it before, either. We need the Lord's help.

Same day, 8:00 P.M. — Journal entry

This morning Linda talked to me and said a special prayer, one that kept me together today. The bishop's blessing repeated some of the things Linda had mentioned. Although I was near tears, Linda encouraged me to show more strength when she asked, "What kind of mother does Marita need when she returns?" I realized that I must fight depression. I need stability and health, maturity and financial security. Antonio left me with no money but plenty of bills to pay.

Tonight the bishop asked me again, "The time may come when there's nothing more you can do to get Marita back legally. Do you think you could accept that and give up trying?"

It is not a question I can even consider. I desperately need this separation and divorce, and I would be rejoicing about my freedom from Antonio if he had left Marita with me.

Bishop Morrill stood up, placed his hands on my head as he stood behind me, and pronounced a priesthood blessing through the inspiration of the Spirit.

As I left the bishop's office, I felt steadied and comforted by the blessing I had just received. I felt loved—accepted of the Lord. I remember from the blessing:

- That this time and situation has a purpose that only the Lord knows now. I should not worry because I cannot understand it.
- The Lord has heard my prayers. He will continue to listen.
- He knows where Marita and Antonio are. Marita is playing, happy, and well.
- The Lord would bless Marita vicariously at the same time I received my blessing. She would be strengthened and protected, physically as well as emotionally, so that this experience would have no harmful effects on her in the long run. She will be returned to me someday.
- I should go to the temple before deciding about seeking full-time employment, and I'd receive direction there.
- The decision to divorce Antonio was correct, and the Lord no longer wanted me to be married to a man who was not worthy of me.

- I am to follow the lawyers' and President Martinez's counsel. After I do all I can to get her back, the Lord will move in his power and by his hand will the work be done. I am to use honorable and lawful ways to get her back.

Tuesday, January 13, 1976

Antonio called my mother from Puebla! Marita was there with his parents. His sister Ana Maria was taking care of her. When I heard this, I thought, *I know Ana Maria is a good woman, but I'm the mother! I should be taking care of her! At Marita's age, she could forget me so easily. I don't want her to think that someone else is her mother. I love her! I want her here!*

For the first time since she left I let myself cry without trying to stop. I cried for two hours.

Sunday, January 18, 1976

The BYU Credit Union allowed a two-year extension on the car loan, a real easing of pressure. My parents sent money when they could to pay the larger bills, but until I could find a full-time job, I accepted food from Church welfare to avoid using government welfare.

All my earning life, I had been paying fast offerings which provide the necessities of life for the Church's "worthy poor." Suddenly, I was one of them. It felt so strange standing in the Orem Bishop's Storehouse with the food order in my hand, utterly dependent on the goodness of others and upon the Lord. Every time I opened a can of Deseret canned beef (my favorite), I felt a surge of gratitude for the donated hours and labor of unseen Saints that made it possible for me to eat.

But eating alone was still very hard for me, and I missed Marita desperately. I called Puebla, but Ana Maria said Marita was sleeping. After that, I spent the evening translating the divorce documents and my lawyer's cover letter for Antonio and the Church's lawyer in Mexico, Lic. Agricol Lozano. [*Lic.* is the abbreviation for the title of *licenciado*, meaning "a licensed lawyer."]

Tuesday, January 20, 1976

For seventeen long days and nights, Marita had been gone. On the eighth call to Puebla, I was finally allowed to talk to her! She sounded happy to talk to me and happy in general. Missing her became more painful—but the reality of her light, happy voice dissolved some of the blacker nightmares. Now that I knew for sure she was in Puebla, the bishop wrote letters I then translated to Antonio, his father, and to President Agricol Lozano, who besides being the head lawyer for the Church in Mexico was also the Regional Representative for Puebla.

The bishop gave me a copy of his letter to Antonio, and the others were similar to it. I hoped these letters would help Antonio respond in a positive way to amend what he had done. Here is part of what Bishop Morrill wrote to Antonio:

Dear Antonio,

You have caused us all quite a bit of concern, especially Mari Vawn. I am sorry you chose to run away instead of trying to settle matters here pertaining to your and Mari Vawn's divorce. I know you feel bad that Mari Vawn's decision is to get a divorce, but you must realize that you have not given her any choice. I have spent many hours with you two and know of her desire to work out the problems in your marriage, but you have just not kept your promises to her nor your commitments to me.

You have broken your promises also to Heavenly Father— remember the visions you have had, especially the first one. From all I can determine, Brother, you never really repented (changed) from the problems you caused in Mexico that made Mari Vawn get sick and leave to return to the United States. Is she not justified in the action she is now taking since you have not kept your promises, commitments, and covenants? I trusted you, Antonio, and you have broken that trust and faith. This most despicable act you have now done, taking your daughter and leaving the country, is by far your worst yet. Are you doing this to punish Mari Vawn and cause her to suffer or because you love your daughter? I cannot believe you, who claim to love your daughter so much, would take her out of her home, her mother's arms, and take her on a trip of several thousand miles with no more than the clothes she had on. Where can your love for her be when you apparently care so little for her physical and emotional health? Had you been honest with me and stayed here as you indicated, I would have tried to help you make the settlement between you and Mari Vawn as good as possible for both of you.

Antonio, you have dishonored the covenants you made with Heavenly Father both at baptism and in the temple. You have mistreated your wife and according to the Apostle Paul she should have been your most valued treasure, even a part of you (Eph. 5:22-31). You have been dishonest to your bishop and friends and your flight to Mexico with your daughter cannot be accepted as morally right. You know the steps of repentance, Antonio; confess to those you've wronged, repay to the extent possible and forsake all wrong actions. I stand ready to personally forgive you when you are ready to confess your transgressions against me and forsake them . . .

Mari Vawn, Linda, and Ron also should receive your apologies and request for their forgiveness. Before asking Mari Vawn's forgiveness, you need to return Marita to her mother as the law has requested, then you and she need to make a peaceful settlement of your marriage.

So far as the Church is concerned, I have taken action to retain your membership records in my ward until this matter is settled. This action is taken until a determination of whether or not a church court is necessary to bring about the necessary process of repentance . . .

Antonio, you have the potential of being a great young man. I respect and love your father and know he will help you understand and do what is right that you might become a great spiritual leader like him. I encourage you to study the scriptures, fast and pray and receive the Lord's direction for your life and confirmation of the things I've taught you before and have written in this letter. May the Lord bless you to do what is right. I'll pray for you and put your name in the temple here. Your brother in the gospel,

Sincerely,
Steven Morrill, Bishop

Saturday, January 31, 1976

I thought I had been strong and had coped well enough with all the problems of this long difficult month, but I learned how vulnerable I was to Marita's absence. I missed her so much.

I had been invited to attend the Merrie Miss Daddy-Daughter

Party although I no longer taught the eleven-year-old girls at church. I decided to go have some fun and arrived at the church a little early. As I waited, however, I thought of Marita, and I began to cry.

People passed me on the way to the kitchen. When I saw one little girl carrying food, I cried harder. I couldn't help comparing her with Marita. The Merrie Miss girl was near me, but Marita was not. She was going to have a good time with her dad at the party, but I didn't know what was happening with Antonio and Marita. It had been a month and I knew so little about how Marita was really doing. I wanted to know what she did every day, what she ate, how she was feeling, if she remembered me, or if she still spoke English.

I dried my tears and cleaned up my face. As I walked out into the hallway, I noticed Bishop Morrill a few feet away. Surprised to see me, he asked, "What are you doing here, Mari Vawn?"

I cringed against the wall and blurted, "They invited me and I wanted to have some fun for a change." I wished I hadn't come and wished I could disappear.

"Please come into my office right now."

As soon as I sat down, I began crying, sobbing, almost screaming out in heartbreak. I wasn't strong enough to see all those young daughters come in with their daddies and know I was there too, but *my* daughter was not! How I cried! Emotions I hadn't known existed inside me spilled out in a painful release. The bishop tried to comfort me and he called his wife and told her he was sending me over. The ward clerk drove me to the bishop's home.

There, Sister Morrill stood by my side as I cried and gave in to my mourning. Finally I stopped. As a distraction, she let me use their electric typewriter to make some dittos for my lessons. I typed for hours and went home when I felt better.

At home alone I wondered how long it would be before I saw Marita again. I tried to think of the positive, of the good things that had happened that month—

- I got the divorce papers in order and sent them to Mexico. I expected Antonio to sign them and return them.
- BYU refunded all of Antonio's tuition, which helped make the house payment.
- My supervisors at BYU allowed me to switch my job

at the computer lab to mornings so I could take another part-time job in Provo in the afternoons.
- I had enough food to eat although I had lost seven pounds from not feeling well enough to swallow it.

Tuesday, February 3, 1976

An emotion-straining, dreadful dream woke me in the early morning. In the dream I was doing everything in my power to get Marita back, and Antonio and his parents were keeping her from me, just out of my reach as I ran after her.

Despair from the dream vanished, however, after a phone call I received from a man who made movies and filmstrips for the Church. I had met Brother Olson at Benemérito when he took slides of my students. He knew the Cruz family well and offered to do what he could to bring Marita back with him from his next trip to Mexico! He was flying there in a week! I decided I'd send some of Antonio's clothes with him as well as a power of attorney to authorize Brother Olson to bring Marita back. This news gave me hope and energy.

Friday, February 6, 1976 — Journal entry

> I took all of Antonio's clothes out of the closet, but I didn't feel a thing for him as I folded them and sorted them into piles. I guess I'm mostly relieved that he's gone. However, I haven't been able to walk into Marita's room since she left. I intend to leave her clothes and things just as they are, in hopes she'll be here soon to use them.

Chapter Five

Monday, February 9, 1976

PAYDAY! OR WAS IT? I got my paycheck from BYU, but other rewards for my efforts and patience didn't pay off as I had hoped. It was the deadline I'd set to receive the returned divorce papers, but no mail came. While I was in the lawyer's office for the power of attorney document, I signed a release to publish a summons in the newspaper. If Antonio didn't respond, then I was on my way to divorce in spite of him.

However, before I signed it, I called the Cruz home to find out what he had done with the divorce papers.

Antonio's older sister Adriana answered the phone cheerfully, but when she heard my voice on the line, her tone changed, and she didn't want to talk to me. In Spanish I asked her if she knew if he had sent the papers. She answered abruptly, "I don't know anything about anything!"

I asked how Marita was doing.

Hard and fast, almost shouting, Adriana spat out, "*¡Muy bien! ¡Muy bien!*" But she wouldn't let me hear Marita's voice.

The hurt began all over again as I put the phone down. I had every right to know how my daughter was and to talk to her, but no one there would let me do that. In spite of a throbbing migraine headache and intense emotional pain, I completed the arrangements to send a suitcase containing Antonio's clothes and treasures, along with the documents for Marita, to the pilot. Brother Olson was flying out the next day.

As I packed, I considered new worries. I felt that Antonio must have told many lies to his family for them to treat me with such caution and hatred. Always before, Adriana was friendlier than anyone else there, and we got along well. From the way she just had talked to me, I wondered if they were also telling lies to Marita to turn her against her own mother. She was still a baby. What could she understand? What would she believe? I just hoped she wouldn't hear much because she would be home with me soon.

It was past 9:00 P.M. when I delivered the suitcase to Brother Olson's friend's house in the Indian Hills section of Provo. He would take it to Salt Lake the next day. As my VW rolled down Canyon Road on my way home, I suddenly realized that I couldn't see anything very well. Then, everything around me grew blacker. Seconds later, I couldn't see where I was going at all. The car hit something—a guard rail or a post.

After that first impact, the car went out of control and raced toward a greater blackness directly ahead of me. A deep ditch? I felt helpless to prevent a devastating wreck. As I went into shock, I thought, *I'm going to be killed! I'll never see Marita or my parents again!*

I don't remember doing anything consciously to stop the accident. I just sat there, frozen behind the wheel. During those moments of terror, I felt a force pushing hard across my foot, pressing it to accelerate on the gas pedal. The car zoomed along, zigzagging, half-on, half-off the road. As it neared the far edge of the other lane, I thought it would go off the other side.

Then again, I felt a strong force on my hands, moving them so that they were guided to turn the steering wheel so that in some way the car got back on the road. In these seconds I realized that one of those angels mentioned in the blessing was indeed nearby, saving my life.

As the car slowed down, I stopped it and sat in silence.

I stepped out to inspect the damage. Nothing had happened to the outside of the car, but the gear shift rasped and wouldn't shift properly. Mostly, my inspection revealed that I had failed to turn the car lights on. The mishap was my fault, but I was relieved beyond words for the protection I had received in spite of my distraught state of mind and exhaustion.

As I backed the car up to the point where I had lost control, the lights shone on a large ditch with a bridge across it. Looking at it logically, I should have been at the bottom of the ditch with half the bridge scraped off and carried along with me. I thanked the Lord for his help.

Valentine's Weekend

My mother, Betty Bailey, arrived on Thursday, two days before Valentine's Day. We shared four days of meals, cleaning, feelings, fun, and being in the same room. It was a reprieve from the isolation I had been experiencing.

On Friday night, she sat near me on the couch watching television while she hemmed my drapes. I kept glancing over at her, hardly trusting my senses of her nearness. The needle flashed quickly through the white cloth. All my life I have seen a needle held in her fingers, especially for quilting. Few women anywhere could make as tiny or as straight a line of stitches as my mother. Her patience, eye for beauty, and skill in creating quilts and flower arrangements have been in constant demand. As a young woman, she qualified to represent Montana at the National 4-H Congress for her fine sewing. She passed many of these skills on to me. I hoped I could pass them on to Marita.

I sat next to her making valentines: one for her, one for Linda, and one for the Morrills. I always liked creating homemade cards and personalizing the sentiments, but telling these people I loved them didn't seem so simple now as it was the year before when Marita was still at home and I was still married.

Not as simple, either, as it is for a child to give valentines. Somehow, after those first few years of grade school, we never give or receive so many valentines again. We become more self-conscious and restricted in our expression of our love for others. We hold ourselves in with silence or play it safe with stock, expected phrases while our hands too often hang down, empty, and our hearts yearn for that familiar joyful feeling.

Is it because we have learned too much about life . . . too much about love and how fragile it all can be? And the older we get, isn't it harder to find cards in the stores that express what we really want to say? Our feelings run deeper than the trite words on cards, and often much is left unsaid.

But I must try. Cold words, hard words, or not enough words all take their toll on tender souls. Kind and thoughtful words do nourish, uplift, and even save lives. I learned during my years living in Mexico that if I knew someone cared about me, even two or three thousand miles away, I could still feel secure and loved. Love shared, even from a distance, helped me endure the loneliness and other voids in my life.

And that night on Valentine's weekend, I wanted to break through some barriers so words would mirror my feelings and communicate a message of greater love than I had known before Marita was taken. I was beginning to understand more about the power of love and how we can live and love forever—if we pay the price.

Early Saturday morning I wrote a verse about love on the valentine I had made for my mother and gave it to her. When she had finished reading it, she walked into my bedroom, hugged me, and held me tightly for a long time. We cried softly together. We talked of the pain of having Marita gone, of how much we loved her, and how much we prayed for her little life. We focused on the last line I had written on the card: *May we be able to hold Marita in our arms next Valentine's Day!*

All day we cleaned house. I was expecting a new roommate to move in to Marita's room soon to ease the burden of the house payment. I spent the time in the safest room, the living room, shampooing the carpet and cleaning the furniture. My mother took Marita's crib down, put away toys and some clothes, and washed the walls, curtains, and bedding. Throwing away reminders of my past with Antonio and working together against dust and clutter gave me a new surge of energy and a feeling of more control.

For lunch, we shared a box of valentine chocolates and tomato soup. One of my Merrie Miss girls arrived in time for dessert with a pie-sized heart-shaped sugar cookie decorated with pink icing and loving words. For some weeks I had felt that people avoided me because they didn't know what to say, but that cookie let me know that someone cared.

By Sunday night, with Mother scheduled to leave Monday morning, I was already missing her even though she was still in the next room. I didn't want my mother to leave, yet I knew I had to go on alone. The feelings deepened and I thought of Marita. What did she do when she missed me? What was our separation doing to her heart and mind?

Monday morning we waited in the parking lot of the University Mall in Orem for her brother-in-law to pick her up on the way back to Montana. It was cold out, my car heater didn't work, and the windows were frosting over. For a few minutes I memorized the details of my mother's face: the bump and freckles on her nose, how the right corner of her mouth lifted up when she smiled, the fringe of bangs across her forehead, the strength I saw in her green eyes. Few fifty-four-year-old women looked as young and lovely as Betty Bailey did.

At 8:15 the Rushtons' car pulled up, and she loaded her suitcase in their trunk, kissed me, and said through her tears, "We pray for you. Just keep living one day at a time."

I couldn't speak. Then she was gone.

Wednesday, February 18, 1976

If I hadn't been sitting in the middle of a row at night Relief Society, I would have left. As it was, I stayed and endured every sentence of Social Relations Lesson number five, "Understanding Those Who Are Bereaved." Objective: "To help each sister increase her understanding of the feelings and concerns of those who are bereaved and to help her become aware of things to do and say that will be helpful."

Of course, the lesson focused on the loss of one's spouse, but I focused on applying the lesson to the loss of my child and wondered how I would adjust because Marita was still alive. She was like a prisoner of war or an MIA in Vietnam. How did the families of those men handle their bereavement? The lesson never touched on what I most wanted to know, and I never spoke because tears were too near the surface.

However, the discussion on the five stages of mourning helped because I recognized that I was stuck in most of them. Keeping Marita's belongings in the same places had been my form of *denial*. Flashes of *anger and resentment* zinged through me every week, usually on weekends. I hadn't done too much *bargaining* yet, but *depression* was an old companion. Would I ever reach the *acceptance* stage, which the lesson described as "a sense of contentment and a feeling that all is well?"

I couldn't accept the lesson summary: *the bereaved will eventually have to look within herself for the strength to face life without the loved one*. I couldn't go through life without Marita. Someday I would see her again.

Sunday, February 22, 1976

With another month's ward newsletter ready to go to press, I slumped down on the Morrills' old gray couch, waiting for the bishop to inspect every page as he always did. I couldn't keep my eyes open, and his wife brought me a faded quilt and a pillow.

After the bishop approved the copy, he looked at me with concern. He pulled a kitchen chair over to the couch. "I've never seen you so run down and worn out, MariVawn. Tell me about your daily schedule."

"Well, I get up at 6:45. First I drive to BYU where I proctor at the TICCIT learning lab from 8:00 to 10:00. Then I have office hours in another building and I prepare for my classes. I usually eat my sandwich as I drive to work in Provo. After a few hours, it's time to return to BYU to teach my 111 Comp. class at 3:00. I go right from that to three hours of graduate classes. After 7:00 I am free to go home again."

"Good grief! How do you keep all your times and places straight?"

"Oh, it's not so hard. The need to survive scares me into going on. I bet you'll never guess what the hardest thing is, though."

"Grading all those compositions?"

"No, I'm used to that by now. But every two hours I have to go outside and try to remember where I parked my car!"

Bishop Morrill uncrossed his legs, folded his fingers together, and spoke in a more serious tone. "MariVawn, I'm afraid for you. I don't know how much longer you can keep up this crazy schedule and stay sane. I'm afraid your inner drive will collapse some day soon and leave you stranded."

"I've been getting through it so far," I protested warily. I hoped that this would show any skeptics that I was stable and able to take care of Marita when she returned.

He asked carefully, "As your bishop I know you'd like me to have faith in the last blessing I gave you. You've been hanging on to the promise that Marita will be returned to you. What if Brother Olson doesn't bring her back in his plane, MariVawn? What will you do then?"

I couldn't say a word. I just sat there.

"And what if he did? You don't have any time for her right now. You're working or studying every waking hour of the day."

It was true. I was too far into the semester to back out, and I needed the money. What could I eliminate without going on welfare?

Bishop Morrill continued as gently and as cheerfully as he could, "Don't you see that it's a blessing for Marita to be in Mexico right now while you put your life back together? She needs to see her mother more often than on weekends. And life would be easier on you if you found just one good full-time job."

I groaned and put my head into my hands and squeezed my eyes shut. It hurt when I thought of Marita down there so far away. Surely it was better for her to be with me, even if I *was* busy. I still couldn't speak because I felt like crying.

Then the bishop cleared his throat and stood up. "What I'm going to say next isn't the bishop talking, so don't take it as inspired because it's not. I'm just talking as Steven Morrill, the man. Still I want you to listen carefully and think about it this week. I've had these thoughts for some time now, and I hope you'll be strong enough to consider a cold reality: in all probability, you will not see Marita again until she is a grown woman."

I leaped from the couch. "NO! that can't be! I must see her soon! She must be with me! I'm her mother!"

Suddenly my strength ebbed. Images of twenty empty years without Marita gathered in my mind. The bishop got me a glass of water after I sagged to the couch.

I asked the bishop to offer a prayer. Then he asked me to pray. When I closed my eyes, it seemed as though I were transported back to the edge of the cliff at Canyon de Chelly near Chinle, Arizona, where I had stood years before, gazing down at the expanse of desolate, sandy beauty hundreds of feet below me. I began the prayer with the feeling that one misstep now would send me falling to my destruction.

As I prayed, I told the Lord that I didn't know which direction to step. My trail had stopped there. I imagined I stood inches away from a cliff's edge, surrounded by darkness that seemed to float up from the depths before me, and the canyon loomed deeper. By the time I finished praying, however, I had calmed down. I sensed that Marita would probably be in Mexico a while longer. But no way could I accept the idea of *years* without her.

Tuesday night, February 24, 1976

I called Brother Olson. He reported that Antonio's parents had told him Marita was in Mexico City where Antonio was staying with his sister. My father-in-law also said Antonio would give Marita back when the courts awarded custody. But how could a court act when Antonio still had the papers? I knew after the phone call that he wouldn't send the papers back.

Marita: Missing in Mexico

Wednesday, February 25, 1976 — Journal entry

Today my mailbox contained the registered letter which held a copy of the divorce papers my lawyer had sent a month ago to Lic. Agricol Lozano—undelivered, unsigned for, unopened. Antonio had either refused to accept it or he never got it.

I knew I shouldn't have felt shocked, considering the mysteries of the Mexican mail system. Truckloads of mail disappear monthly and packages rarely arrive.

Once my mom had sent me a heart-shaped, purple-foiled box of Valentine's chocolates. I paid a near ransom-sized bribe (AKA *duty*) and was allowed to take it home. When I reached in for a chocolate, however, all I found were empty white paper cups. Some postal clerk had enjoyed my candy. Still, I had paid for the box, so I kept it to hold keepsakes and to pass slips of papers around to my students.

Nevertheless, today I felt dumbfounded. I knew they usually handled registered mail with more respect. There was no clear explanation for this returned envelope. The second disturbing news was that the judge of the fourth judicial court in Utah County refused to sign my release for the newspaper. Now I could not advertise the divorce instead of serving papers on Antonio.

So, all in all, I was right back where I was two months ago: Marita was still missing in Mexico. I could not serve Antonio with papers. My divorce still had not really begun.

Thursday, February 26, 1976

One piece of good news was a job offer. The Church Educational System would pay me to tutor Benjamin Parra, the Church real estate agent for Mexico and Central America. My job was to teach him grammar every day for an hour and take him to the devotional on Tuesdays. Other tutors would handle pronunciation, dialogues, etc. The job would last for one month.

I couldn't refuse. Benjamin Parra was one of the greatest LDS missionaries Mexico had ever known. Among the three thousand he had baptized was Antonio. He was the most eloquent orator I had ever heard speak in Spanish. He was a Regional Representative. How could I turn down a chance to teach Benjamin Parra?

Sunday, March 21, 1976

The bishop and the stake president spent all month deciding whether to summon Antonio to a church court. In the end, they decided not to. Also, we finally received a letter from President Agricol Lozano responding to the bishop's January letter. The implications from the letter's surprising comments changed our approach to finding a solution. Some of the major points from the letter:

> (1) Antonio had received the papers I had sent him and had consulted with Lic. Lozano. In spite of Bishop Morrill's request for him to give Antonio some ecclesiastical counseling as a Regional Representative, President Lozano had confined himself to legal advice.
>
> (2) Antonio didn't have to sign the papers because they were not valid in Mexico. Publishing notices in the U.S. paper was not recognized as a valid procedure either.
>
> (3) Lozano summarized by saying divorce proceedings should be commenced in Mexico because that is where we were married, where Marita was born, and where she is now.

After the bishop let me read the letter, we had another long chat. I suddenly realized why the Cruzes told Brother Olson that Antonio would let me have custody of Marita when the courts awarded it to me. He felt relatively sure that I would never go to Mexico or proceed by Mexican law, thus leaving me with very little more I could do. A few days earlier, Benjamin Parra had said that he would be happy to help me, once I told him exactly what he could do. Bishop Morrill wanted to write some more letters to leaders in Mexico, but he didn't know what to say that wouldn't be misinterpreted or spawn additional problems. No one I knew had heard of a similar case. Bishop Morrill settled back into his office chair, rested his head in his hands, and looked down at the letter.

"Sometimes we get answers to our prayers that we don't want or expect. If President Lozano is right about this last point, then you have not gone through the worst yet in this whole experience. If you should be proceeding according to Mexican law, then you will need someone to give you Mexican legal advice and perhaps you might have to go to Mexico . . ." His voice faded.

I stared at him. I remembered the Glasgow lawyer's warning: "You must not ever step into Mexico again. You could disappear." My mother actually feared for my life. I whispered, "I don't know if I could go there again."

Bishop Morrill's eyes shifted to mine. "Mari Vawn, you're going to have to decide how far you're going to go to get Marita back. Just what is the limit? And when there is little you can do anymore, could you accept that and adjust your life and go on living without Marita?"

Through my tears I said, "I don't feel I've yet done what the Lord had in mind for us or completed my mission as her mother, either. There has got to be more, but I don't see how I can do more if she spends much of her life in Mexico. I feel that *I* am her mother because there is something I can teach her or offer her that perhaps no one else can. I don't know what I'm going to do now to get her back, but I am not giving up!"

Wednesday, March 24, 1976

I went to the Provo Temple several times in one week, motivated by a desire to know how far I should go in trying to get Marita back. As I sat in the sacred silence of the Lord's holy house, the Spirit repeated many times to my mind, *She has to feel your spirit, to know you.*

I was surprised to hear these words because I didn't think it would be safe for me to go to Mexico. Yet now I knew I had to go there if only to be with her so she could know me and I could see her and talk to her. I would have to find the strength to leave her there if I couldn't find a way to bring her back.

Before I left the temple, I put Marita's name on the prayer roll—and my name, too. And Antonio's. We all would need the extra prayers, faith, and help.

Mari Vawn Bailey

Saturday, March 27, 1976 — Journal entry

    Today was especially difficult because I had to go into Marita's room and get it ready for my new roommate, Rosalyn Wolff. I opened the drawers and looked at Marita's clothes. I had to touch them again, hold them, and fold them neatly into storage boxes. Every item I picked up brought tears. Her little white shoes, bought only a week before her disappearance, broke my heart. I held a navy blue sweater, a Christmas gift that she had never worn.

    I still dream of Marita. In the dreams Marita is always standing there, unaware of me. I scramble toward her, but the Cruz family whisks her away. I pray that the Lord will bless her to remember me, perhaps through her own dreams.

    I dug deeper—I found my maternity clothes, Marita's tiny baby clothes, her baby book. I read the notes I had taken the day she received a name and a blessing in our Madero Ward and was reminded that she was blessed to have strength in spiritual things. I take comfort in the promises of that blessing and in those others I have received.

    Tomorrow the bishop will give me another blessing to assist me in making wise decisions that have to be made soon. I have felt paralyzed by the need to make decisions. Should I quit my master's program and get a full-time job? What about teaching? If Marita comes back to live with me, who will watch her while I work? Did any of this matter if I need to go to Mexico? Would I be down there for years, too?

    I carried the boxes of clothes out to the storage room by the garage. Time is passing. Signs of spring brighten the backyard—poplar trees are budding. There are two more weeks to teach, three of graduate courses, and I will be out of work on April 24. I have already advised the department that I won't teach next semester. General conference is only a week away. Many of the Mexican

Church leaders will be in Salt Lake for conference. Perhaps I can make some appointments to talk to them.

Whatever—I will be free in three weeks, once finals are over.

Tuesday, March 30, 1976

I decided to go to the Provo Temple and meditate, to see what reaction I would get with the decision *not* to go to Mexico. I finished dressing and sat in the chapel with everyone else dressed in white. As the company left the room to go to the session room, overwhelming gloom swept through me. I couldn't suppress the tears. As much as I tried to stay with the decision not to go, my mind kept sorting other possibilities, the problems I would encounter in Mexico, possible solutions.

I reviewed the priesthood blessing I had just received. I was told I'd have some soul-stretching tests ahead that would be for my good and progress because I would learn about human nature more deeply. However, in the meantime, I had to study things out in my mind and ask the Lord in the temple to find out what I must know in making the immediate decisions that faced me.

So as I sat in the session, I slowly realized that I would have to go to Mexico to see Marita, no matter what the peril, no matter what the sacrifice. As much as I tried to concentrate on the ceremony in the session room, my thoughts wandered and I remembered my mother's valentine's visit—how much it hurt when it was time for her to go and she left me alone again. Yet, to be honest, I had more positive effects from her visit than bad. I knew she had done what she could to be with me and show her love to me.

Likewise, I felt the experience of making lasting memories and impressions of myself on Marita would be worth it in the long run, even if I had to leave her again. I didn't want to be a complete stranger to her in the future. I knew Marita must come to know me through my visits. I decided I would continue to fight for her custody. More than anything, I wanted Marita to know her mother.

With this decision, I felt a greater peace than I had in weeks.

Chapter Six

Friday night, April 2, 1976

PRESIDENTE PARRA SPOKE dynamically to a large crowd of former missionaries and their dates or spouses at a missionary reunion. We tutors had also been invited. It was the highlight of the year so far for me. As I sang hymns in Spanish, I felt homesick for Mexico. The prayer in Spanish brought me a special intimacy with God, as such prayers alway had for me. Those eternity-old stirrings for the people of Israel touched my soul again as they had so many times in the past . . . the same strong stirrings I felt when I was ten years old in Montana and I told everyone that I was going to Mexico when I grew up.

I remembered—

> • The spirit of awakening that overwhelmed me at the BYU Fieldhouse in 1967 as Elder Spencer W. Kimball spoke about the American Indians and related peoples and their need for help. During his discourse, I heard another voice, speaking audibly to my mind that told me to prepare to teach them, for my mission was to the descendants of the Book of Mormon peoples, the Lamanites. I had grown up around the Native Americans in Montana, but my heart more easily reached out to the descendants of Abraham and of the prophet Lehi who lived in Mexico and South America. I prepared.
>
> • The confirmation I felt as I heard Quintana, an Indian princess on the stage during the BYU Indian Week Pageant, ask, "Who am I?" During the answer, "You are a daughter of

Israel," I promised myself that I would be a champion for Israel's people and teach them and love them.
- The total euphoria that surrounded me during the summers I spent in Mexico with BYU Travel-Study in 1967 and 1968. Forcibly, I felt I had come home, that I belonged there and was needed there. I was in love with Mexico, its people, contrasts, adventuresome atmosphere, colorful history, and promising future.
- The total happiness I experienced my first year of teaching at the American School in Torreón, Coahuila, in 1969.

At the missionary reunion I forgot my present circumstances for a while as I considered the future. I knew I would go to Mexico again sometime soon.

Tuesday, April 6, 1976

Disappointment swiftly replaced my joy. In spite of all our efforts, no meeting with Mexican leaders materialized before the worldwide conference in Salt Lake had ended. Nothing good happened except for the phone call I made to Elder Thomas Fyans at the Church Office Building in Salt Lake. Elder Fyans was the area administrator for Mexico and Central America, and he lived in Mexico City. He agreed to talk officially to the Regional Representatives, Benjamin Parra and Agricol Lozano, soon.

I hit bottom. There was only a blank before me and behind me . . . the cliff, the black hole, the emptiness of the void. After three months of doing everything I could think of, nothing had worked out. I stood again where I stood in my empty house on January 4 when I discovered Marita was missing. By the time conference ended, I had no idea of what to do next.

Linda suggested a priesthood blessing. I felt the comfort of the Spirit as Ron put his hands on my head and gave me a powerful blessing, clearly inspired of the Lord. Then I wished I hadn't doubted so much when things hadn't gone as I had hoped for. As I walked home, I thanked the Lord for sharing more perspectives with me.

The blessing reassured me that the Lord was pleased with my efforts to do his will. The Lord had a purpose in all this incomprehensible to me now. I was assured that Marita would come back to me in the Lord's own due time—which I would know about ahead of time. I learned that a season of testing and the refiner's fire awaited me, a time of trying me with great sacrifices in my life. Hearing this, I felt apprehensive, but I was next assured that I would be able to stand up to the refiner's fire and learn of his will.

Wednesday, April 7, 1976

Bishop Morrill had an appointment to talk to Elder Fyans in Salt Lake. We also had hopes that President Arturo R. Martinez could meet with us. The bishop had been trying to locate any Mexican Church leader who might want to meet with us informally to kick around some ideas of what to do about Marita's situation.

Arturo R. Martinez was the first Lamanite to be called as a mission president, and until recently, he had been the Regional Representative to Puebla. I had been a part-time missionary in Torreón while he was mission president there. Marita's first name, Andrea, was for Sister Andrea Martinez, his wife. He had been very concerned about Marita, as though she were family to him.

The bishop and I pushed our way through the brass and glass revolving doors into the world of modern Italian Renaissance inside the Hotel Utah. After glancing around the massive gray marble columns, I spotted President Martinez in a dark business suit near the reception desk.

My friend was nearing fifty, and time was graying and thinning his hair. We greeted each other and I introduced him to Bishop Morrill. We had chatted together a few minutes when another Mexican Church leader emerged from the revolving door. Brother Abu Sado joined us. I hadn't expected he would come to talk to us, but I was pleased to see him again. It had been a couple of years since I had seen him in Mexico. Businesslike at first, our stiff introductions and formal smiles remained until each person knew the name and status of the others.

Brother Abu Sado's intense brown eyes bored into mine as he asked four times how I was. I replied each time positively, "*¡Muy bien! ¡Muy bien!*" At last he seemed convinced that I was doing all right in spite of my situation, and he led the group to a small round table in the lobby.

After we sat down on upholstered chairs around the table, Brother Sado continued asking me more questions in Spanish. Then, our visitor's demeanor changed and his eyes shifted to Bishop Morrill. The preliminaries were over.

As Bishop Morrill explained the major things we had tried to do, Brother Sado understood the English, but answered in Spanish. President Martinez translated. Brother Sado sat rigidly at first, listening attentively and speaking decisively and crisply. We hadn't expected much from our visit with him . . . just to greet him and get to know him a little better and have him meet us. I thought we would leave in a few minutes, but Brother Sado continued looking at me from time to time until gradually, he thawed.

Suddenly a change in the tone of the meeting flowed from him to us. He started telling me exactly what steps I must take in Mexico if I wanted Marita. At last, specific, direct answers from Brother Abu Sado convinced me that I must go to Mexico!

I had felt it in my heart at Parra's reunion, spiritually in the temple, and intellectually from President Lozano's letter, *but right then, all at once*, the testimony forged from a unified heart, mind, and spirit shot through me with undeniable force.

Brother Sado asked us not to mention the meeting to anyone else. We all promised. Then, abruptly, he stood up. Again, he searched my eyes and declared, "*Ésto require valor. ¿Tiene Usted valor?*" [Do you have the courage required to do this?]

I assured him firmly with newborn conviction, "*¡Sí, tengo valor!*"

He grabbed his briefcase and said, "*¡Adios!*" and disappeared through the door. I remained standing, marveling that he had told us so much and that I had told him I was brave enough to do what he suggested in going after Marita in Mexico.

Friday, April 9, 1976

During a break from work at BYU, I attended the "Expanding Church Symposium" in the Wilkinsen Center where I met a friend, Lavina Fielding. Seven years before, we had been English majors, attending the same BYU ward. Now she was an editor/writer who had been sent to cover the symposium. She had not changed much in the last few years. Her short, brown hair still framed her round face in a simple uncluttered hairdo.

After the symposium, we sat outside the Y Center as we talked. She casually asked, "Well, Mari Vawn, what are you planning to do when the semester is over next week?"

I looked away a short time, wondering if I should unveil my secret plan. No one else outside that circle of people in the Hotel Utah knew about it, and I didn't know when I'd tell my parents. Still, Lavina had understood my feelings every time I'd gone to Mexico, so I told her of my new decision to go there again. She wasn't surprised at the news, so I expressed my apprehensions.

"This time, my trip to Mexico will be different. I won't cross the border so matter-of-factly as I always did before. This trip won't be as a tourist or as a professor, but as a mother with her life in danger. During this past month my parents and the bishop all told me they would never let me go there again . . . at least until I'm divorced and there is no danger."

"Why are they so worried and why do you plan to go anyway?" Lavina asked.

"Antonio could serve me with papers if he found out I was in Mexico and legal entanglements and red tape could force me to stay there for years," I explained. "I also have reason to fear Antonio. He has hurt me before and has more reason to hurt me now."

"And the old Murphy's Law of *If anything can possibly go wrong, it will* could affect your negotiations, right?" she concluded. "You're afraid you'll get into predicaments there that will be hard to get out of alone."

"You're right," I continued. "I have already suffered from quirks inherent in the system in Mexico. The simplest transactions escalate into nightmarish difficulties. You wouldn't believe what a person has to go through just to get mail out of the post office, let alone to get a visa renewed."

"What could possibly happen?"

"Well, once while I was at the border to renew a visa, they confiscated all my documents and told me they weren't going to let me back into Mexico. The lawyer who sent me to the border for new papers had told me it would take only a few minutes to get them. I believed him and rode the bus up there taking only my sweater, purse, and my journal. I was caught in a sort of no-man's-land between Ciudad Juarez and El Paso for three days."

"So how did you get out of that?"

"Finally, with some pressure and extra pesos from Antonio's

wealthy cousin, one man told me to go to El Paso for a certain document and pass through the border check at a certain time and place where I would least likely get hassled. It worked. I returned to Mexico barely in time to attend my own wedding," I finished, frowning. I hoped that I would never find myself without visa papers again.

Lavina smiled gently. "But the worst is that you can see yourself down there this time following a lawyer's advice to get Marita back and still, in the end, after spending time, money, and heartache you may not be able to bring her home with you. Am I right?"

She was. My voice wavered. "All I know now is that I have to go there and do whatever is required, and when I pass the tests, I hope I finally get to bring her home." An ominous feeling of fear struggled against the faith I had held onto. I knew how illogical and patient and flexible one had to be in order to live in Mexico. I felt brave, but I also recognized reality. Still, there didn't seem to be any other way.

Lavina put her arm around me. "It will be a true test because here in the United States you are more protected—your friends, your family, the bishop, the temple are all here to help you. You have a home and our laws protect you. But there . . ." Her voice trailed off.

We both stared down at the cement squares and patches of grass between the library and us. Then, Lavina blurted out some words I never expected to hear, "I'll go with you, Mari Vawn."

I raised my eyes to hers. Half-believing, I asked hesitantly, "Oh, Lavina, do you really mean that?"

"Yes, Mari Vawn, I mean it." She hugged me reassuringly, and I didn't feel so alone.

We talked schedules. The semester ended in a week, but I would have to go to the Mexican consul in Denver for seals on documents and letters to be officially translated before I could take them for use in Mexican courts. We probably could leave in May. Suddenly, the dreaded but accepted necessity of going to Mexico was sorting itself into a series of manageable tasks.

Sunday, April 18, 1976

My roommate Rosalyn surprised me with a bowl of dyed eggs, mints, and chocolate eggs hiding in Easter grass. It added a festive note to an otherwise dreary day. I supposed Marita was with the Cruz family at Tecolutla on the Gulf of Mexico where they always went for Easter week. How I hated being separated from her.

I thought of Heavenly Father, willing to endure separation from his Son. Recently I had borne my testimony in church of our Heavenly Father's love. He has allowed us to leave his home, to come far away to a world where we hardly remember him at all. (What could Marita remember of me after all these months?)

My list of things I needed to do to prepare to leave for Mexico was shrinking. I finished all my graduate projects and turned them in. I took the bus to Denver to get the documents and letters of character reference ready for the Mexican courts. Professionals and others had attested to my psychological soundness to be a fit mother. My lawyer's affidavit swore to the facts of the case. While I was at the consul's office in Denver, I talked to a lawyer who used to work for a law firm in Mexico City. He said a divorce there cost around $1,000.00. That was more money than I had.

Wednesday, April 21, 1976

As I administered the final to my English 111 class, I was surprised at the tears that came to my eyes. As usual, teaching had been magic for me and my students had been some small substitute for Marita. I could express my concern for them and maintain a sense of control over at least one area of my unstable life.

One by one, the students said good-bye and left their tests on my desk. Only three students lingered behind the others to polish their final compositions. Finishing at about the same time they turned in their papers, and grabbed each other around the waists and whooped and danced as they laughed and shouted with joy to be free of finals.

I sat behind my desk and watched them as I cried inside. I was lonely. I was also worried. Where would I find $1,000 for the divorce and custody lawsuit in Mexico City? One thousand dollars was as much money as my parents had spent on my entire college education my freshman year at BYU—tuition, books, food, rent, travel—the works! How could I pay that, plus traveling and living expenses in Mexico until I got Marita? I didn't want to go into debt, but I had no choice. That last day of finals was the last predictable day I had until the whole mess was over.

Chapter Seven

Sunday, April 25, 1976

THREE YEARS AGO ON THIS DAY, Marita was born in Mexico City. I wished I could be with her on her birthday, but instead, my mother and sisters, Tana and Kim, were with me, filling the hours with lively conversation and avoiding any mention of Marita. I was on the verge of tears most of the day.

About 6:00 P.M. the phone rang. It was Marita's little voice chattering on the line, quite happily it seemed. It didn't sound like English, but it wasn't anything in Spanish that I could understand either. The gibberish continued as I asked questions in English, then Spanish. Then, all too soon I heard muffled sounds, and Antonio's voice came on the line.

I asked where Marita was living. In English he said, "Puebla. I have to hang up because I can't afford any more money for the call." The line went dead. The call hadn't lasted one minute, yet hearing Marita's voice for a few seconds consoled me.

Recently I had told my mother about contacting an excellent law firm in Mexico City that charged between $70-$100 an hour. My dear mother said, "I've said to Daddy many times, 'Wouldn't it be good if we could borrow money and pay a ransom to get Marita back?' We'll borrow the money for you, Mari Vawn."

Although I had yet to mention a trip to Mexico to my mother, having their financial support, I knew I could make more definite plans. If all went well, we could return in time to celebrate Marita's birthday next year—with the Baileys around the table sharing her smiles and her cake.

Sunday, May 9, 1976

I couldn't face going to church in our ward on Mother's Day. It would have been a martyr's day, not Mother's Day. All the little children and everyone talking, singing, and thinking about mothers would have been too much for me to bear. My mother sent me a card and some money to buy "whatever you want." But money couldn't buy the only gift I really wanted: to hold Marita in my arms, to talk to her, to have a *normal* day with her once more, the kind most mothers take for granted.

I hoped to see her soon in Mexico, and the waiting to go there had become terribly painful. I had decided not to buy the ticket and leave until I heard from the law firm in Mexico that Brother Sado recommended. In the meantime, I accepted a scholarship from the Linguistics Department for spring classes. I attended halfheartedly because my mind was already in Mexico.

I decided to attend church services at a BYU singles' ward on Sunday because no one brought children. It helped, but I couldn't escape the pain of having a missing child. I was fine until the rest hymn. Hearing the words of "Lead Kindly Light" unleashed a wellspring of tears because each verse reflected so forcibly my situation. I couldn't see the distant scene and had to go one step at a time until some morn I would see that angel face "smile which I have loved long since, and lost awhile." Well, John Henry Newman, your song was to become my new theme song as I let the Lord guide me on.

Wednesday, May 12, 1976

Were things going wrong on purpose? I called Brother Sado in Mexico City. I had sent him documents my lawyer had drawn up to be taken to the law firm he had talked of. Brother Sado sounded so surprised that I had wanted him to do that and reported that he had returned them to me by mail just the day before. Why?

I was seething as I drove to Provo to see my lawyer.

He called the law firm in Mexico City to check on the letter we had sent them. They said they had answered two weeks ago—they handled only corporate legal problems and referred us to another law firm there, Rivera Ugalde Y Asociados. Then we called the new firm and left a message.

Across the street from Mr. Becker's office stood the Utah County Courthouse, an impressive, white stone building covering half the block. As I walked toward it, I wished that this American hall of justice could hear my legal problems instead of the Mexican system. The bubbling water fountain on the north corner of the courthouse faintly reminded me of the glorious fountains in every park in Mexico. How I loved to visit fountains with their geysers of rising and falling water. I sat down on a bench near the deep-set curbs full of irrigation water flowing down the street, so typical in Utah towns.

While I listened to the water, a tall Mexican approached me. Robert, a man I had met in Mexico City nine years before, had married one of my BYU friends, and they had lived in my high-rise apartment building in Tlaltelolco the first year I had taught in Mexico City. Robert had accompanied me home every night after work to make sure I arrived safely from the one hour's journey from Benemérito to Tlaltelolco at 10:00. Both his advice and his presence had saved me from dangerous situations in the past. I was startled and happy to see him again.

He shook my hand, and with a few well-chosen questions, he deftly extracted my predicament. He looked me straight in the eye. "What are you doing *here*, MariVawn? Antonio is making a fool of you in Mexico. He's been there for four months with the opportunity to set things up legally with no interference from you. Why are you still *here*?" he asked urgently.

Indeed, why *was* I still here? Fear. Lack of money. Ignorance. Too much patience and hope. I painfully realized that Brother Sado had indirectly told me the same things Robert was saying.

Robert's directness left no doubt: I would leave for Mexico as soon as I could. I drove to the Utah Job Service for a scheduled typing test. With adrenalin surging, I typed a lousy twenty-three words per minute. I did it on purpose. I didn't care about finding a job anymore. It finally dawned on me that no one had hired me yet because I needed to be free to leave for Mexico. Strange blessing in disguise. Was I too late? What if Antonio already had legal custody of Marita through the Mexican courts? What if I were already divorced down there and didn't even know it?

Thursday, May 13, 1976

My lawyer received a phone call from the new lawyer in Mexico City, Alberto Rivera U. They talked for fifteen minutes, and Lic. Rivera said he would take our case and help get custody of Marita but that I needed to be in Mexico to help him. He told Mr. Becker what additional documents we would need from Utah. One was a certificate of good conduct from the Orem City Police! The phone call was all I had been waiting for.

A thought by Dag Hammerskold guided me through the day:

> To be free—
> To be able to stand up
>   and leave
> everything behind
> without looking back—
> to say Yes.

I called Lavina and we agreed to leave in a week. We could drive to Phoenix in her car and fly to Mexico from there. It would save on air fare. That sounded fine to me. I knew I would need a few more days to collect documents, pay bills, drop out of school, and pack.

Next, I called my father. Although I hadn't talked of going to Mexico, he had expected my news and told me not to worry about the money for the plane fare. He was more concerned about my health and state of mind. I told him that I felt drained and tired, yet uplifted and determined. I would not look back. I only looked forward to whatever my time in Mexico might bring.

Sunday, May 16, 1976

Part of my preparations included asking for another priesthood blessing. As each hour passed, my nerves ganged up on my stomach, and I was woozy and jittery when I arrived at Bishop Morrill's office. He asked if there were any special considerations concerning the blessing.

I had two: that the Lord not withdraw his Spirit as an added trial while I was in Mexico and that when I had done all I could I would know when to quit.

Bishop Morrill lifted his hands to my head and began. I wrote the major messages from the blessing in my journal:

- I would be protected by special beings from on high.
- Doubt not! I am not to let Satan's tool of discouragement get to me. I am to pray daily—morning, noon, and night; reporting to the Lord what I've done and plan to do.
- I would be successful. I had a three-fold mission: to try to get Marita back, to let others know of my feelings, and to tell others of the atonement of the Lord. I will know when I can do no more and when to leave the rest in the Lord's hands.
- The Lord won't force people against their wills. I must accept it if I've done all I can do and I still can't bring her back. The Lord would not then hold me accountable any longer for trying.
- It will be a short trip.
- People will befriend me and I'll be blessed.
- I must read the scriptures daily to understand principles upon which blessings are given. I'll be tried on a principle, and after I have passed the test that a certain principle is based on, the Lord will answer my prayers immediately. I won't have to wait a day, a week, or a month, but I'll have an answer immediately.
- I am to listen to the still, small voice of the Spirit. I will have the power of discernment—to know when people are lying, etc., so I can turn away from them.
- I will be blessed with physical and emotional strength. People are to feel my honesty and integrity. I am to stand tall and unafraid in the presence of those who would do me harm.
- I will be blessed with a clarity of mind and of heightened intellectual capacities to understand the laws of Mexico, to discern truth from error, and to discern what I *can* do. I must think carefully through it all with my lawyer and read everything carefully.
- If I manage to bring Marita back with me, we will be blessed on the trip. I will be blessed temporally when I arrive here.

The bishop closed the blessing. But he had barely said "Amen" and had taken his hands from my head when he said, "There's more to the blessing. It's not finished yet." The addition to the blessing was for my parents so that they might feel comfort while I was gone and know that I would return safely. He closed with, "It is right that you go now."

After the blessing, the bishop sat down again behind his desk and assured me, "I also feel you'll be safe down there and now is the right time to go. Just remember Joseph Smith and Job and how they were blessed in their trials."

Then he pulled out his silver pen and began to write out the affidavit the new lawyer had asked for. He paused often. He couldn't write of many instances when Antonio had been cruel to me because Antonio had told him those things in confidence. However, he wrote that the information about Antonio's behavior in my journals was true and that when he had discussed many of those things with Antonio, Antonio did not deny them. The bishop warned me to protect my journals as valuable evidence while I was in Mexico.

My mother called. She had been struggling with her fears ever since Thursday but finally accepted that I had to go. She had hoped that I could be going under safer conditions, with more legal arrangements to protect me. She agreed to support my plans anyway. A second call came from President Martinez. He had arranged for his friends, the Morenos, to pick me up at the airport and take me to their home for a while. I could trust them, he said. What a relief to have a good place to stay for a while. Brother Sado had estimated two weeks so I packed enough clothes for two weeks.

Tuesday, May 18, 1976

Oh, it felt so good to be doing something concrete for Marita at last! I called the law office in Mexico City to say I would be there in twenty-four hours. The secretary gave me an appointment with Mr. Rivera at 8:30 Thursday morning. Next I picked up Bishop Morrill's affidavit and took it to Joann at Mr. Becker's office for her to rewrite in legal terminology and type up before it was notarized.

I tried to rest, but I was too nervous and excited. Finally I got up and finished packing. Sister Morrill brought me the bishop's signed affidavit and the mailman simultaneously brought my papers by registered mail from Brother Sado. They came in five days! A miracle! Usually it takes three or four weeks for mail to arrive from Mexico. I stared at them a long time, wondering just how they could have arrived in time to take to my new lawyer who could make good use of them.

Finally, I had everything I needed for the trip: my tickets and traveler's checks, a stack of affidavits, support from my parents, a good roommate to look after the house while I was gone, a faithful friend to accompany me, and the knowledge I was doing what needed to be done immediately—go to Mexico for Marita.

Lavina pulled up in her light-green Buick, and I loaded my big blue cloth-sided suitcase into the trunk. We had supper at Arby's, but I was too excited to enjoy it. We left Provo at 6:30 and drove in two-hour shifts.

As our trip began, I talked on and on about things I had saved up to tell Lavina. And I shared what I remembered of the blessing I had just received. When I told her I had been warned I would be tested on a principle but that I didn't know which one it was yet, she speculated, "I thought of 'honor and integrity' when you told me that." I had wondered myself if that could be it.

As night fell, Lavina fell asleep easily in the backseat when it wasn't her turn to drive. I felt exhausted, but the stress kept me awake, and I slept only about three hours the whole night.

Wednesday, May 19, 1976

By the time we reached Phoenix, I had diarrhea, swollen glands, pain in my right ear, and some huge cold sores at the corners of my mouth. My eyes burned. My head ached. And my face had broken out in large pimples from the anxiety I felt about re-entering Mexico.

After eating breakfast at Tempe, we drove to the airport. Around 11:15 A.M., we were in the air aboard Areonaves. Before long we approached the Mexican border and terror almost overwhelmed me. Lavina's presence calmed and reassured me, her clear thinking giving me a reference point for my own stress-distorted reasoning. I thanked her again for being there with me because I felt like a limp doll crumpled up and laid in a woven basket she was carrying into Mexico.

Mari Vawn Bailey

The flight to Hermosillo was very rough. I was nauseated when we landed at the airport. As I stood on the highly polished stone floor and felt the land of Mexico beneath my feet again, memories of other trips into this land of great contrasts displaced the reality of the United States. Mexico had always welcomed me into another reality, and I could feel myself responding with unexpected joy.

We passed under the *¡Bienvenidos a México!* sign and boarded the plane for Guadalajara and on to Mexico City. In this silence above the clouds I wrote on the last page of the first journal I had begun for Marita almost five months before. I had come to the end of the journal and of what I could do for her in the United States.

For years, I had always begun a new journal by writing the date and a new quote on the inside front cover. I usually chose a quote that emphasized the essence of my life at the time or a theme to guide me. I copied a quote by M. Louis Haskins into my new green journal because it fit my life so well at that time:

> I said to the man who stood at the gate of the year:
> Give me a light that I may tread safely into the unknown.
> And he replied: Go out into the darkness and put thine hand into the hand of God. That shall be to thee better than light and safer than a known way.
>
> M. Louis Haskins

Chapter Eight

THE PLANE CIRCLED DOWN through the clouds until I again glimpsed the outskirts of Mexico City, or simply *México* to the natives. We were approaching from the south. Squares and patches of the city appeared—bright yellows, blues, and pinks—but mostly drab, gray concrete squares. I recognized Chapultepec Castle from the air, and soon we were skimming above the neighborhoods near the airport. Then we were down. I glanced east toward Puebla. I was only one hundred miles away from Marita, two thousand miles closer than the day before. A peace accompanied me as we deplaned. I knew that at last the time was finally right to be there. We found our luggage and struggled with it to the other end of the airport where Hariella Wright and Marilyn Moreno's son, Dave, were waiting for us. Hariella rushed up to me, enfolding me in a big hug. I was glad to see her jolly round face with metal-framed glasses just like mine. It was so good to see a known face from Utah in a crowd of so many strangers.

I felt comforted by Hariella's warm and enthusiastic down-home personality. She and her children had arrived in Mexico City only a week before us to join my friend Steve Wright for his first job out of graduate school. Both Steve and I had studied in the same master's program and we both had tutored Benjamin Parra in the spring. And that day, May 19, was Steve's first day of teaching at the Instituto de Relaciones Culturales. Somehow, the Wrights and the Morenos had met.

Marilyn, a tall smiling woman with snappy hazel eyes and short brown hair, was waiting in a large brown station wagon in the parking lot. I liked her on sight and thanked the Lord that she didn't mind having two strangers in her home for a few days.

Marilyn drove us south into a part of Mexico City I didn't know well. Another blessing. I had always worked and lived in the northern part, so it wouldn't be safe to go there. Too many people could recognize me and pass the information on to Antonio. We turned off the traffic-thronged Boulevard Tlalpan to the Morenos' house in Colonia Xotepingo, a nice, upper-middle-class suburb, or "colony" in Mexico.

Behind the usual massive stone walls and metal gates that most Mexicans had built for protection and privacy, rose an impressive three-story, dark stone building that reminded me of a mission home. Its dark, mahogany built-in furniture contrasted with the polished, white marble floors. After climbing an open stairway to the second floor, we crossed a colorful homemade area rug of pieced carpet scraps on the way to the guest room.

Marilyn introduced us to her other sons, Marcos, Marty, and Mike, then returned to her work. After a refreshing shower, we left to make a trial run to determine how much time it would take us to travel to the lawyer's office for our appointment the next morning.

The orange trolley made regular trips up and down Tlalpan. We rode to the end of the line and boarded the metro, a key to traveling easily anywhere in Mexico City. I remembered riding it for the first time in 1968 when the city proudly opened it to the public. My roommates and I were the only ones in the car, and we rode it from one end of the line to the other and back again. The cars, shiny and unscratched, had just arrived from France. The only flaw was the overheated air, not needed in Mexico. After all these years, they still hadn't fixed it. A blast of hot air poured on us until we stepped out at Insurgentes, the hub of pleasure spots and high-class commerce in *La Zona Rosa*, or the "Pink Zone" of the city.

As Lavina and I walked south on Insurgentes, we passed the poor and the maimed, those unescapable street people found in nearly every section of the city. Everyone seemed so tired, poor, and dirty. I had almost forgotten. The noise was horrendous—screeching, roaring, blaring bumper-to-bumper traffic from the multilaned main street a few feet away. Caught in sensory overload from the trip and the rush hour traffic, I staggered down each block until we found the office building.

By the time we went to bed, I was exhausted. Nothing could keep me awake that night.

Thursday, May 20, 1976
Colonia Xotepingo, Mexico City

I woke promptly with the morning light, nervous, excited, and anxious about our meeting with the lawyer. I didn't know anything about him. Was he intelligent, dependable, and competent enough to help me in all the ways I needed? The Mexican public regarded typical lawyers as glorified thieves. What was Alberto Rivera U. like? Would he understand the North American mentality and my position?

We were prompt for our 8:30 appointment and entered the tall, gray corner building where we took an elevator to the second floor. Down the hall to the left we read in gold letters on a wide gray door, Lic. Alberto Rivera U. y Asociados, Bufete. I wondered why they didn't call a law firm or a lawyer's office an *oficina*, but lawyers used the word *bufete*.

Directly opposite the entranceway stood the secretary's desk, and on the wall behind her desk, rows of windows opened out to Insurgentes Avenue. The secretary, a young Mexican woman not much over five feet tall, rose to greet us as I stated my name. She asked us to sit down. Of course, it was like an American to arrive at the appointed time. But Mexicans, especially those with more money or influence, would not be expected to arrive for at least a half an hour after that.

The view from the couch revealed a tastefully decorated office with pleasant pictures on the walls, healthy plants, mint green walls, and strong dark wooden furniture. At 9:00 a man in his middle thirties walked briskly into the office and greeted the secretary. He was fair-skinned and had no moustache; I guessed he was American or European—too young to be a lawyer. I was alarmed. I needed an experienced pro to get this job done. But the next instant, intelligent-looking brown eyes looked into mine through large, black-framed glasses as he extended his hand. Lavina and I stood up.

"Señora Cruz, I'm happy you arrived safely. I'm Licenciado Alberto Rivera Ugalde, to serve you," he said in a warm, yet businesslike manner. As he ushered us into his office, I noticed the confidence of his stance, his perfectly tailored suit, the subdued, expensive whiter-than-white silk shirt, the classy masculine decor of his office. Expensive walnut trim and paneling lined the room's walls and blended with custom-made bookshelves. Law volumes and reference books, sculptures, mementoes, diplomas, and certificates—all were placed just right. The atmosphere in the room hinted to me that money was no object.

Mr. Rivera invited us to sit down on the burgundy sofa upholstered in leather and studded with brass brads. A matching wingback chair facing the sofa was positioned a few feet away in the middle of the room. To the left was a large desk. Obviously pleased, he flipped through my little bundle of affidavits, deeds, and certificates. He asked a few questions about my background, and for details about Marita's situation.

Incisively, he outlined: "There are three possible ways to get your daughter back: civilly, penally, and through immigration. I will study these papers you brought for a few days and look up laws related to your case. I have some friends in immigration I'll check with, too. I want you to know that there is hope. Antonio has done some pretty stupid things, and now that you are here in Mexico it will be harder for him to get away with it all. However, cases such as this one are difficult to resolve, and I must admit that I haven't handled one like this before. Please don't worry about that though. I will consult with my colleagues and I'll do everything possible to help you."

I wondered if he could do it all quickly enough that I could fly home in a week or so. "Could you give me an idea how long this all might take and how much it will cost?" I asked.

"If you would come in again Monday afternoon, I'll have the fees worked out by then. As far as the timing goes, there is nothing that can be done legally until June first or so because everyone is on spring vacation now. It will all take more time after that, of course," he replied.

Spring vacation! How could I have forgotten? Every year the students on all levels were free to roam about the country (or use the time to study) for two weeks until final exam time began in June. Government workers didn't have tests in June, but they had a long vacation every year in May, too.

My anxiety turned into anger and confusion. Why hadn't I realized this before we left Utah? Why was I told in the blessing that *now* was the right time to be here in Mexico?

Marita: Missing in Mexico

Mr. Rivera noted my disappointment and continued, "Actually, we will need these next two weeks to prepare these documents for use in court. I can't submit most of them the way they are now. The Mexican courts only accept documents originated here or those with a consul's seal on the page where the notary's seal is if they come from the United States. You will have to send most of these to the consul in Denver. I'll return them to you now so that you can mail them soon."

I stuffed them back into my purse.

He settled back into his chair and gave more instructions. "Actually, it will probably take more than two weeks for them just to get to Denver. Also, you'll need to arrange for some additional affidavits and their seals. One will state the exact address of your home in Orem. Have three neighbors sign it, saying that you, Marita, and Antonio had lived there for at least a year. Also, get a copy of your house contract."

I took notes and agreed to get the things he needed. The anger subsided when I realized that without these documents in order, I wasn't ready to go to court anyway. Lic. Rivera wasn't finished: "I also want the most recent photos you have of Marita so that it will be easier to prove she is really your daughter. Besides, I want to put Antonio under surveillance, and pictures of her will help the detectives to find and identify Marita."

He picked up Marita's Mexican passport. "I'm going to try to renew or revalidate this passport. It is important because Antonio did bring her into the country illegally without her documents. The law actually protects you as the mother because in Mexico all children up to the age of seven go with the mother. Also, in 1975, just last year, Mexico passed a law giving women equal rights as citizens. You are actually protected because he took Marita away without your knowledge, permission, or consent."

I felt a sudden surge of hope, though I knew that in reality, I would *not* receive equal treatment even though I was still married to a Mexican citizen. Before we left his office, Mr. Rivera suggested that we go to the American Embassy for help and additional advice. After an hour, my hope had not diminished. Mr. Rivera had obviously thought through my case in detail. He seemed not only competent but also interested and sympathetic. I wondered where he had learned to speak almost flawless English.

My taut nerves eased and I felt the anxiety of the past few days subside. The overall impression of meeting Mr. Rivera was one of comfort because something in his manner and deep voice seemed so familiar to me, as though I had met him before. Out of the hundreds of lawyers in Mexico who could have been recommended to me, I silently thanked the Lord for whatever influence it took to get this one.

Lavina and I walked the few blocks to the American Embassy after leaving the lawyer's. I had been there to register Marita as a dual citizen when she was eight months old. It took my pleading with Antonio the first eight months of her life before he finally gave me permission, and I had gone the next morning before he changed his mind. What if I had never made the effort to ensure that the U.S. government viewed Marita as an American citizen, too?

We passed the Marines stationed outside the tall, white stone building, picked up our passes to see the consul, and soon found ourselves upstairs taking a number to wait our turn. This time I was not a mother registering her baby, but a mother looking for her baby. Apparently the consul had seen far too many mothers of both kinds, and I was just one more problem for this busy, tired, wrinkled woman who didn't really help at all.

"You are wasting your time and money," she said, not ungently. "The American women usually give up and go back to the States without their babies. These things happen all the time, and our government can't do anything to help you. *Rarely* does the American woman win custody through the Mexican courts. We'll be happy to do whatever your lawyer thinks will help, but it's pretty hopeless for you. If you stay, you'll need lots of stamina because it will take a long time to get your daughter back. My only recommendation is for you to kidnap Marita back and hold her until the courts can settle the custody." She was the second to suggest that solution.

I learned that the embassy could not do much more than give legal advice or check on the health of American children held hostage. I basically would have to proceed according to Mexican law with no help from my own government.

She had never heard of my lawyer. When she took his card around to the other consuls, neither had they. Mr. Rivera had said there was hope. The consul said it was hopeless. I wanted to believe my lawyer.

With the most important matters for the day behind us, we became tourists for the rest of Lavina's stay in Mexico. On our way to the

Metro I stopped to have my scuffed-up brown shoes polished for three pesos. They looked brand new after a little Mexican magic. The friendly shoeshine man spoke English and directed us to the native handicraft market Ciudadela, a few blocks from the Balderas Metro stop. Lavina bought an embroidered dress and a blanket. Next, we walked through the artisan building by Bellas Artes and admired the handiwork.

About 5:00 P.M. I succeeded in reaching Elder Fyans, the area administrator of the Church in Mexico, on a pay phone by the Alameda Park. He gave me an appointment to see him in his office. Elder Fyans told me that nothing much had been done yet to help me. He had only told the brethren to try and work it out. I wondered what that meant.

As we rode the trolley down Tlalpan toward Marilyn's house, Lavina asked how it felt to be in Mexico City again. A little surprised, I realized that it felt as though I had never left.

Home to thirteen million people in 1976, Mexico City expanded daily with hundreds of new babies, rural immigrants, and others hoping to make a new life in a new place. Easily the largest city in Mexico, it would soon be the largest city in the world—if only because no one knew how to stop the urban sprawl that covered nearly four hundred square miles. A city built on the mud of Lake Texcoco thousands of years ago, the capital had expanded beyond the mountains that surround it on every side. The suburbs were full of commuters and factory workers beyond the official borders of the federal district [*distrito federal*, or *D.F.*] itself.

I loved Mexico City because contrasts were everywhere and instant adventure was daily fare. It was a challenge to adapt to so much available cultural, mental, and linguistic stimulation. I had never grown tired of this city, even though I disliked such elements as the thick smog created by the exhaust fumes of thousands of vehicles and the smokestacks of the prolific factories. The ring of mountains held the smog in, and it only disappeared during the few weeks of the spring rains.

But I was different than I had been in previous visits in one important way. I was tense—tense from the pain of an unremitting headache, braced against the fatigue that came more easily, wary of the lack of clarity in my own thinking, haunted by the dreams that troubled my sleep, on guard constantly against the possibility that Antonio would find out that I was in Mexico City.

Sunday, May 23, 1976

Lavina and I didn't go to church because too many people would know me. Instead, we enjoyed the morning performance of the Ballet Folklorico and I thought of Marita. How she loved to dance! Everywhere we went, I saw little girls playing and thought of Marita and wondered what she was doing. Lavina was going to leave the next day, but I felt steadied by her companionship. She bought some *cajeta* candy and several varieties of Mexican cheese to take home as souvenirs. On Friday we had mailed the money for the documents to Denver from the National Post Office, an ornate building that looked more like a renaissance theater than a post office.

After we left the post office, we walked over to the Congressional Library which was crammed into a remodeled church. I enjoyed checking out the libraries of every city I visited to see how they ran things. My visits to each Mexican library so far had truly amazed me, and this one topped them all. We were escorted through both floors of the library by a foolish old gentleman who couldn't see or remember very well. I knew enough about Mexican history and national heroes to know that most of what he told us on the tour was misinformation.

That didn't seem to bother him a bit. Before we left, he told us that there wasn't very much new information being printed anymore. All the books were about the same because the authors just copied each other. I asked, "Are you a writer?"

He laughed, "What for? I'd just copy the others!"

That man was the highlight of my day Friday. I bet he prayed every night to the patron saint of mediocrity and was outrageously blessed.

Monday, May 24, 1976

Lavina left at 6:00 A.M. I went to see my lawyer and helped Marilyn translate some Relief Society materials and tried to keep my mind off the fact that now I was really alone in Mexico. But at least Marilyn had become my friend and I still clung to the belief that it wouldn't be very long until I'd follow Lavina back to the states.

Marita: Missing in Mexico

Wednesday, May 26, 1976

Out of the darkness of early morning, a voice woke me from a deep sleep saying, *There will be a disaster.* The voice was calm, male, authoritarian, and very real. It did not occur to me to doubt it. I only wondered *what kind of disaster.* I dressed and left to meet Elder Fyans at his office/home in the Lomas Colony. Since he was a General Authority of the Church, he lived in one of the best areas of Mexico City.

Most Mexicans envied those who lived in Lomas, a suburb that belongs to the rich, the old families, and to the foreigners in charge of large companies. The Church's mission home and the residence of Mexico's President, "Los Pinos," were located there. I passed the more elaborate homes and yards as I rode the bus down Reforma to the street where Elder Fyans lived in a new condominium.

Tall and graying with calm eyes, Elder Fyans was direct. "It looks as though you have done all you could so far. I feel that going through your lawyer and a civil court is your best course of action now. Remember, the law is on your side as a mother. You should be able to get her back all right."

Our visit was brief, and I left feeling comforted yet frustrated. I could see I wouldn't get much help from that quarter. I caught a bus back to the Zona Rosa. After window shopping aimlessly, I stopped at my favorite flower shop. I ate tacos for lunch and sat in a hotel lobby to write letters while I killed time before my appointment with Mr. Rivera.

I was too tired to walk to the lawyer's office from there, so I took a bus those few blocks. As I sat down in the middle of the bus and opened my purse to put away my change from the fare, I was shocked to discover that my coin purse and travelers' checks were missing! I asked the man behind me if he had seen anyone who could have taken my money.

He pointed to two young men that had just stepped off the bus. I sprang to my feet and grabbed the cord to ring the buzzer. The bus driver glanced at me, glanced away, and drove on. Fortunately, the next stop was only a block away, and the thieves were standing on the other side of Insurgentes. I jumped off the bus. As I waited for a chance to cross over several lanes of traffic, one turned and saw me. They began running down a side street.

Fueled by the energy of anger, I began running after them but soon lost sight of them. I looked around for several blocks and asked others if they had seen the men, but I had no luck. I searched the area for my driver's license, my BYU I.D. card, and other important papers and tickets in case they had just taken the money and discarded the rest. Again, no luck.

Completely disheartened, I began walking south again. I didn't have enough change for a bus ticket—less than a peso. I didn't cry, but I wanted to. I had always been careful, so why had I been so foolish to have carried *all* of my money with me this time? And I had no more identification with me after that, either.

As I described the robbery to Lic. Rivera, his eyes widened and he swore. Why had I tried to follow them? he demanded. I could have been hurt. He lent me fifty pesos and called the First National City Bank to tell them that all my traveler's checks were stolen. They said I could be reimbursed the next day. We both agreed it would be useless to go to the police.

At least he had some good news for me. Some detectives were investigating Antonio in Puebla. I signed some documents for court when it opened on Monday.

I realized that there are things more precious to lose than my money. I had already "lost" Marita for six months. I still had my life and senses. I wondered if the stolen money was the disaster that I was warned of. Or was there something worse still to come?

Chapter Nine

Friday, May 28, 1976
Colonia Xotepingo

I COULDN'T FIND MY TOURIST VISA ANYWHERE. Had it been stolen too? Was it with the papers I had given Mr. Rivera the first day? I hoped so. I wouldn't be able to leave the country without it. Always before I had carried a Xerox copy of my visa with me to avoid losing the valuable document itself. Why hadn't I made a copy this time?

During my appointment with Mr. Rivera he told me, "I don't have your visa." I felt desperate. Only the thieves knew where it was. I lamented, "What can I do about it now?"

He reminded me, "You know how *gobernación* is. You will just have to get an exit permission to leave the country, and that won't be easy." He smiled grimly.

The word *gobernación* sent extra adrenalin through me, and I dreaded going there again. It was the last place in Mexico City I wanted to meddle with, and now I was forced to return to the large gray stone building by the Alameda Park with the innocent title "Secretary of Tourism." That referred to the maps, handicraft displays, and tourist information housed on the bottom floor. Most tourists probably never knew that most of the building was something like the U.S. National Archives and immigration offices combined. Files for each foreigner needing more than a tourist permit shuffled through piles on desks on the second and third floors, always taking longer than expected to be processed.

I had been there to register myself each time I had moved, and I had experienced disgust as I tried to wrest my immigration papers and other permissions from the worst bureaucratic bottlenecks, hassles, and legal entrapments I had ever encountered. *Gobernación* held utmost power over my life once more, and I knew I wouldn't be leaving Mexico very soon at all.

Mr. Rivera sympathetically told me the rest of the bad news: his fees would be approximately $2,000. Not pesos, dollars! In 1976 that was a considerable amount. It was the right opening for the reason I had asked to talk to Mr. Rivera. I humbly approached the subject:

"I know that here in Mexico paying bribes, stretching the truth, telling lies, and falsifying documents is all a part of everyday work for lawyers. It may not be legal or acceptable, but I know that if bribes aren't paid in many places, the work won't get done. In my particular case, I must ask you to avoid doing these things. Everything must be done aboveboard and right. If I do not use honorable means to get Marita, then how can I expect success? We will not stoop to lies or deceit to get what we need. I know I will get Marita back, someday, some way. But we must do things right."

Mr. Rivera seemed dubious but agreed.

I left the *bufete* and went to the bank to get the refund on my lost travelers' checks. It was important to me to be able to pay Marilyn for the food I had eaten during the last week; but when I put a 100 peso bill in her hand, she gave it back to me, explaining, "I can't take your money. You need it. But I know that there should be some exchange of services while you stay here. Would you be willing to tutor my children half an hour every day in Spanish until their annual tests are over?"

For the first time that day, I smiled. "Of course I'd like to do that!"

Pleased, Marilyn added, "Then, you can tutor them in English after they pass their Spanish tests."

What a relief to know I could stay as long as I needed to without feeling that I was imposing.

Monday, May 30, 1976

Going to *gobernación* took me four hours—a trip that normally takes less than two hours round trip. I was feeling ill and tired. But I had to go in person to fill out the forms to report how I lost my tourist visa. I discussed the form with an official just back from vacation who seemed interested in helping me. He assured me that I could pick up the exit paper that same week on Thursday at 10:00.

I rested at Marilyn's after that, and then I began a letter in my journal for Marita to read later:

My Dearest Marita,

I pray often that the angels of the Lord tell you that I am near you, yearning to come to you. Do you feel that? Perhaps this separation will help me understand on a deeper level what it means to be a mother. I am the first and most important teacher you will ever have, but how can I teach you with the gulf of miles between us? The home is the greatest school of all but neither one of us has a home together now. What are you learning in the Cruz school? I pray daily for your well-being and protection.

Especially this week I have prayed that the powers of darkness will not succeed in separating us again. There are too many ways to lose a child besides kidnapping. How many hearts have been eternally broken because of poor communication, drugs, alcohol, sin, or deception and poor choices?

How many children have been separated from their parents for months and years, yet they live in the same house? How many people will never learn how to go Home again?

Good night, my daughter. May the angels stay near about us until the day we walk together and go home again.

With a greater love than before, I close with a greater desire to use righteousness and truth as tools to regain you.

Thursday, June 3, 1976

Typical? Yes! Aggravating? Absolutely! My frustration at *gobernación* should have been expected, but I had hoped for "normal" according to U.S. standards and hadn't counted on all the shouting I'd have to do. I arrived at 10:00 to pick up my tourist card as directed. After waiting in lines and reception areas for more than an hour, a woman told me I couldn't get a new tourist card until they had checked with the airport in Hermosillo to make sure I had really entered the country when I said I had.

I glanced down in disgust at the stack of file folders and papers on the desk in front of me and saw a paper sticking out of a folder with Antonio's name on it! They had my *expediente*, a manila folder with a record of all their dealings with me since 1969—permissions, visa renewals, changes of address, and documentation concerning the legality of my status in the country. I panicked. That file represented my life, and it controlled my life in Mexico.

"Señora," I said urgently, "this is my file. Here's my husband's name. I don't want him to know I am here. He took my little girl, and I followed him from the United States so I can get her back. I came as a tourist because I don't plan to be here long. The tourist visa was stolen. I'm sick. I should be in bed. I can't keep coming here for you to tell me to come back in a few days. Tell me absolutely when you will have my exit papers ready." My voice steadily rose until I was almost shrieking.

The woman shrugged and turned away. I scowled at the great hall filled with desks crowded together and semiprivate compartments. I moved on to other officials, my rage undiminished. I tried to kick up some action until finally someone assured me that my visa would be ready Monday at noon.

I was too ill to protest further. My head was spinning and I barely made my way through the stone corridors and down the wide stone steps without collapsing.

Gobernación stands on a busy street corner across the street from the central park, the Alameda. Winding paths lead past fountains, statues, park benches, and food or balloon vendors. Hedges and trees provide an oasis of green in the city, and the peaceful atmosphere of the park promotes strolling and relaxing. With my head throbbing and my legs shaking, I wavered to a park bench and sat for a long time before I could make my way to the metro.

One good effect of the battle was that I no longer felt worried that Antonio would know I was in Mexico. The battle with *gobernación* was, ironically, the last homecoming ritual. Now I felt really at home in Mexico again. Somewhat recovered from my rest and new perspective, I stood up and found I enjoyed freely doing the other things I needed or wanted to do that day. Some of the fear I had brought from Utah was gone, and I felt more in charge.

Marita: Missing in Mexico

Monday, June 7, 1976

I woke up with diarrhea and went downstairs to take some medicine. A sudden wave of vertigo made me grab the sink to keep from falling down. *I must be sicker than I thought!*

Then the realization hit me: earthquake! Everything was shaking. I ran into the street. The telephone poles were swaying, the wires tightening and loosening like maypoles dancing. The quake lasted for more than two minutes, and the newspaper reported it registered six on the Richter scale.

In spite of the quake and my illness, I left for my appointments. First, I picked up the fee schedule from the lawyer's office. The huge total disheartened me—$2,200. The fee breakdown included costs for appearing before the familial court in Mexico City and the civil court in Puebla, for documents, for locating Marita and Antonio, and for travel expenses for two people.

"What two people?" I asked Gloria, the secretary.

She replied, "Licenciado Flores works with Lic. Rivera."

So, he was Rivera's partner, but why did he have to go to Puebla? And where were they going to eat to run up a bill like that? Of course, some of that fee was padding for bribes the lawyers were paying regardless of what I had said. They knew what I had yet to admit—in Mexico absolutely nothing happens without bribes. But it seemed like all the money in the world. I had existed on so little money for so long that the fees upset me. I tried to calm down before I left the lawyer's office, remembering costs are relative things. Marilyn said it would cost $1,000 just to get her house painted, and it cost that much to have a baby in a hospital in the USA.

Next, I dragged myself down Reforma and to the desk in *gobernación* for my promised tourist permit. The secretary saw me, whispered to the man at the next desk, and sent me over to talk to him. With a look of great authority he haughtily informed me, "You'll have to come back tomorrow. We still don't have any news from Hermosillo that you actually entered there."

The next blow of the day came when I arrived at Marilyn's and heard her news: her mother was coming to stay with them for three weeks. I would need to vacate the guest room. Marilyn had arranged for me to house-sit for the Johnson family while they went on vacation. She helped me pack, and we attended the women's Relief Society meeting in her ward.

For years I had heard monthly cultural refinement lessons featuring a different country each month, but until that night I had never heard one on the USA. Besides hearing interesting facts about New York City, I saw stacks of postcards of Chicago, Los Angeles, Miami, and San Antonio—the main cities besides Salt Lake that most Latins had heard about.

When I told them where I was from hardly anyone knew what Montana was or whether it was a country, state, or city. By the end of the lesson, the discussion centered on lifestyle, and just as the Utah women wondered in these lessons what it must be like for a Samoan woman to live without a refrigerator, the women in Mexico asked the teacher if most of the women in the USA really had dishwashers in their homes and if dishwashers really got the dishes clean.

I could tell from the discussion that most of them felt it wasn't fair that North American women don't have to spend as much time in the kitchen as Mexican women do, even though Mexican women often have maids to help them out. I agreed silently. It wasn't fair. And my counterparts at home didn't have to deal with *gobernación* either.

I had been in Mexico for only three weeks, but it already seemed that the USA was only a faraway place featured in the pages of a book.

Wednesday, June 9, 1976
Monte Athos in Las Lomas

The Johnsons lived in the posh colony of Las Lomas. From my perspective, its chief advantage was that it was easier to get to *gobernación*. Taking just one bus down Reforma, I showed up at noon and was told to come back at 2:00. I sat there, waiting, instead. The officials noticed and sent me to another office on the other side of the building where I continued to wait in a room with other foreigners.

A woman from Argentina who sat next to me told me of a Canadian woman whose husband had taken her child. She lost the case in court and pretended to make up with her husband. About six months later, while he was at work, she took the child, bribed her way out of Mexico, and went back to Canada.

Here was another reminder of what I'd heard continually since I'd arrived: the foreign woman rarely gets the child back from the Mexican husband through legal means alone. When I considered what some women had done to get their children back, I just hoped that I wouldn't be required to do as that Canadian woman. I didn't think I could do that.

One by one, each foreigner's name was called. At 3:00, I sat alone in the circle of chairs. It was closing time, but at last I heard, "Bailey Hansen de Cruz." I stood up and went for my paper. It was good for only thirty days! I knew by then that would not be long enough. My stay in Mexico would not be short.

Chapter Ten

Thursday, June 10, 1976 — Journal entry
Lomas de Chapultepec

    It's my birthday today, and there's no one to celebrate with except the maid. I'm twenty-nine years old. I called my folks at 6:30 A.M. to report the lawyer's fee. My mother is very concerned, but my father is inclined to have faith in the lawyer and pay the thousand-dollar retainer. They warned me that I cannot count on an unlimited bank account. I know.

    Then my mother gave me a disturbing message. Antonio called Mom and told her to tell me that he still loved me, to not cancel our temple sealing for another two years, that maybe we could live together again. I'm flabbergasted! What can he be thinking? That I'm missing him? That I'll pay the bills in Utah and keep things together while he does who-knows-what? And what will change during two more years? I feel nothing for Antonio, unless it is pity. My mother sounded worried. After my anger subsided, I began worrying, too.

    Living with Antonio again is the most horrible thing I can think of. Could I do it—even for Marita? Could this be part of the refiner's fire and testing ahead—to see if I will do it, for her? My worry quieted when I remembered my April 6th blessing that told me I will pass the tests. And I remembered the scripture, "After much tribulation come the blessings." I spent several hours today pondering what I knew about trials and the refiner's fire.

Several points stand out to comfort me. A righteous person cannot assume that just because she is living diligently she will not be tried or persecuted. To the contrary. More tribulations come to forge godly qualities within the person. The promise is that she will be blessed even though the blessing may be strength and patience to endure the suffering. The righteous who suffer have the assurance that they will not suffer in vain but will see their sufferings turn to work toward their eternal good. The tribulation could be seen as a gift and as a time of opportunity.

Today I realized more forcibly that my time in Mexico would be filled with suffering, tests of faith, and enduring until I learn what I have to learn, do what is required, and pay the price to have Marita with me again. Peace comes with the idea that the strength must already be there somewhere in my soul to do these things required of me, or else I will gain the strength in time.

That peace is turning into quiet determination. I *will* meet the tests. And a year from now, I *will* be free with Marita in the United States to celebrate my birthday. I won't worry about having to live with Antonio or being married to him.

Saturday, June, 12, 1976

All night I had nightmares again of going to Puebla, begging and begging for Marita, and getting refusals. The family wouldn't let me have her. In each dream, I would stop begging and promise I'd come back for her. How I prayed that these dreams were only products of my worries, not any indication of what would happen.

Tuesday, June, 15, 1976

During my time at Lomas I had little to do but wait. I finished writing my life story up-to-date. The last section told the truth—that my life hadn't gone as I had hoped. I wanted to put it all behind me—the bad years and feelings connected to Antonio—so I started on the forgiveness process. At church they always told us to forgive others but never went into much detail as to "how" to do it. The only specific help I'd received was in President Spencer W. Kimball's *The Miracle of Forgiveness*. I had some time on my hands to do some soul work, and I began trying to forgive Antonio.

I also read good books from the Johnsons' library, and I made some "chin-up" collections of good quotes for Marilyn to read when she felt depressed. Three of the quotes I illustrated for her pages also appealed to me in my situation: Henry Van Dyke wrote, "The best rose bush after all, is not that which has the fewest thorns, but that which bears the finest roses." Some anonymous person said, "There will be no crown bearers in heaven who are not cross bearers on earth." The Prophet Joseph Smith wrote, "If there is no conflict, I cannot gain a victory; If there is no victory, I cannot gain a crown of reward."

When I talked to Marilyn on the phone, her news altered my plans. I had planned to stay at her house when the Johnsons returned on the 26th, but now Marilyn's family was leaving for the United States, and I would have to find somewhere else to go.

Thursday, June 17, 1976

Mexicans have a lot of holidays, maybe because most people have to work six days a week and only have Sundays off. With a variety of commemorative holidays sprinkled into each month, they get a break. It was the day of the "Manuels," symbolized by brightly decorated miniature stick and straw mules sold in the streets as a reminder of the All Fools' Day. I had heard of practical jokes played on June 17, but with the bad news I heard from Mr. Rivera, I wished he were joking.

He wasn't. President Echeverria had tightened down on easy Mexican divorces. For me to do anything in the courts, I was now required to be an immigrant.

I signed a power of attorney to start a change of status from tourist to immigrant. It would have helped if I had my FM booklet [*Forma Migratoria*] showing my past immigrant status in Mexico, but I hadn't been able to find it or my American passport. I still wondered if Antonio had them. Mr. Rivera said it would be quite difficult to get a

Marita: Missing in Mexico

new FM form because it is against the law to lose them. At least I still had my *expidiente* number, and they could use it to find my file at *gobernacion* to create a new FM form.

He also told me about the six-month waiting period they observe in Mexico concerning separations. Apparently, after six months, Antonio could serve me with papers if he could find me. Antonio could also claim I had committed some crime since Mexican law is based on the Napoleonic Code, "Guilty until proven innocent." But if I didn't do anything at all during a certain amount of time, then divorce became automatic.

And last of all, I learned that Lic. Rivera's private investigators had entered the Cruz home posing as officials from Infonavit, a government housing authority. Although they asked questions as though they were collecting data about the people living in the home, no one mentioned Marita or Antonio. They did not see her. If they weren't in Puebla, where were they?

Monday, June 21, 1976
Colonia Xotepingo

I had spent the weekend house-sitting for Marilyn and quilting while I kept an eye on the maid. When Marilyn returned from Vera Cruz, her friend Marta came to visit her. We all sat around the quilt working while the two women talked and I listened. Marilyn had told me a few weeks earlier that Marta had recognized me. Her husband had worked with Antonio once, so during a lull in the conversation, I asked her, "Have you told anyone I am here in Mexico? I have good reasons for keeping my presence here a secret."

"No, I haven't," the plump woman assured me as she looked up from her needle. "Marilyn told me about your problems. I'm sorry it all has happened like that. I wish I could help you."

I ventured another question, "Well, there's something I've wanted to know for a long time. I was told a few months ago that Antonio was living at his sister's house. I know that you used to live in her ward before she moved. Do you know where she lives now?"

Her eyes rolled to the right as she tried to recall. "I saw her two little boys at church the last two Sundays, but I didn't see her. I'll try to find out more for you."

I thanked her and we continued quilting. The conversation drifted on to other topics until she started talking about a relative of the Cruz family who lived only two blocks away from the Morenos. Because she was a good friend of theirs, she jumped up and left immediately to go find out what she could about Antonio.

About forty-five minutes later Marta returned with a contented smile. "You'll never believe this," she chirped. "The *concunyo* says that she only knew that Antonio had been divorced in the States, had brought Marita back with him, and was working in Mexico City."

"*¡Que Mentiroso!*" I exploded. What a liar! Is that what people here thought? That I divorced him and so nicely allowed him to return with his daughter to raise alone?

Wednesday, June 23, 1976
Monte Athos, Lomas de Chapultepec

Mexico no longer fascinated me. Finally, I could remain calm and patient no longer. I woke up shaking with anxiety. I couldn't concentrate on anything except my worries. Where was Marita? How would I get her back? When? Where would I go to live in two days? Would my money hold out? What trials were coming to test me? With these thoughts, I was driven by insufferable tension all day as I fretted, paced the floor, and called Marilyn on the phone.

She was kind enough to listen to me. On the fifth phone call, I told her that the pieces of news and the actions to get Marita seemed to come only a drop at a time. I wanted a bucket to come pouring down and drench me—soon!

Finally, that night, Mr. Rivera called. He had gone to Puebla the day before with the detectives. Excitedly, he declared, "I saw Marita!"

"Where?"

"Outside on a tricycle. Antonio and his mother had gone out with her to take the trash out to the garbage truck."

"How do you know it was really her and not one of the cousins?" I asked cautiously. She looked so much like them.

With assurance, Mr. Rivera answered, "Señora, the pictures of Marita and the documents arrived from Denver just before we left for Puebla. We took the pictures with us. There is no doubt that Marita is in Puebla. And no doubt that we saw Antonio. He was out in the street wearing a

T-shirt and has put on quite a bit of weight since those pictures were taken."

I drew a long, shaky breath. "Thank you! Thank you for going. Thank you for calling! This means we can proceed in court now, doesn't it?"

"Yes, of course," he went on. "I plan to go personally with the messenger who takes the papers to the judge in Puebla, pay him a bribe, and make sure the papers are handled quickly. If I don't, it would take more than a month to get things going there. And now we have these new affidavits, we can proceed in the Mexico City courts, too." I didn't even bother to reply about the bribe. I was learning it was no use.

I wasn't sure what he planned to do in the courts, but it had something to do with proving my innocence and showing my worthiness to have Marita's custody and asking for it. I had already waited for her longer than I thought I could stand, but I asked anyway, dreading the answer, "Do you have any idea how much longer this is going to take?"

"We don't know what Antonio has been doing or what we'll find when we go to court, but I would say you will probably be here for another month. The judge may only give you custody if you agree to live in Mexico with Marita. But you could agree to that, then leave later," he explained.

After the phone call, the turmoil ebbed, and I relaxed the most I had since I arrived in Mexico a month before. In less than two weeks, the six months waiting period required for a Mexican legal separation would be over. Pressure had mounted in me from the fear that Antonio would find me before I had found him. My stomach had actually hurt from fear, but at least once I knew where Marita was, I no longer felt like a prisoner.

Chapter Eleven

Sunday, July 4, 1976 — Journal entry
Virrey Antonio de Mendoza
Lomas de Chapultepec, Mexico 10, D.F.

It was six months ago TODAY that Antonio left me! Today is the USA's two hundredth Birthday and Bicentennial Celebration! Marita and I have been separated six months!

It must be significant that I am here in Mexico. From within a foreign country, I probably have a deeper love and appreciation for my country than many citizens who are up there celebrating right now. The life I have known in the USA is still by far more blessed than life in Mexico. Yet, I feel at home in Mexico.

Today I went to church in the English-speaking ward where there was a continuation of the quiet celebrating we did as a ward at a hacienda yesterday. In our Sunday School class we talked about faith, and we were reminded of the Prophet Moroni's words: that the witness, the knowledge, the signs, and the miracles come *after* the trials of one's faith.

The last person to speak to the congregation today was Elder Thomas Fyans, who is also a member of this ward. He bore his testimony of the reality of Jesus Christ and that he lives. Elder Fyans often sat in the Church's leading councils with apostles, so his witness was especially heart-felt. Then he declared, "I bless you that the desires of your hearts will be given unto you. Peace be in your hearts." His words touched me personally, and I felt he was especially blessing me. The congregation sang "My Country, 'Tis of Thee" for the closing song, but I couldn't sing through my tears because each phrase of the song meant more than usual when I was so far from my country.

I'm house-sitting for a family vacationing in the States. Their lovely home is only a few blocks from the Johnsons', so it was an easy move. And my days go about the same here. Although it has been frustrating to spend my time resting and reading good books because I have no deadlines and nothing required of me, I have noticed that I am healing. The paralysis of despair I used to feel at the thought of Antonio is being erased by hope.

More of my old self, the true me, is slowly but joyfully emerging. I am feeling freer, surer of myself, happier, less afraid, and more thrilled to be alive in this world. Our wedding anniversary was this week—the best one yet—because I haven't seen my husband for six months!

Monday, July 5, 1976
Virrey Antonio de Mendoza, Lomas

As I awoke slowly, I was aware of a new feeling of peace in my life. I had been in Mexico six weeks, and no one from the States had written to me. Sometimes I felt alone and forgotten as the days stretched into the unknown. Nevertheless, I had not often succumbed to depression or discouragement. I was trying to make something happen. I knew my parents wanted to do all they could, but there was nothing they could do but wait, worry, pray, and pay the bills. I'd been telling them for a month that I should be seeing the judge soon. And Antonio hadn't been served papers yet, either. Why did everything go so slowly?

The only explanation was BIG FIVE, of course. That's what Marilyn said once when I complained to her about the lack of significant action. She exclaimed, "Welcome to Mexico! It's just BIG FIVE!"

"BIG FIVE?" I had never heard that expression before, and I had only been gone from Mexico for two years. "What does that mean?"

"Oh, it's what the missionaries say when something screwy happens that doesn't make any sense and could never happen again if you wanted it to. Hold out your hand and I'll show you what it means."

I held out my hand, and her index finger touched the tips of each of my fingers. As she touched each finger, she said a word: "You Are In Mexico Now!" Five fingers, five words. She continued, "It means that there is no explanation anyone could understand other than *you are in Mexico*, and here you have to stop thinking things will happen predictably or by the book or by a certain time. We usually say 'BIG FIVE' when things are beyond our control and we just have to let things run their course."

"You're right," I added, glad to learn an expression that gave a name to that common experience.

"And getting angry or impatient or frustrated won't do you any good in a BIG FIVE situation. So . . . welcome to Mexico!" She concluded as if there were no more to say and I would just have to adjust a little bit more to Mexico's version of Murphy's Law.

By July, I could see that lots of things weren't going as I had hoped. My permission to stay in Mexico would expire in three days, and after that I wouldn't be there legally even though they were processing new documents in *gobernación*. I didn't want to make a trip to the border to renew my tourist permit. And how could I? I only had six dollars.

Thursday, July 8, 1976 — Journal entry
Lomas de Chapultepec

> I don't spend all my time underlining scriptures or reading. Sometimes I go up and sit on the roof and watch the clouds or the maids across the street swishing water down the driveway with their brooms. This posh colony is like a never-never land of exquisitely manicured yards and hedges, elegant homes, quiet streets, and classy cars and residents. The maid here fixes the meals and cleans the house. It seems unreal to me to be in this cocoon day after day, living without strain or work or worry. Everything is lovely, and I know this hedge time is provided to

help me unwind and rebuild my inner strength before the harder trials come.

A phone call set today apart from all the others. My friend Linda called from Utah! She was worried about me. I assured her that I am OK, but sometimes I get anxious about everything taking so long to happen. I still haven't seen the judge and I need my visa.

I asked her if she ever found my passport at her house. She still has not seen it and thinks Antonio must have it. Then she told me that people in my Orem ward would like to write to me but nobody knows where to send things since I move so much.

I hadn't thought about that. My lawyer gets upset when I move so much too. It isn't good for my file at *gobernación* when I keep reporting a change of address every three weeks. And I'll have to move again because the husband will return by the end of the month while his family continues their vacation in the States. So I told Linda to tell people to send mail to my lawyer's address as long as I'm in Mexico.

Tuesday, July 13, 1976 — Journal entry

Mexicans consider all Tuesdays the thirteenth to be unlucky instead of Friday the thirteenth. But today was a good day for me. Mr. Rivera called to say that my name and the time I can appear before the judge would be in the following day's judicial newspaper. Most judges hear forty to fifty cases a day, but my judge was scheduled to hear sixty-nine cases on the day my case was scheduled.

Wednesday, July 14, 1976

Mr. Rivera showed me a few documents during our appointment. "These papers will be ready soon to serve on Antonio. Once we have decided on a course of action, you must trust me, support me, and cooperate with me one hundred percent."

"What do you have in mind?" I asked.

Mr. Rivera settled back into his leather chair and enumerated the steps of how he envisioned we could get Marita. "We will go to Puebla next week. Decide what you can say and do to persuade Antonio to let you be with Marita a little while."

I agreed to think of something. Mr. Rivera continued, "I strongly advocate your kidnapping Marita back and going to the States as quickly as possible *before* we serve papers on Antonio. That way, he can't hide her again during the proceedings and drag things on for months and months." He paused.

Others had suggested this solution, but I had always pushed it aside. Now, I had to face it. "After I get her out of the Cruz house, then what?"

"Then I will make sure that you get on the plane and out of the country safely. When she is safe in the USA, then I will continue the case here. With her out of the country, there isn't much your husband can do to drag out the case, and you will have custody," he explained.

"And what if I am caught before we get out of Mexico? Could I be put in prison or something?"

"Don't worry," he assured me. "There is no problem because Marita is your own daughter and nobody has legal custody yet. She has just as much right to be with you as she does to be with Antonio."

Well, that made sense. And since I agreed to consider his advice, I spent the rest of the day trying to figure out how I could convince Antonio to let her be alone with me for a while. When I called my folks about the plan, my mother immediately got upset, wondering if I could be put in jail if I were caught. They called President Martinez in Salt Lake and asked him what he thought of the plan. He agreed with the lawyer. On the next call my parents said they would send more money for plane tickets. Imagine! But first I would have to find the magic key to persuade Antonio. What would it take?

Thursday, July 15, 1976

I went back to the consul again. This time, I saw a younger, sassier woman. After hearing my story, she told me to get three passport pictures of Marita ready. They would add one of her pictures to my passport. She also gave me an emphatic piece of advice as she waved her hands in the air and ordered, "If you get your hot little hands on her, honey, you get out of the country as fast as you can!"

Marita: Missing in Mexico

Saturday, July 17, 1976

All the time I stood at the bus stop, swayed on the bus, and walked to the lawyer's office, I reviewed my suggestions for persuading Antonio. My tools would be humility, kindness, and understanding. I would take two roses to remind him of his vision and of his vow to make up for the mistakes, to help me find happiness, to help our family progress, and to give love. Perhaps with the power of the roses, the force of the vision would touch Antonio's soul again.

Since it was a Saturday, Mr. Rivera was informal. I met his associate, Mr. Flores, a short, wiry man, bristling with energy. He seemed like a friendly puppy, eager to get started. I felt good about working with him.

First I told them my plan to approach Antonio. Mr. Rivera seemed pleased and added, "If you can talk to him in a friendly atmosphere where he won't get upset and defensive, then he may not suspect you have lawyers and documents backing you up."

Mr. Flores suggested, "We know it is more dangerous for you to show up in Puebla to see Marita on a friendly visit, but we must try it this way first. If you can manage it, you should try to take Marita out for an ice cream cone or something. If someone else wants to go with you, fine, but just act natural. Then get permission to take her to your hotel to sleep overnight with you." He made it sound so easy.

I protested, "What if I can't persuade him? I don't think he will let me take her overnight. I really don't know how much he has changed these past six months since I last talked to him or if he'll even be there the day we go to Puebla."

The wrinkle between my eyebrows furrowed deeper as the worry crept in and I feared I would fail in carrying out my part of the plan. I had the hard job; all they had to do was pick us up, get us out of the country, and serve papers on Antonio later.

Mr. Rivera understood my unspoken fear. He responded to my hesitation and answered, "It's true—it will be difficult to persuade him because he is feeling safe now. He's had six months to rationalize everything to the point that he has everyone else convinced that you are the one to blame. He won't want to let Marita go. Nor will his family. And we can't forget we are dealing with his machismo. Yes, it will be difficult, but ninety-nine percent of our success depends on this first visit."

Mr. Flores put in, "Señora, we realize it will be a sacrifice for you to do this, but remember, Marita's value is very great. You will have to fight for your daughter and perhaps lie a little, but it will be worth it when you have her with you again."

Sacrifice? Lie? What was he talking about?

He continued, "Antonio will probably say that you can go places with Marita if you promise not to leave Mexico with her or if you agree to live with him again. It would make things easier if you agreed with him. You could leave with her later one day when he didn't suspect it."

The exact scenario the Canadian woman had followed! Did Mr. Flores counsel her too, or was this standard operating procedure for retrieving babies from Mexico? My stomach turned at the thought of living with Antonio again or even lying to him.

I pled with my eyes and my voice, "Please don't ask me to lie! I won't lie! I can't. If I lie, others can see it in my face and hear it in my voice. I just cannot plan to tell a lie and get away with it." Both lawyers looked at each other and back to me. Mr. Flores sighed. It was not going to be easy.

Mr. Rivera reminded me that the *exhorto* would be ready to serve on Antonio on Tuesday; even temporary custody wouldn't be granted until the court appearance nine days later. They wanted me to go to Puebla the next weekend between business hours when no one would be at court to take any action. My tension increased as the importance of my first visit became more apparent.

Mr. Rivera explained soberly, "There are no guarantees that we can get physical possession of Marita even if we have a stack of court papers giving you custody."

I stared at him bleakly, "Why not? If the court says so . . ."

"The papers won't matter if Antonio hides her. There is nothing we can do to stop him if he leaves with her as he did in Utah. He can also drag things out in court, and we can respond, but I hope things work out on your first visit."

Before I left the office, they showed me the judicial newspaper listings. I saw my name there, misspelled as usual. However, this was evidence that some decisions had been made to move our case along in court in Mexico City. As I rode the bus down Reforma, I realized that more tests were beginning. Everything would be easier if I lied. But I had to think of another way.

Chapter Twelve

Later on Saturday, July 17, 1976

MY STOMACH STARTED TO ACHE BADLY, then my head. I kept swallowing past a knot in my throat. My hands trembled. To fight my case of nerves, I began to read books borrowed from Brother Schofield in the English-speaking ward. A few of Eric Hoffer's aphorisms spoke directly to me:

- The wisdom of others remains dull til it is writ over with our own blood. We are essentially apart from the world; it bursts into our consciousness only when it sinks its teeth and nails into us.
- One of the best reasons for guarding ourselves against doing harm to anyone is to preserve our capacity for compassion. For we cannot pity those we have wronged. (Will Antonio have compassion for me?)
- It is waiting that gives weight to time.

The phone rang while I was still reading. It was Brother Schofield, a Harvard-trained lawyer who worked with the diplomatic corps at the U.S. Embassy in Mexico City. Although he had called about his books, I found my fears spilling out as I talked with him.

He sighed, "Sister Cruz, I think it will be impossible for you to convince Antonio if you couldn't do it last January with the bishop and your friends there to help you. He has his family all around him now. They are probably expecting you to show up sometime, and you'll have to find a different way than you tried before to convince him to let Marita go."

"I don't know what else to try," I admitted.

"What about Elder Fyans?" Brother Schofield suggested. "Perhaps he could go with you to Puebla since no one else in the Church here wants to get involved. If he doesn't succeed, then you could send your lawyers in immediately to serve Antonio with papers before he can disappear again."

It took several hours to reach Elder Fyans. "I'm going to Puebla tomorrow to dedicate a chapel there. I could go with you to the Cruz home then," he reported.

It was good news and bad at the same time. I had an awful feeling it might not be the best day to go, but I was pleased he wanted to help me. "I'm afraid to go there without the legal papers," I pointed out. "They won't be ready for a few days still. What if we don't convince Antonio? Then he could just disappear."

Elder Fyans understood. "My weeks are very full, but call me when you get your papers in order. I will try to arrange my schedule so I can go to Puebla with you."

I thanked him and called my parents to report that the check had arrived the day before, just in time before I moved back to Marilyn's. The idea of receiving help from Elder Fyans calmed my parents' jitters and my own.

Monday, July 19, 1976

When Marilyn returned from the market this morning, she backed the station wagon up to the gate and yelled for us to come help her. The back part was heaped with piles of green and golden ripe pineapples—fifty of them! I guess she couldn't help herself at a bargain twenty-seven cents each.

Soon Marilyn began a Mexican version of canning day with the help of Marta, the maid, and me. We manned our stations and passed the fruit along to the next person. I was a hacker, whacking away at the scaly sides until the sticky-sweet yellow fruit lay bare in my hands. The knife was stuck—welded to my hand soon after I began chopping pineapple into chunks that would fit a canning jar. By the time the jars were filled, my feet were glued to the pool of juice on the floor. After the canning, we made fruit leather with the leftover ripe fruit until all the screens out on the patio were filled with fruit and the last pineapple was chopped to pieces.

It felt wonderful—working at something physical, producing visible results, and especially working with Marilyn. We had a great deal in common and our instant friendship had only deepened over the weeks. She was a buoyant, tough, spontaneous, and capable woman. I loved her unconventional nature and views on life.

Marta went home to clean up, and Marilyn sat across the table from me while we rested. We began talking about the things that matter to both of us. She was feeling great because after years of learning skills in Salt Lake, she was able to share those talents with the sisters here in Mexico. Many learned how to can, sew, and dry foods in her classes. They loved her and accepted her. I understood that because my students loved me for teaching them English.

But there was another reason why we found living in Mexico so fulfilling. It was more than just the opportunities available to grow culturally, spiritually, or professionally. It was more than the international flavor, the subway, the climate, or the variety of people we found there. All these elements enhanced that "Mexico feeling" I got when I was there—that I missed when I was in the States. I loved the adventure of Mexico. But more than anything, I loved the beauty of Mexico, its stimulation to help me generate ideas, feel deeply, and learn new things.

I explained to Marilyn that my constant image of "walking on a Trail of Beauty" had been there for seven years ever since I read *Laughing Boy*. It gave me a sense of what I wanted in life and how to get it. I am a seeker of beauty. It seems that in order to get beauty, one must walk towards beauty and strive for better things. *That's* why I tried so hard all these years—I had been trying to bring beauty into the lives of others and into my own in all the ways I could.

Beauty to a Navajo means peace and harmony and living at one with God's ways and with nature. That concept of beauty is the result of living as one who strives to pluck that fruit, white above all others. I wanted that fruit. My Trail brought me to Mexico, but I didn't know where the Trail would lead Marita and me when the waiting was over.

Marilyn had a better idea of where she was going. In a few weeks, after they got back from the States, she and her family were moving to Cuernavaca where her husband was planning to set up his new company. She was excited about going to a place of new beginnings. I was happy for her but a little sad for myself. I didn't know what was ahead for me. Are we rarely satisfied, we frail humans who cannot see much beyond the present hour?

But as usual, Marilyn had a response to this. "Isn't it incredible how much the Lord loves us? We do our part and he watches out for us. *No* "sacrifice" is *ever* enough to pay for his blessings."

Wednesday, July 21, 1976

When I called Mr. Rivera's office, his secretary Gloria reported excitedly, "Today we got the *exhorto* papers!"

"Wow! Finally! Now we can go to Puebla with them!" I rejoiced. I had waited two months for this news. The joy lasted only a moment, however, because Gloria's next announcement was so unexpected.

"You can't take them the way they are."

"Why not?"

"Because they need another seal on them from the city, and we can't get it until Friday."

What a disappointment. She had told me also that Mr. Rivera would be out of town until Friday and gave me an appointment to see him then.

I phoned Elder Fyans to see how soon he could go to Puebla with me. He was leaving for Vera Cruz Friday afternoon and would not return until August 4. We talked for an hour, trying to find a solution. At one point he said, "If only you had gone with me last Sunday when I did have the time. But I also realize that you have done the right thing waiting to get all these legal papers and support behind you. I think the Cruz family surely must know by now, somehow, that you are here."

I agreed.

"You must be prepared for hostility at first, but I suggest you go to Puebla and get on a communicating level with the family again. Especially with your father-in-law. Everyone must feel your spirit, get to know you again, and realize how much you love your daughter. Be completely honest and open with them," he counseled.

As we discussed possible plans, Elder Fyans agreed to ask President Parra to go with me. The family knew and respected him and President Parra knew me better than Elder Fyans did.

Marita: Missing in Mexico

Thursday, July 22, 1976

When I kept the appointment I had made with Elder Fyans, I learned that Brother Parra would like to talk to Antonio, but he was not available. Elder Fyans suggested I take his secretary, Chave, instead. She used to work at the same place Antonio and others in his family worked. At one time, Antonio's brother-in-law brought her to Puebla for a weekend. She knew them all and could go with me to Puebla. Since she was a nice person and Elder Fyans' secretary, we hoped that the family would be comfortable and hospitable with her. With Chave, at least they should let me into the house. I agreed to take her with me. With that decision made, Elder Fyans continued, "As I see it, there are three courses of action open to you: (A) Kidnap Marita back. (B) Go peacefully and maturely and talk over the problem to arrive at a solution that would be acceptable to everyone. (C) Try a reconciliation with Antonio."

It was easy to reject plans A and C. So we focused on B. In the discussion he clarified his thoughts, "Only by getting closer to the family again and sincerely trying to find a solution will the Lord be able to soften their hearts. I feel the Spirit of the Lord will be there if you try plan B. And the time will come that everyone will feel good about the solution. However, it may take a long time for this to happen. Don't worry about Antonio taking off during your visits. He isn't working right now and is just going to school. I don't think he would take Marita too far away."

Elder Fyans discussed the idea with her, and Chave agreed to go with me to Puebla. I sized her up. She stood shorter than I, was vivacious and friendly, and she seemed to be the sort of person I could work with. We left the office together at closing time. We chatted on the metro, and I hoped this perky Mexican woman with the bouncy, thick hair would indeed be trustworthy and helpful. I felt I was plunging into darkness with only my hope and faith to light the way.

Saturday, July 24, 1976 — Journal entry

After preparing my heart and two batches of cookies for a trip to Puebla, it fell through. I waited at the lawyer's office for three hours yesterday to make final plans for our trip. He called to say he had problems with *tránsito* and couldn't come. Numbness spread through my mind and body, and by the time I arrived at Marilyn's, my head was pounding so hard I could hardly function.

For the past seven months the same cycle has repeated itself far too often: I discover a way to get closer to Marita, I make plans, I get my hopes up that, by a certain day, *something* is going to happen, and I program myself to be patient for that time. But all too often, when the day comes, nothing happens as I had hoped. A big zero. A letdown. The disappointment spreads into anger, emptiness, and hurt. Tears follow with depression, and I feel vulnerable. I am weary of so much stalling and waiting.

But I have to remind myself of BIG FIVE and try to adjust to living with delays. I'm learning that we don't know how much we can endure until we are actually in a situation where we can do little else but endure. I don't like to admit it, but this is the part of the challenge in learning more about myself that I'd just as soon skip over. At least yesterday I held the *exhorto* papers in my hands. After two months, they are ready. My mind is at rest knowing that Antonio must be served papers soon to give him the nine days' waiting time to appear before the judge here in Mexico City on August 6 at 9:15 A.M. Circumstances can't put me off any longer than that.

When I wished Marilyn a "Happy twenty-fourth of July" this morning, she opened a bottle of home-canned dill pickles for our version of the annual Mormon Pioneer Day celebration of when the Saints entered the Salt Lake Valley in 1847. Then she invited me to go with her and Enrique to Cuernavaca.

Leaving Mexico City for the day was just what I needed! I could actually *see* a blue sky once we left the smog of Mexico behind us. The vegetation of the passing countryside was a comforting lush green. I breathed in fresh, clean air as we wound along the curves on the old highway to Cuernavaca.

Cortez knew a favored spot on earth when he saw it,

and he built his summer palace there. Lying between Acapulco and Mexico City, it is dressed in semitropical trees and flowers every day of the year. Balmy, warm, or hot weather are the standards. Being in Cuernavaca is as close to paradise as I've ever been.

The home the Morenos are renting for a year is a dream. Colored glass built into the walls filters the sunlight into hazy patterns of hues and shadows on adjacent walls and floors. The view from the balcony opens to the swimming pool, fruit trees, banana trees, and poinsettias in the backyard. And the bougainvillea clambers in orange, fuchsia, and red splashes of color over the stone walls surrounding the property. The only sinister note is a tiled-in box of a mini swimming pool that runs along the wall of the master bedroom and bath and through a hole in the wall into the next room. That end looks like the end of a coffin and makes a visitor's trip to the bathroom unforgettable.

Enrique took us to the industrial park where he was building a new plant for his company. Then we left the city and traveled on a narrow, winding highway to Amecameca and Chalco, passing through Cuatla, Portales, and Cocoyoc. Popocapetle, Mexico's sleeping warrior transformed into an impressive snow-topped volcano, loomed ahead of us everywhere we drove. I found myself laughing and talking freely as we went along.

By dark, we pulled into Amecameca and bumped through rutted, unpaved streets until we stopped in front of the home of Richard and Marla Moore. He is in charge of translating Church materials into Indian dialects, mostly Mayan. Richard showed us the camera-ready copy of the sacrament prayer in a dialect I couldn't even spell. Because my master's degree is in linguistics, I found every minute in his presence more instructive than weeks of college courses.

He and Marla had chosen to live like the natives of the area, and he joked about the termites falling out of the roughhewn wooden beams above us. My professors had us simulate fieldwork in exercises as we listened to tapes, but it was hard to imagine what real fieldwork was like. Now I have a better idea. It is bringing your wife and family to primitive areas while you work with yet another exotic language. It is catching hepatitis in a whitewashed adobe home with no centralized heating. And it is teaching your kids to cope, no matter what the circumstances, and hoping they can pass college entrance exams later on after such a varied international education.

The Moores have been married eight years, and their six children have been born in the United States, Fiji, and Tonga. Their seventh will be born in Mexico. Marla tutors them at home but works hardest at teaching them learning patterns so that they can teach themselves both from books and from the situations they find themselves in.

Listening to them talk, I felt an instant kinship. Wasn't this, in a way, what I had done in coming to Mexico to teach and marry? Won't Marita also benefit ultimately because she is in Mexico again? Won't we both survive better in life later on because of all we learn now?

Monday, July 26, 1976

Mr. Rivera hadn't considered using Church contacts and was pleased about my new plan when I explained it. Known and loved by many people, Antonio's father was the stake patriarch. Antonio might not respond to Elder Fyans or President Parra, but I believed "Papa Dan" would.

I explained, "Papa Dan is the key person in that house who could help me get Marita back. He is a good man. Will the papers be ready to serve this week so he will know I am trying to do things in an honorable way?"

Lic. Rivera assured me, "Yes. I'm sending Lic. Flores there tonight. He'll be at court as soon as it opens in the morning. All the seals will be ready, and I'd like to serve the papers on Friday."

Doubt mixed with hope, I asked, "Friday? Are you sure we can see Marita this Friday?"

"Definitely. We could leave here about 7:00 A.M. Also, I want you to have a copy of this letter I sent to *gobernación*. It explains your lack of migratory status in case anyone tries to give you a bad time. Do you know how blessed you are to get papers from court as soon as you did?" I shook my head, and he went on, "Most judges stop all processing until the client gets all the migratory status cleared up . . . which usually takes months. Then, they go on to other minute points to delay action. Since you don't have any status at all at this point, it's a miracle you have papers to use in Puebla this week!"

"How did you get them for me?" I wondered.

He smiled and responded in a casual tone, "Since the judge is my friend, he didn't cause any problems and finally signed them. I paid a bribe to get the seals and signatures I needed to take the papers to Puebla quickly. If I hadn't done that, it could have still taken a month to get these papers ready."

My strength returned after I left the office. I could smile again, and I made plans to prepare one more time for my reunion with Marita. But in the meantime, my next problem was finding a place to stay. Marilyn and her family were leaving for a vacation in the States in two days; then they would be moving to Cuernavaca.

When I told Marilyn I would be in Mexico a few more weeks, she suggested I call Steve and Hariella Wright. They had an opening in their boarding house with room and board for 300 pesos, or about $25.00, a week. The gorgeous house they were subletting was in Churubusco, within walking distance from the metro. A glamorous newer neighborhood with movie lots and resident movie stars, it was viewed as the Hollywood of Mexico. It had a different sort of prestige to it than Lomas. The Wrights' home was more expensively and tastefully decorated than any I had stayed in so far. I was excited at the idea of moving there and staying with friends. With a phone call to Hariella, I made arrangements to join the other boarders in two days. She sounded happy to have me come.

Chapter Thirteen

Thursday, July 29, 1976
338 Cerro Gordo, Colonia Campestre Churubusco

I WENT WITH HARIELLA TO THE *TIANGUIS*, the transitory open air market whose vendors always arrived at the same empty field on Tlalpan every Thursday morning. The produce and meat were fresher and less expensive than in a supermarket, and most people I knew always bought their weekly food supply at a *tianguis*. It took some haggling over prices and lugging plastic mesh bags of food from stall to stall, but it was worth it. Hariella bought and prepared the food for six of us boarders and the maid, in addition to her own family.

While she bartered for oranges, chickens, and vegetables, I searched the flower vendors' wares at the west end of the market. To my delight, I found just what I had in mind—a potted red rose with a double bloom on the main stem. For whatever Antonio might read into it, I was ecstatic with it, hoping he would remember the Vision of the Rose when he saw it.

I was afraid to see Antonio again, but I longed to hold Marita. I bought a coloring book and a puzzle for her, and when we returned home I made her some carrot cookies. I read the scriptures and prayed fervently. And I waited. There was nothing more to do to prepare.

Friday July 30, 1976

I left the house a little before 7:00 A.M. and walked to the metro with my arms full. Chave met me by the subway and we prayed together. About 8:00 A.M. we met the lawyers and drove east to Puebla in Mr. Flores' car. *Puebla de los Angeles* . . . City of the Angels, so called because centuries ago the workers on the central cathedral there were having difficulties finishing the top spires and other basic work on the building. One morning they awoke to find the hardest work done. Everyone says that the angels came during the night. Children have scanned the balustrades and top porticos for decades, wondering which ones the angels touched. Indeed, heaven had always seemed closer to Puebla than most other cities. Its sky was bluer and clearer. A sense of the past lies thickly in the valley formed by four volcanos, the Iztacihuatl and Popocapetle looming larger than the others. Long before the Spaniards started building a city in 1532, the Aztecs, Mixtecs, Zapotecs, and other tribes had fought, planted, and erected homes and temples in the area anciently known as the home of their god, Quetzalcoatl. I had first visited the area as a BYU student in 1967.

Maquey plants lined the country roads leading to the hills of Cholula, a town just outside of Puebla. The Spaniards didn't realize that the Indians had built seven pyramids—temple complexes—one on top of the other to form the largest hill. Excavation had uncovered these levels. Standing on the bottom temple layer underneath a thousand years of religious dreams and deaths, I had felt in touch with the oldest fibers of life I had ever known.

This feeling of antiquity had followed me to Puebla. Mr. Flores' car pulled into the main streets of Puebla about 10:00 A.M. Puebla's Fort Loreto commemorates its decisive battle with the French each May 5. Instead of being a nice place to visit, to me the city seemed transformed into the site of another battle of Puebla. Only I had no idea how long the battle would last or what day I would commemorate forever the day I had won and could take Marita walking free into a new life.

He parked the car a block from the Cruz home, and Chave walked to the house to see if Papa Dan were home. She crossed the street and passed the home on the corner. From the car I could see her approach the Cruz property and disappear under the rolled up metal door that covered the outside entrance to the family business. An inside door at the back of the shop led directly into the home of Ana Maria, Antonio's sister. Their parents' home was built above and beside it, in a typical Mexican duplex opening into a shared patio east of the shop.

Antonio's mother, Mama Rosita, always had one part of the home under construction, adding rooms for all the in-laws, children, and even boarders who wanted to live under her roof. This family was no exception to the Mexican tradition of living near one's parents, and the extended family visited the old home place en masse on weekends. She had room for everyone, and from the street, I could see she had made some obvious changes in the last two years.

The outside stone walls extended higher on the house than they had before, with a new apartment above the *zaguan*, or wrought-iron gate attached to two large portals, through which cars could enter the courtyard. Sheets of metal behind the bars blocked the view to the patio with only a peephole where the two doors met and locked. Was this action mainly for my expected visit?

Chave wasn't gone long, but my nerves tightened. Then she and Papa Dan emerged from the *despacho* [shop or office] door. I got out and started towards them. Antonio's father smiled warmly and said, "Hola, Mari."

I gave him a long *abrazo* [hug], tears in my eyes from my memories and from the relief. After the hug and the "Buenos días," I said, in Spanish, "I came to see Marita, but I don't know how the family will receive me."

With a smile he reassured me, "Mari, I think of you, as always, as when I first met you—with respect. What has happened doesn't change that. But it would help me to know if there is any chance you could ever live with Antonio again."

I did not even feel tempted to mislead him. "No. I cannot do that."

Disappointment clouded his face, but his hospitality did not waver and he replied, "You are always welcome in our home. Please come in." Chave joined us and we walked closer to the pink, gray, and white stone walls surrounding their home. He opened the padlock on the *zaguan*, and we entered the patio, passing Ana Maria's living room and kitchen doors on our left as we entered Mama Rosita's living room door straight ahead of us. I greeted Carlos, Antonio's tall older brother, who stood by the doorway.

While Papa Dan went upstairs to tell the others I had come, I glanced around the living room. Not much had changed since I had seen it last. Just sitting there gave me the sensation of going back in time at least twenty years. The designs and colors of the furniture, art work, and curtains all reminded me of rooms I had visited when I was a little girl. Although nothing was worn out, nothing was new either, but would probably last until the Millennium, just like the old cars that Mexicans repaired and used for decades. Custom-made shelving lined the wall facing the couch, and the stairs turned L-shaped along the north wall behind the curved end of the brown couch. Potted plants filled the corner under the stairs and were placed on each ascending step as well.

All of Ana Maria's children came in to greet me, and I gave each of them one of the carrot cookies I had baked.

Suddenly Marita bounced happily down the stairs wearing a long pink dress. I held my breath, hoping she would remember me but without expecting her to. I ran to her and quickly gathered her into my arms. Tears of joy, relief, love, and thankfulness for the blessing of holding her poured down my face. My tears didn't frighten her. She just nestled into my arms.

I sat down on the couch with her in my lap. I was surprised how short and prickly her hair was. It is traditional to shave Mexican babies' hair off when they are a year old. Then their scalps are rubbed with egg yolk, supposedly to help the hair grow out thicker. I had refused to let Antonio shave Marita's head, but he must have done it once he got her home. Her dark hair had grown out long enough to make her look like a little boy.

I looked her over carefully. Seven months had changed her, and she wasn't a baby any more. Oh how beautiful she looked to me. We began looking at the book I brought, and her cousins crowded around us. Antonio came downstairs and sat on the other end of the L-shaped couch, across from me. He held a book and pretended to study.

Next I gave Marita the Sesame Street puzzle. It delighted her more than anything else. She slipped off my lap to put it together on the floor. I watched every move and listened to every sound she made, absorbed totally in her. My in-laws and Chave left the room during this time, and Antonio sat reading, avoiding my glances for the first half hour. At last I sighed and asked Antonio, "What are you studying?"

"History. I go to the Normal Superior so I can teach high school someday. I also have a card to attend the *tecnologico*."

"Do you go to classes every day?"

"Yes. I only study right now so I can spend more time with Marita every day. I don't have a job."

Little by little, we eased into other topics, the ones we needed to explore. I was afraid he would leave for classes and take Marita with him, but he explained, "I've decided to stay around while you are here. I know I have to be careful with you. I'm afraid you will try and take Marita out of Mexico. Just so you know, I will allow you to come see her in the house, but you can't leave the house with her unless I go with you. By the way, I want to see Marita's passport."

"I don't have it," I asserted.

He looked at me suspiciously, took my purse, and rummaged through it. I brought the pot of roses over and explained the symbolism I saw in the roses. He simply stared and shrugged. I set them on the bookshelf by the door, hoping they would soften his heart.

The conversation turned to the past. When I mentioned his lying to Bishop Morrill, he acted surprised. "I had to lie in order to leave the country. You were such a fool, Mari Vawn. You trusted me. And you were a fool not to pull some dirty tricks yourself."

"Antonio, I am an honorable person. I do not believe in lying to get what I want. And I don't believe in asking friends to lie either, as you did with Juan."

Antonio smiled and waved his hand. "What are friends for?" he countered. "Those lies didn't hurt. In fact, I know they helped because they were part of how the Lord helped me bring Marita to Mexico. I know the Lord wants her to be in Mexico right now. We got out of the States so easily." He was obviously pleased with himself.

"You did get out easily," I agreed. I tried to keep our talk on a non-threatening level. "It looks like the Lord does want her to be here for now. I can see that she is well taken care of and healthy. She's more well behaved than any three-year-old I've seen all year. I'm glad she can stay where there are so many people who love her. She is happy, bright, active, and quite self-assured. I can tell that her stay here has been good for her so far."

"Thank you. I have done my best to take good care of her."

"But didn't she suffer on the trip?" I asked. "Veronica told me that on the way to Las Vegas she kept begging for Mama and wanting to see me. I have felt such agony over our separation."

Antonio was quiet for a moment. Then he admitted, "It was hard for her at first. When we first got to Mexico, she was afraid of everything. She refused to talk for quite awhile and she wouldn't eat very much at all. But you can see today how well-adjusted she is." He smiled again.

I decided to try another angle. I reminded him of his struggle to finish vocational school with grades good enough to enter college classes. In the version of his life story that I had read, he had lamented the sufferings and errors created in his life because he had been separated from his mother during his formative years when she enrolled him in the new elementary school the Church Education System had just opened in Mexico City.

At that time, many parents had held the dream that by taking their children to a central school taught by a totally Mormon staff—a school that allowed LDS students from every state in the Republic to mingle, their children would enjoy a higher level of education. These children would then return to their own areas after graduation to strengthen the Church and their home towns. Little by little, the prophecies of the Lamanites blossoming as the rose in the desert would be fulfilled. An educated, more purified body of Saints would grow in Mexico so Zion would flourish sooner.

It may have worked that way for many students, but Antonio had bragged to me many times that the first thing some kids at Benemérito had taught him was how to pick locks. I had seen him in action, and he had learned well. He had needed guidance and love but spent too many years alone at the boarding school. Later on, when his mother got a job there to be near him, he graduated from middle school and returned to Puebla to attend the vocational school. But he was actually out on his own at sixteen.

As I recounted some of these details to him, I reached the part I hoped would touch his heart: the words he himself had written at the end of his story, *"But one thing I do know is that a child needs his mother while he's small. That's why I don't think I will ever let Mari Vawn work outside the home while we have young children. Because if someone that loves you doesn't help you, then no one else will help to form you and make sure you understand things."*

Antonio scowled and was silent. Hopeful, I continued, "Little girls need to be with their mothers. When can she be with me so I can teach her?"

He stared across the room before he responded, "Well, she can probably go to BYU when she is old enough for college. Or, if you remarried and came to live in Mexico, I would let you see her on the weekends." He was serious.

I didn't roll my eyes in disgust, but I stared back at him, not sure what to say. His next comment ended the conversation. "I would die before I would let you return to the United States with Marita."

I decided to go play with her in some other room and asked Marita if I could take some pictures of her with her cousins. They all lined up on the couch and smiled. Then Antonio's sister Teresa and her husband arrived with their two boys. Teresa looked more like her mother than the other girls, but she was shorter and quieter. She also taught classes, English mostly. We chatted a while, and then Adriana came into the room.

Adriana had always been my favorite sister-in-law. I admired her intelligence, her drive to excel, her superb teaching and mothering skills, and her lyrical abilities with Spanish. We had taught together in the Normal Superior of Puebla the summer Marita was born. She was happy to see me, and I enjoyed hearing her infectious laugh.

Marita needed to go to the bathroom, so I went with her. I put my arms around her and kissed her and said, *"Te quiero, Marita, te quiero"* [I love you].

She put her arms around my neck and hugged me tightly. I felt that she did know who I was again. Perhaps it was hearing my voice or seeing me move around that brought recognition. Then I decided to go out front to the *despacho* where Chave was talking to Papa Dan and tell them it was time to eat. Marita began crying because she thought I was going to leave her. I promised to stay a while longer.

I found Papa Dan standing behind the customer counter of the shop, and we had time to talk. From where we stood I surveyed the street beyond the customer counter. Where were the lawyers? We had been there three hours—plenty of time to serve papers.

I asked, "During all the time I talked to Antonio this morning not once did he seem repentant or ask forgiveness for any of his actions. Did the stake president ever talk to Antonio?"

Papa Dan stared past me out to the street, and with a voice tinged with sadness, he answered, "The stake president asked me to talk to Antonio. But every time I try to talk to him about what happened, Antonio gets defensive and rebellious. He tunes me out. He's over twenty-one and as an adult, he figures I can't tell him what to do."

"I've had a hard time talking to him myself," I added.

Marita: Missing in Mexico

"I wish you two could reach some sort of agreement. We've had a lot of problems having Antonio back home, but I put up with him for Marita's sake. She was sick for some time when he took her to Mexico City until he decided to settle here. I want to have Marita where I can keep an eye on her and know that she is being taken care of properly." He faced the street, looking away from me.

My breath stopped. Marita sick? Dragged from one strange house to another? Humbly, I thanked him for his efforts and asked one more question before we went up to eat lunch, "Do you know if Antonio has done anything about divorcing me?"

"No, I don't know anything about it." He turned, shaking his head, and walked past me. With still no sign of the lawyers, I followed him out the door to join the others.

Marita sat at the small round table in Mama Rosita's new breakfast nook eating a hamburger. As I helped Marita with her food, I teased her by touching her teeth with my fingertip and saying, "*Dientitos.*" Every time I mentioned her little teeth, she laughed and giggled. Tears came to my eyes, tears of joy to experience such simple acts of life as talking, laughing, and eating with a loved one. Her voice caught my ear every time she spoke. I had never heard her speak in full sentences before, and never in Spanish, so I loved listening to her quick light voice.

After lunch I invited Antonio and his parents to sit down with me to explore the situation. His parents hoped for a reconciliation, but I was clear and direct. The marriage was over. Our job now was to find a solution for the present and the future. I reminded them that little girls need to be with their mothers. The laws of Mexico sustained this fact. Antonio looked smug. A triumphant look flashed at me as he exclaimed, "You'll never get custody, Mari Vawn!"

"Why not?"

"We are already divorced! I started the action two years ago when you abandoned me in 1974. All I had to do when I returned to Mexico this year was resume the paper work. I got the divorce in May by publishing in the papers."

"Show me the divorce papers, please." I thought fleetingly how revealing it was of our marriage that I simply assumed he was bluffing. I would only believe if I could see proof of his claims. I was shocked to hear him say I had abandoned him the summer of 1974. It looked as though I would have to prove in court that *he* had abandoned *me*. I held out my hand for his proof.

He refused to talk about it anymore, and our conversation died without any conclusions or agreements. Yet I was glad that I'd tried and that his parents had been present. I hoped they could see that Marita should be with me. Since she was still sitting on my lap, I asked her to show me her things, and we left the living room.

First we climbed the flimsy metal stairs to the roof where four or five dogs and some chickens lived. The animals had free run of the flat roof, and all the dogs except Marita's pet were watchdogs. Marita excitedly showed me Ven-Ven [Come-Come], a little white poodle as nubby as a lamb. Ven-Ven was the only dog I had ever seen that Marita wasn't afraid of. I was glad she had a pet to love.

Next she took me to the dining room to dance with her. Moving to rhythm was as easy as breathing to her. She copied my movements exactly as we danced and laughed together. We found the puzzle again and put it together countless times before she took me by the hand and led me to her bedroom upstairs. There was a twin bed for Marita and a small dresser for her clothes.

Tears brimmed in my eyes when she showed me her clothes. Except the dress she wore, all were hand-me-downs: faded, torn, and wrinkled. Rags! All of them! All her young life, she had loved pretty clothes more than toys. I determined to make her some lovely new clothes as soon as I could. How sad she must have felt to wear those rags! My heart hurt for her.

About 4:00 P.M. Mr. Flores arrived at the *zaguan* asking for me.

We walked away from the house to talk. My patience was gone. I blurted, "Chave and I have been looking for you all day! Where have you been?"

"We did have the person from court here to serve the papers, and we were waiting out in the car with him."

"Well, why didn't you come do it then?"

"We didn't know what you had found out or what arrangements you were making. So, after a while we took the paper server back to court. Now, it's too late to serve papers. I'm sorry."

I was furious. "Why couldn't you walk half a block and see how things were going?" I hissed. Mr. Flores didn't say much except that they were ready to return to Mexico City. I walked back to the house to say good-bye to Marita.

Antonio had put her in the bedroom and was holding the door shut. I pushed past him and opened it. She was crying. I kissed her and told her I had to go but that I would come see her on Sunday. Both of them followed me down the hall, and Antonio held Marita's hand tightly. They looked down over the wrought-iron railing on the edge of the dining room that overlooked the stairs as I walked down the stairs.

Mama Rosita stood at the bottom of the stairs. So the tall, stocky matriarch had decided to speak to me! Once a very beautiful actress, Marita's grandmother was usually outgoing, making friends immediately with strangers on the bus or at the market. She loved to tell jokes and have people feel at ease around her. Her rippling laugh and winning smile were her trademarks. But during this visit I had seen none of that. Even sitting in the same room, she had avoided me.

Lifting the pot of roses, I held them out to her. She thanked me, chatted about some paintings she was making, and said good-bye. Papa Dan walked out to the street where I gave him a hug and thanked him. Lic. Rivera introduced himself, and we left immediately.

The ride back to Mexico City was silent. I was still angry at the lawyers, but I offered a silent prayer to the Lord to thank him for the comfort of seeing Marita and holding her again.

Chapter Fourteen

Monday, August 2, 1976
Campestre Churubusco

ON SUNDAY I TOOK AN EARLY BUS to Puebla in hopes of spending a lot of time with Marita and sewing her a dress out of the material I brought. But when the time came for everyone to leave for church, Antonio refused to go with us or let Marita go. I feared a beating or unpleasantness if I stayed alone with him, so I attended church with my in-laws. His sister Ana Maria sat silently in the car, glaring my way. This was completely out of character for her because she was usually exuberant and ever-smiling. I determined to change her perception of me.

Our first meeting was Relief Society. Mama Rosita, Ana Maria, and I were the only ones there and they continued to ignore me. After the meeting the silence was broken by the arrival of old friends of mine from Mexico City who were happy to see me again.

After Sunday School, Papa Dan took me back to the house, but Marita wasn't there. While we waited for about three hours, we talked, trying to find an acceptable solution. "Antonio has suffered," he kept saying. The family thought I should give him a few more years to grow up and take him back when he was ready for marriage. Impossible. By the end of our talk, we agreed for trying for an out-of-court settlement in Lic. Rivera's office. This seemed to be a more mature action than fighting in court and would save time, money, and any number of problems.

When Antonio brought Marita back about 4:00 P.M., it was time to eat. Delighted to see me again, Marita wanted me to sit by her. She blessed the food impishly, "*Alimentos, Amén,*" and began showing off and acting silly as we ate. Suddenly Antonio whisked her off for a nap. I had barely seen her at all. I decided to leave for Mexico City.

Antonio stopped me at the gate and insisted, "Please don't go yet. I want to talk to you."

I agreed to stay.

"Listen to me. I want so much for us to be a family again. It was killing me to have all of us sitting there at the table as though nothing was wrong. But there's too much wrong. For example, you're selfish and only think of yourself," he said.

"How so?"

"This morning you left for church when you could have spent your time with Marita and me," he complained.

"I don't know how much you have changed in seven months, but I remember some scary times on Sundays when we were alone at home in Utah," I explained.

"You are the homewrecker because you won't give me any more chances when I'm ready in a few years," he snapped.

With all the sincerity I could muster I informed him, "I have truly forgiven you of all you have done to hurt me, but that doesn't mean I want to begin another nightmare."

As we talked more, I realized he was highly unstable, alternating between being open and sincere and being defensive and intimidating. It was obvious that he needed much help and love, and he wanted it from me. I had pity but no more love. I remembered that Mexicans in general cannot back down. If they do, they are looked upon as untrustworthy because they do not stand by their original convictions and loyalties.

By 8:00 P.M. we had reached no conclusions or agreements, so I started gathering up my things for the trip back to Mexico. The Cruz family asked me to stay overnight since the streets of Mexico City would be dangerous after 10:00 P.M. when I would arrive.

I stayed, and Antonio set up the sewing machine for me to make a dress for Marita. Awake after her nap, she spied the sacks holding surprises for her. She pulled the purple polka-dot material out of the sack, held it ecstatically up to her face, and danced with it. She loved the border design of red roses splashed along the bottom. I let her have the paper sack with the tape, ribbons, and elastic in it to play with while I cut out the dress and sewed it up.

Marita kept asking me if I were almost finished and she told me she wanted to help me as she handed me the pins. The sewing went slowly because I kept looking at her and talking to her, deeply comforted by being close again. We were actually in the same room together! The dress fit perfectly and she loved it.

I called my folks so they could talk to Marita. They only heard her say her name, but my mother needed to hear Marita's voice.

All too soon, it was her bedtime. We had a little prayer together. I kissed her three times, and she kissed me. As Antonio took her away, I told her I loved her. He kissed my cheek, but I turned my face away and left the room.

The next morning he left the house with her early and no one knew where he had taken her. I stayed until 1:00 P.M. to see if he would bring her back or if the papers from court would be served, but nothing happened. Papa Dan took me to the bus station. A month ago, he said, Marita had wanted to speak to the congregation, so Antonio took her up to the microphone during fast and testimony meeting. The first thing she said was my name and continued with what she usually said in her prayers. Since it is a rare occurrence for children so small in Mexico to bear their testimonies, everyone sat up and listened to her. I was thrilled to know she had remembered me after seven months.

Back in Mexico City, I called Gloria to inform the law office of my visit and what the Cruz family wanted. Lic. Rivera called me back, in a cold rage. He reprimanded me. I was a fool not to offer the hope of reconciliation. I should trust no one—not Papa Dan, not Chave. There was a good reason for not serving the papers on Friday, but he said he would only tell me in person. There would be no meeting about an out-of-court settlement until after the papers were served. He would do it himself Wednesday morning and then check for Antonio's claimed divorce in the Puebla courts.

His words flowed on, and I said little, but stood listening numbly. I thought I had done well under the circumstances in Puebla, yet he let me know I might have blown it, especially when he learned that Antonio had taken Marita away again. He had wanted me to string Antonio along so he wouldn't get scared and take off. His parting words were given sternly, "Don't talk to anyone at all about this case, especially this week. It is a very delicate situation."

"All right," I murmured. Then I called my parents right away. My mom had been waiting to hear if the papers had been served and reacted with some hyperventilation when I told her they hadn't been. Oh, how we both wanted something to happen soon!

I felt so sick inside after those phone calls that I could not eat. The tongue lashing stunned me. The only bright moment was that Papa Dan called later to report that Antonio had brought Marita back.

Wednesday, August 4, 1976 — Journal entry
Colonia Campestre Churubusco

> I began fasting Tuesday night that the papers would be served soon. I sat by the phone all day reading a book while I waited to hear the news. The ending of the book, *Til We Have Faces,* by C.S. Lewis, fascinated me in light of my own struggles and prayers. In it the queen had finished writing her book which was a complaint to the gods that they hadn't answered her for how they had messed up her life. Then she discovered that the book she had written was her answer. She wrote:
>
> *I saw well why the Gods do not speak to us openly, nor let us answer. Til that word can be dug out of us, why should they hear the babble that we think we mean? How can they meet us face to face til we have faces?*
>
> Indeed, isn't it through a refiner's fire that our faces and souls are formed? Will the Lord give me understanding about this ordeal only after I write about it?

Mr. Rivera called at 8:30 P.M., speaking vigorously, "I did it! I served the papers on him this morning!"

Overjoyed, I demanded, "Tell me about it!"

"Well, as I stood at the *zaguan,* I could see Marita playing in the wading pool with all the other kids. When he came to see who was at the gate, I served him. He was too shocked to say a word."

I gave a half-laugh. I didn't know how tense I had been until I felt the relief. What he was so sure could not ever happen to him, being served with Mexican papers, had happened—exactly eight months to the day that he had taken Marita away.

Friday, August 6, 1976
Churubusco

We went to court for the first—but certainly not the last—time, but I didn't feel I had been to court because there was no hearing after all. The lawyers parked the car outside high-rise offices in downtown Mexico City, and we hurried up the steps of a modern building that didn't fit my preconceptions of a courthouse. The inside didn't either. In a small office with only a chair for the clerk behind the desk, my lawyers rummaged through a pile of papers that Antonio had already dropped off.

The *exhorto* served on him had given him only one day to prepare a defense and appear in court or else bring the documents that disclosed his legal activities of the year to date. He brought the documents. With this new information, the judge suspended court action for awhile. My lawyers quickly read through the documents, taking notes on important dates and names. I looked at some of the forms myself and saw that Agricol Lozano had signed some of them. So he had advised Antonio legally! He also was the Regional Representative of the Church for Puebla.

We learned that Antonio started a divorce case on January 15 on two grounds: He claimed that I abandoned him (in Puebla!) and that I was suffering a "sickness." Somehow, my father-in-law was Marita's legal guardian—yet Papa Dan had told me that he knew nothing about any divorce action!

The divorce proceedings had not been completed, so it was possible for my lawyers to appeal Antonio's illegal procedures. I would still have a chance to gain custody of Marita if I won the divorce case. Since the *pleito* [lawsuit or litigation] must be fought in the D.F. court, an appeals court, and the court in Puebla where Antonio first filed, I could expect to spend at least six more months, maybe longer, in Mexico for several different court cases.

Before we left the court, we signed a document stating that we had shown up for action. On the way to the car Mr. Rivera surprised me by the delighted way he exclaimed, *"Se va a poner bueno el pleito!"* [The court battle's going to get exciting!] He seemed to be looking forward to it. And I thought, *Yes, and it's going to put fat on your bankroll, too.*

All the way back to the office, Mr. Rivera chided me about trusting the Cruz family, especially Papacito. He had lied to me, and Mr. Rivera didn't let me forget it. I suppose I was naive in some ways. I prefer to think the best of people and give them the benefit of the doubt. But then I had hoped a man with his high calling in the Church would have told the truth. I responded to the chiding with, *"Le va a ir mal,"* meaning some punishment would come in consequence to their lying and illegal procedures.

Agreeing, Mr. Rivera added, "Maybe Divine Justice will be done along with Mexican Justice."

Back in his office, Mr. Rivera outlined what I must do. Give him a list of witnesses who could go to court to prove that Antonio and I had lived in Utah, that he abandoned me, etc. Ask Antonio's boss in Provo for an affidavit stating how long he had worked there and reasons for leaving, etc. Get documents from the embassy about Antonio's immigrant papers to the United States. Get a copy of the paperwork showing a transfer of ownership when we had sold our home in Acueducto in 1974. Ask for Utah phone bills with his name and address on them. Visit Marita. See if they would let me in and make note of how they treated me.

It felt great, despite the scolding and my money worries, to be taking action. Somehow I felt a peace in spite of wondering, "What am I going to do to survive the next six months?" I knew my parents couldn't keep sending money too much longer. I'd need a coat for the winter months. Obviously I needed to find work. Back in Churubusco, the Wrights were surprised that I took the news from court as well as I did. Instead of acting depressed, I felt a peace and a curiosity to find out how it all would be resolved.

Steve and Hariella suggested I apply where Steve worked: the Instituto de Relaciones Culturales. My BYU advisor was a good friend of the school's director and had helped Steve get a job there. I settled in for the long haul and called Montana to report the court news and my plans to stay in D.F. and be available for court hearings. My mother was relieved to hear most of my news, and we decided my sister Kim could live in my Orem house with Rosalyn since she was going to attend BYU. I spent the rest of the day at the typewriter preparing requests for help I needed from people in the United States so I could get a job, more documents, and more clothes and makeup.

The letters were hand-carried to the border to be mailed in the States.

Linda and Joann called me from Orem to see how court went. They were as amazed as the Wrights and my folks were. Of course, they could get a long list of signatures to prove that Antonio left me. Before we hung up, Linda passed on wise advice, "Mari Vawn, from now on you need to protect yourself even more. Live missionary standards. Take a witness with you when you go to Puebla. Follow the Spirit. If there is something you shouldn't say, stop in midsentence if necessary. Please be very careful! I love you."

Saturday, August 7, 1976
Churubusco

Most of my prayers for the day were answered. I got up early and traveled more than an hour across the city north to Acueducto to catch my former bishop and visiting teachers at home before they could go anywhere. They all agreed to testify in court as my witnesses about my life with Antonio. One of them, Ann, also agreed to go with me to see Marita. From her house, the trip took all afternoon, and we arrived in Puebla by bus about 5:30 P.M.

A no-nonsense American with snappy eyes and short white hair, Ann may have been intimidating to some Mexicans, but her witty comments made the trip fun for me. She had married a Mexican twenty years earlier, and I met her at Benemérito the first day I taught there. She became a mentor of sorts because she taught English in the room next to mine and we used the same language lab for our students. I had shared much of my heartbreak with her about my marriage before I left for the States in 1974. As my visiting teacher in 1974, she urged me to divorce then and had offered to help me. I was glad Ann had known me back then and was still in Mexico.

After we left the bus, we took a taxi to the Cruz home. As we approached the customer counter, Papacito looked up. Suspicion and displeasure clouded his face. He turned away from us and attended a customer. We waited without saying a word until it was obvious that he didn't want to talk to me. I finally said, "I have come to see Marita."

He glared at me and snapped, "But, Mari, things have changed so much now. What a drastic turnabout you made!"

Ann protested, "But she's Marita's mother! Let us come in!"

Only then did Papacito leave the shop and walk down the street a few feet to the *zaguan*. He dug in his pocket for the key to the padlock on the gate. Just then Antonio and his mother met us at the gate. Their shock and reluctance were palpable, but they opened the gate, shook hands, and let us in. His parents went upstairs, but Antonio stayed in the living room.

I repeated my request to see Marita.

Antonio promptly lied, "She left last night to go on a picnic. And she won't return until Monday morning."

"I want to go upstairs and look around." (Everyone else who lived there was there. Who would she go on a picnic with?)

"No, you can't," Antonio said. "My mother will get nervous and upset."

"Then, I will look for the necklace Marita was wearing when I left," I stated.

"No. She has lost it by now."

He guarded the bottom of the stairs like a wolf. Ann and I listened for sounds of Marita, but there was nothing.

Antonio growled, "Remember what I told you before—you cannot come see Marita unless you definitely have decided to live with me again. If you really want to prove your love for Marita, you will give me another chance."

"Well, if I can't come just to talk things over, it will be harder to figure out the best things to do," I reasoned.

"You should have thought of that before you served papers on me! Now that we have a *pleito*, you aren't welcome here unless you stop fighting me in court," he threatened.

I was curious about the documents I had seen in court, so I queried, "What did you have in mind for grounds of divorce based on '*enfermedad*'? What sickness?"

"Oh, your epileptic fits! It's not safe to have a child around a mother like that," he complained.

I looked at Ann. She looked back in astonishment. I calmly asked, "Could you give me some idea of when I have had such a fit?"

"Oh, you'd get upset and go running out into the streets at night, crying and carrying on."

What? Fits of anger and crying spells are not epileptic fits. I didn't know if he'd ever seen a grand mal convulsion. I hadn't seen one either, but I knew I'd never had one during our marriage. What evidence would he have to prove it, unless he'd paid bribes to some doctor to manufacture some false reports? I continued, "Antonio, you get upset thinking about my supposed fits. I get upset about Marita staying with a man who mistreated and beat her mother."

His defenses flared up. "I never beat you! I never laid a finger on you! Just when do you think I did that?"

"The last time was just before Christmas," I recalled.

"I didn't!"

Obviously, our two definitions of what constituted mistreatment didn't match, or else he had blocked it out of his mind. I remembered being seized, spanked hard, dragged to the bedroom, thrown on the bed, and raped on that occasion. It was true, he had never blackened my eye or hit me with his fists, but he had wrenched my arms so hard that sometimes I had bruises.

After twenty hostile minutes, we left. Antonio's parting shot was, "Marita's better off with my loving family. You 'cool' Americans don't show as much love and affection as my 'warm' Latin family. And I don't want her at any babysitter's!"

Ann and I both countered, "It's being with her *mother* that counts, even if it isn't all day."

We walked out without saying good-bye to anyone.

Thursday, August 12, 1976

This morning I talked to Elder Fyans again. "I tried really hard to do what you suggested, and the Cruz family still turned against me. And my lawyer has been upset because I followed your advice about being open and honest."

He asked, "Would things be any different now if you had just served the papers and hadn't gone to talk first?"

"No, they wouldn't. At least I saw her twice," I realized.

"What are you going to do now?"

"There's no turning back. I must proceed in court."

Elder Fyans suggested, "I think you should still go to Puebla every chance you get, see Marita all you can, take her gifts, and talk to the family. Take a witness every time. Do your best to wear down the wall built up after the papers were served. Good luck!"

Marita: Missing in Mexico

I saw Lic. Rivera that afternoon. He had tried to switch the hearings from Puebla (against what Antonio had requested) to Mexico City. But we still had to examine the court files in Puebla Monday and find a way to nullify what had been done against me so far. The Cruz family's reaction to my last visit there was pretty much what Mr. Rivera had expected, but he encouraged me to keep visiting Marita.

He explained, "Antonio has been caught with both hands in the pie. He wishes you'd never come to Mexico to stop him or discover his indiscretions. Yet, at the same time his ambivalence draws him to you. He loves you and hates you at the same time. Take advantage of that ambivalence. Even though he says you can't go there unless you take him back, go there anyway at least once a week. Take presents. And go with a witness."

I blinked. At last Elder Fyans and Mr. Rivera agreed on something. I shared some good news. "I had a job interview yesterday at the Instituto de Relaciones Culturales, but I can't be hired until I have my *no-imigrante-visitante* papers. With that status, the school can get me working papers. In the meantime, I need to take their methodology-teacher course, and if I do well, they will hire me in October. And I have a scholarship! I have to go to classes every afternoon for two hours."

Mr. Rivera smiled and congratulated me, "That's a good school. I hope you get the job." He also commented that he had lived in the United States during his high school years. No wonder he could speak English so well.

Sunday, August 15, 1976

A BYU professor visiting in Churubusco offered to take the other boarders and me to Puebla. We left at 6:30 A.M., stopped to take pictures, and still arrived in time to get people out of bed at the Cruzes. One of the boarders had served part of his mission in Puebla and was Benjamin Parra's secretary. He had come along to help his brother find a place to live. This legitimate reason got us all in. I had hung back a bit, and Papacito hadn't seen me when he came to the gate.

Everyone was being very nice to President Parra's secretary; and when I said, "I want to talk to Antonio and I have some presents for Marita," they invited me in. I had asked my friends earlier not to leave me alone, but after an hour, the tourists were ready to move on. My roommate Cheryl agreed to stay with me and take the bus back.

Marita came downstairs for her bath, and they let her sit on my lap. I gave her some candy, a pink plastic bracelet, and four photographs of me on a card to help her remember me better. I held her and touched her and listened to her, trying to make every minute memorable. I didn't know how long I could be with her or when I would see her again, so I tried to love her and play with her all I could.

Cheryl gallantly stuck with me all day, even when Antonio insisted on talking to me while everyone else went to church. Since Cheryl had just arrived from the States, she didn't understand much Spanish yet, but she listened attentively. Antonio somehow had the idea that I would be returning to Utah to start school in two weeks. He was sincere, humble, and warm. He told me he had prayed I would return one more time so he could talk to me. He had prayed that my heart would be softened. I listened, making mental notes.

He said he was proud of me for coming to Mexico alone, showing love and courage to get Marita back. He wanted me to finish my M.A. at BYU and remarry him after he graduated in three to five more years, to give Marita a home with both parents. He admitted that he was young and immature when we were first married. Yes, he'd made mistakes—but so had I. He reminded me that he had recommended hormone treatments so that I could be more responsive sexually. Rage flickered, but I reminded him quietly that any woman who had been abused as much as I had would find it hard to respond freely and lovingly. He said nothing but invited me to go to Vera Cruz with him and Marita before school started.

I was there for five hours and he told me repeatedly that he still loved me. He confided in Cheryl that our parents helped to break up our marriage, but he told me to "really pray to see if the Lord doesn't want us back together—eternally—sometime." When I was noncommittal, he gave me an ultimatum: I could continue the court battle and never see Marita again unless the courts gave me custody, or I could "humble" myself and "accept the Lord's help" and be welcome to return anytime to see Marita.

I smiled thinly and thanked him for communicating with me. I knew by then that very day was the last I would be with Marita for a while. We spent an hour on the roof with the dogs and Ven-Ven. We looked over the edge, down to the street, and talked about the cars and people. We read stories. Down in the patio, I watched her pedal her trike around. We made her bed and put on handcream. She looked in my purse. She had no toys at all, so we couldn't find much to entertain ourselves with. What did she do all day? I wished I had a lovely little doll for her to play with.

About three o'clock I knew we had to leave before the rest of the family returned from church. I kissed Marita, told her I loved her, that I had to leave on the bus, but that I wanted to see her again soon. I left her at the table eating. She didn't cry.

As I stepped through the metal gate to the street, Antonio seized me, and holding my head in his big hands, gave me a long passionate kiss. I gritted my teeth and fought down nausea. As soon as he let me go, I wrenched myself away and hurried down the street, wiping my mouth. Even the Mexican courts seemed clean and straightforward by comparison.

Chapter Fifteen

Tuesday, August 17, 1976 — Journal entry

 My lawyers and I left Mexico City today at 7:30 A.M. in Mr. Rivera's sporty silver Mustang. In spite of the rain, he drove quickly, and we parked outside the Puebla Fifth *familiar* court in Puebla by 9:00. Its thick, carved, wooden doors opened to a true courtyard. Built in the Spanish colonial style, it probably had been a convent a century ago. The rain bounced down upon the stone slabs and splashed into the gray stone fountain in the center of the courtyard. Stone columns topped with white arches scalloped the perimeter of the courthouse, and they provided shelter above the corridor that ran past office doors placed every thirty feet around the open courtyard.

 We ducked under the arches to our right and entered the middle office to court number five. Beneath incredibly high arched ceilings painted white, women in the steno pool were jammed into one large room with the desks only a foot or two apart. At each manual typewriter a typist plinked at someone's *expediente*. Every inch of floor space was crowded with office boys, legal aides, and lawyers standing up or leaning against desks or walls. With no room for more than a few chairs, the clients stood up as well. All the typing and talking made it difficult to hear the person only a foot or two away, yet the work went on.

I stood near the door while Mr. Rivera requested our file, and then we all stood near the door reading pages from it. The more I read of *expediente* the more I fought down nausea. My stomach roiled to read lies, false testimony, and false accusations. After the lawyers had read the file, they took it to get the most important pages copied. I wrote down what I could of the major developments of the case from the court record:

Antonio declared me to be the guilty party, losing all rights to any privileges in my marriage. The record said that our ties are dissolved, and I had lost custody of Marita since she was in his dad's care. Antonio asked for custody. Antonio said that we had established our legal married residence at an address in Puebla (it was the same as the home of his parents, an obvious lie). He claimed we had problems from the beginning in our marriage because of my epileptic fits, my demands for more luxuries than he could provide, and my constant threats to leave him.

Besides those farfetched deceptions, he swore in court that on 18 July 1974 I abandoned our home and took a rented car for an unknown destination while he was at work, leaving Marita alone in the house. (We were both still in Montana on 18 July, about the day he received his Vision of the Rose.) The record said that he tried to find me to convince me to come home, but his efforts were in vain because it seemed that his wife had forgotten all about him and their little girl.

Well, by the time he had filed in January of 1976, according to him, more than the allotted six months had gone by, so he demanded a divorce on the basis of my unjustified abandonment of our home and family. He even accused me of infidelity and being a prostitute! He swore he was telling the truth, that he didn't know where I was (in January), that he wanted me to pay the costs, and he wanted the divorce edict to be published in the papers.

By 16 February the judge answered him, and on 15

March the edict was published in *Novedades*. I saw three clippings of it attached to the court file. On 11 March the judge gave me until 21 May to respond in the 40 days final margin of time. On 19 April Antonio began introducing a batch of proofs against me. (But because of the spring vacations and other delays the final sentence was delayed until 30 July since I never showed up at any of the court hearings that I never knew anything about. But that day was when my lawyers were nosing around court there supposedly getting a paper server while I was in the Cruz home visiting Marita. I never did find out why they didn't serve papers that day, but maybe this final court day—30 July—had something to do with it and they found out in time.)

The 30 July entry of the court record showed that the judge needed to send routine queries about my location and status to *gobernación* and the emigration authorities before he could dictate a final sentence.

And the last entry to date was 13 August with the documents and affidavits establishing my side of the story, explaining why I had started action in the Mexico City courts asking for Marita's custody. My three witnesses were listed in the record as willing to testify, along with my request for the judge to nullify Antonio's proceedings and to accept my proofs.

Before we left court, the lawyers added more sections to the new documents prior to introducing them in court, based on the additional details we had just found. I signed more papers to start the action of nullifying the divorce action illegally brought against me.

Outside the courtroom, Mr. Rivera pondered my close call in May. As we passed by the fountain, he declared, "The Cruz family had almost completed the divorce action against you, but *gobernación* saved you. During those days when they were looking for records on your whereabouts to answer the judge, I submitted papers announcing you were in Mexico."

Humbly I added, "And a few days after that the thieves

stole my wallet and visa. What a blessing in disguise! I was forced to go to *gobernación* in person to report it and to ask for a new visa. They saw me with their own eyes, and that was enough to stop everything and give me a chance to do something."

Now that I am home from Puebla, shivers still pass through me when I think of nearly being divorced in May. Because of what I learned, I appreciate *gobernación* for the first time in my life, and I feel more deeply how much the Lord loves me. He knew about the necessary robbery and warned me. Today, for the first time since I came to Mexico three months ago, I understand *why* I had to come when I did. It had seemed ill-timed to arrive during vacation when I could do nothing in court. Yet, in the blessing, I had been told it was the right time to go to Mexico. The Lord has not failed me, and I am thankful for his protection and help.

And more good news came my way today. When I called Rosalyn to ask for another affidavit, she told me that she had just found my FM2 forms! No wonder Antonio hadn't discovered their hiding place that day he left Utah. My passport and the FM forms had somehow slipped behind the top drawer of my dresser and were stuck lower down, back between the drawers. Tonight I thanked the Lord again for that extra protection then. Now I can avoid any more problems at court, at the school, and at *gobernación* because I have found my migratory forms.

Wednesday, August 18, 1976
Edificio Donato Guerra, Tlaltelolco

My mother called me, very upset. Her words rushed out, "Antonio's looking for you! He called us at 1:30 A.M. demanding to know your telephone number!"

"What did you do?"

"Well, Daddy gave him the Morenos' number by mistake."

"Good. They're on vacation."

My mother urged, "He's up to no good to call us like that. You've got to go somewhere safe."

After I told her what I had just learned in court, I assured her I would move soon, and she felt more comforted. I explained to Steve and Hariella why I needed to leave, grabbed the newspaper, and looked for an apartment in the Zona Rosa where I had classes every afternoon.

I took the Metro to Tlatelolco to get a copy of the records of our house transactions and proof of living in Aqueducto. No one would give me the papers, even though I saw what I needed in the file. I had no money for a bribe, so I left. Discouraged, I decided to visit some old friends who lived nearby in Tlatelolco. They invited me to stay there until I could find a more permanent place.

Back at Churubusco, the Wrights told me the news while I packed up. Antonio had called twice but wouldn't leave a message. I decided to leave for Tlatelolco in a taxi immediately and not tell anyone where I was going. Antonio would have a harder time finding me that way.

Tlaltelolco . . . a self-contained city within Mexico City . . . a city of Aztec ruins within towering skyscrapers and high rise condominiums . . . a city that captured my romantic fancies on the first visit and held a prominent place in my favorite memories of Mexico for years afterwards. The site of incredible power and riches, it was from this place that Cuauhtemoctzin ruled the Aztecs when the Spaniards arrived in 1519 and changed their course of history forever. The Spanish ravaging of that city of the gods left another stone cathedral and monastery in the place of a major Aztec temple complex.

In 1971 I often walked among the Aztec ruins, wondering what it had been like there a thousand years ago. But just three years before, in October of 1968, a thousand federal troops fired on students demonstrating on the Plaza. The massacre of at least three hundred young people had created a Plaza of Sacrifice. I had watched mothers lighting candles there on an anniversary October night years later, and I could still see bullet holes in my bedroom window sill and closet door from the killings.

Sunday, August 22, 1976 — Journal entry

This morning, I attended stake conference for the Mormons who attended church in the northern part of

Marita: Missing in Mexico

Mexico City. In every row of Saints, I saw many people I had worked with, taught, laughed, and cried with. Today they were smiling, sitting with their loved ones and children. I sat alone, struggling with the bitter feelings of betrayal. I visited with an old roommate before the meeting started. She looked at me with surprise and then with relief. "I thought I would never see you alive again!"

"What do you mean? I'm fine. I wasn't sick enough to die."

She insisted, "Two years ago people told me that you had a brain tumor and had left to die in the United States."

I am shocked to learn of this rumor. There was no basis for it. I feel angry at the forces beyond our control that step out of the evilness of mankind to affect our lives whether we deserve them or not. Gossip destroys as much as bullets do, and often we are less able to heal the wounds of it.

On Friday, someone opened my purse at the Balderas Metro stop when I was being shoved into a subway car by the entering mob. Luckily he only stole my address book, and I learned not to take my purse on the Metro anymore—just my tickets and a pen. How vulnerable I feel! And after conference today, I feel it isn't good for me to stay in Tlatelolco much longer. Too many memories and deep feelings are surfacing here.

I have a copy of Oliver LaFarge's book *Laughing Boy*, and I reread it today for the tenth time, weeping at his prayer of a man going alone to battle:

> I am thinking about the enemy gods, the enemy gods, among their weapons I wander.
> A-yé-yé-ya-hai! Now Slayer of enemy gods, I go down alone among them. Touched with the tops of the mountains, I go down alone among them,
> Now on the old age trail, now on the path of beauty walking, The enemy gods, the enemy gods, I wander among their weapons . . .

> Forever alone, forever in sorrow I wander
> Forever empty, forever hungry I wander
> With the sorrow of great beauty I wander
> With the emptiness of great beauty I wander
> Never alone, never weeping, never empty,
> Now on the Trail of Beauty I wander, Ahalani
> BEAUTIFUL!

Wednesday, August 25, 1976 — Journal entry

Beautiful! This entire day has been beautiful. After a week in "hiding," I decided it was safe to move back to Steve and Hariella's. I'm doing well in class, and I made myself some new clothes.

I heard from Mr. Rivera that the Puebla court accepted my document that I signed a week ago. The court will serve Antonio with more papers requiring him to present his proofs, stating that what he said in the *demanda* is true. Mr. Rivera was in a good mood. "Antonio has contradicted himself so much that he won't be able to extricate himself," he said.

Marilyn came to see me today after her trip to the States and brought me some survival supplies. She's moving to Cuernavaca this weekend. And I heard by the grapevine that I am the new teacher to be hired in October if all goes well. It feels so good to have a happy day for a change.

Wednesday, September 1, 1976 — Journal entry

President Echeverria's State of the Union message lasted five hours today, but the crucial information took about thirty seconds to repeat as he pulled the stability out from under an entire nation with words no one misunderstood: the peso is being devaluated! I got a headache just thinking about all the problems the devaluation will cause.

By the time I got to the institute, everyone was talking about it. One girl said she had gone to buy a dress, and the store had upped the price one hundred pesos. Another woman said that most stores were closed because they didn't know what prices to charge. I've also heard that the exchange rate for dollars will be around twenty pesos for a dollar instead of the long-standing $12.50. A lot of the teachers are discussing the idea of quitting and returning to the States to work. I am stuck here for now. At least I don't have any savings to lose. It is the destitute Mexicans that will suffer the most from all this.

Tuesday, September 7, 1976
Goldsmith 38 Colonia Polanco

Sunday after church we sat around the long table together for Hariella's good dinner, and Steve sadly announced, "We have decided that we can't survive here economically with the devaluation. My father has located a job for me in Idaho and a house for us, rent free. We plan to leave at the end of this month."

Although I had expected this news, I still wasn't prepared. I loved living in their beautiful home with so many people who cared and shared in my life. I felt alone. Marilyn was in Cuernavaca, the Wrights would leave soon, Ann had no phone, and other friends had no room for me. I didn't want to live in the north or anywhere I'd have to make Metro connections through Pino Suarez. I hated that Metro stop because so often I was caught there in the vise of pressing bodies dragged by the current of trampling feet toward the ticket turnstile. I feared entering that vortex. As I began searching for a place to live, I quickly learned that landlords didn't want me because I didn't have a job, I wasn't a regular student, and I wasn't a tourist. When I wouldn't freely explain, most people concluded I was a spy, perhaps a lowlife, or simply someone up to no good. I couldn't tell anyone how long I needed to rent for because I didn't know how soon I would leave with Marita. However, I made an appointment to see an apartment in Polanco, a fifteen-minute bus ride up Reforma from the Zona Rosa and the school.

I got off the bus at the Fuente de Petroleros and cut across a small grassy park with struggling, smog-choked trees. It all seemed familiar at first view . . . the small shops on Goldsmith Street under condominiums and apartments, the kosher butcher shop next to the address I was looking for, the synagogues and expensive homes in this area—Mexico's Jewish colony. A doorman let me in after checking through the intercom to confirm that I was expected. I climbed the wide, gray stone steps of the entry hall and passed the elevators as I started up the stairs to the third floor. Each step after that was placed with feelings of *déjà vu* because I had seen it all in a dream some time ago. I knew I would live there.

As I walked around each corner and down each hall, I knew what I would see next. Soccoro, a saucy, well-dressed young Mexican woman, showed me her clean, contemporary apartment with a balcony overlooking the street. Three career girls shared it and were looking for a fourth. American Hallmark plaques and needlepoint groupings accented the walls. A full bookshelf, a desk, and plants made the entryway inviting. Beyond that, I saw an L-shaped living room with a dining area next to the kitchen. To my left a hall opened to the bedrooms and bathroom.

Despite my unconventional situation, they decided to take a chance on me. I could move in immediately. Rent was $60.00, or 1300 pesos with the devaluation. They expected me to cook my own food and to share a bedroom with Lupe, a twenty-four-year-old secretary. I could make a down payment of only 300 pesos on the rent because the check I expected all week hadn't come from my folks. I had very little money left for food or bus tickets.

When I called my parents to give them my new address, I found out they hadn't even sent the money yet! Rosalyn hadn't sent the suitcase of warmer clothes, either, because her car didn't work. My theme lately seemed to be "hurry up and wait." And whenever I thought of Marita, I cried. Sometimes I cried a long time.

Sunday, September 12, 1976

Lupe's birthday party lasted until 3:00 A.M. Sunday morning. I had felt so alone since I moved to Polanco even though my roommates seemed to be nice girls. The oldest was thirty and the youngest was twenty-three. Four single girls living alone in an apartment is commonplace in the United States. But in Mexico in 1976 such living arrangements were seen as brazen and unprincipled. Although the custom was slowly changing, most "decent" girls were expected to live at home where they could be protected until marriage.

During the first of Lupe's party, I attended a "spectacular" show at the National Auditorium featuring Sergio Mendez and Brazil '77. When I got back, all twenty guests were smoking and drinking, listening to music and talking, or dancing. I sat on the flowered couch and made small talk. After a while I joined a large, partnerless circle dance, but when someone put on slower music, Lupita's brother pulled me into his arms. He'd had quite a bit to drink, and I didn't know if he even knew who I was, but he obviously enjoyed the closeness. And so did I. How long had it been since I had been in a man's arms without wariness or fear?

But at the end of the dance, I slipped away to my bedroom. The complications of getting involved with a man were more than I needed in my already complicated situation. Besides that, I had no real way of appraising how Antonio's treatment of me had affected my capacity for intimacy, and I wasn't about to experiment with a casual flirtation with a stranger to find out.

Church for Polanco residents was held in the chapel where I gave my first sacrament meeting talk in Spanish nine years ago. I attended the Condesa Ward, a regular Mexican ward. After the services, I hung around to talk to Bishop Ruiz. He had been a leader for some years. I remembered seeing him walking with some of the twelve apostles and the prophet at the area conference in 1972. His clean-cut, well-dressed appearance had always impressed me. He looked distinguished with his full, bushy black moustache under a beaklike nose. He gave me his telephone number in case I needed help.

Wednesday, September 15, 1976
Mexico's Independence Holiday

I welcomed a four-day holiday after I finished an easy midterm. I started it by enjoying a free performance of the American Symphony Orchestra a few blocks from home at the National Auditorium. First they played the Mexican National Anthem and then the American National Anthem. I stood for both, tears in my eyes. Then I attended the Noche Mexicana my new ward had planned to celebrate independence and give the ward members a safer alternative than being trampled or robbed at the capital's principal celebration at the Zocalo.

The party was typical: it started two hours late, wasn't very well organized, and consisted of parlor games, food, and a dance. Family members of all ages attended.

During the dance I met an American woman who lived a few blocks away from me in Lomas. Nancy had accepted the calling of pianist although all she could do was pick out the melody with one hand. I sat by her as she practiced hymns and we got better acquainted. Nancy had long, light-brown hair and a pleasing smile, and she glowed with the beauty of her first pregnancy. I didn't feel so alone with this newfound friend, and I relaxed more.

Yet, for one of the few times in my life, I felt some of the daily desperation that many Mexicans felt from childhood—the worry about having enough food and wondering how long I'd have to stretch my few pesos until I would have more. I had been growing weaker and hungrier as the days passed, and still the money from my father had not come. I had eaten nothing all day, saving my money for bus fares, for I knew that I could eat at the church party. I stood in a long line for the food and realized that this was probably the biggest meal some ward members would be eating for a while, too.

After waiting in line for a half-hour, I was served a heaping plate of pozole and tamales and a warm drink of atole. I sincerely thanked the Lord for it. I had spent only fifteen pesos at the market that week for food. That was less than a dollar in 1976, and it was all I could afford so I could still pay for bus tickets.

Since my roommates had all left for the holiday, I returned to an empty apartment and spent two days and nights writing. Mostly poetry. The first poem, inspired from Lupe's party, covered the struggle I had meeting new people and trying to explain to them why I was in Mexico. I called the poem "Multiple Choice," and it listed some obvious answers, then:

> And if you must know more, only for the very persistent, those with ears to hear:
> - I have come for my princess, my daughter.
> - I have come back for my real self, the person I used to be.
> - I have come for my freedom and a better life for the future.
> - I have come to learn about human nature more deeply.
> - I have come to endure to the end of the refiner's fire.

Now, do you comprehend what I am doing here in Mexico?
And does it make any difference to you?
To the Lord, Marita, and me,
it makes an Eternal
Everlasting
Difference.

I MUST BE HERE NOW.

Saturday, September 18, 1976
Cuernavaca

Marilyn invited Steve, Hariella, their kids, and me to Cuernavaca. I couldn't afford a bus ticket, but the Wrights generously paid for me, and we traveled by first-class bus for an hour through scenic mountain passes. It was a wonderful day of making bread in Marilyn's white-tiled kitchen and talking. Hariella and I were homesick, and Hariella was anxious to go back to the States, but Marilyn had just returned from Salt Lake.

As she shaped the bread into scones, she reflected, "I don't miss Salt Lake anymore. I used to miss the temple, the malls, and things like that, but now I mostly miss my family. It would help if we could see each other more often." Then Marilyn asked me seriously as she gave the bread another punch, "Where is home for you, Mari Vawn?"

I couldn't answer, and I spent the next few hours thinking about her question. Where was home?

In the past ten years I hadn't been back to Montana more than a few days every two years. Yet I supposed I still thought of Montana as home. Living in faraway places, I rarely could enjoy the comfort reborn in my soul each time I walk under the big sky, listen to the rustle of the cottonwoods, and see into the next county. No matter where I went, I was always a Montanan. Eighteen years there had indelibly shaped me for good.

How much was Utah home? That's what I had in mind when I said, "Get Marita and go home." We had a house and friends in the ward there and ties to BYU.

But what about Mexico? Wasn't it my home, too? I had spent almost all my adult life in Mexico, and I loved it. It had an untold impact on my perceptions and reactions, and undoubtedly it would still have a part to play in my future.

Marilyn broke into my reverie to hand me a pile of supplies and explain a project she wanted help with. "On October 16 there will be a regional Relief Society Exposition at Churubusco. We need enough displays for half the cultural hall in the stake center. I'd like you to take over Marla's project since she is returning to the States. Your main emphasis will be to help the sisters understand the role of Relief Society, Visiting Teaching, and how mothers can prepare their sons to be good missionaries."

Pleased to do something meaningful, I accepted the assignment. She went on, "The leaders from fifteen stakes in Mexico City will come for ideas so they can put on a similar exposition for their own stakes. Then we can polish our displays so that by November 16 they will be even better."

"What happens then?" I asked.

"Visitors from Church headquarters in Salt Lake will be there in Churubusco for a special meeting, and they will see our displays."

I agreed to do the October exposition, but I hoped I wouldn't be in Mexico in November and told her so. I enjoyed creating displays, signs, and handouts. The project gave me a real goal and something fun to do. When I got back to the apartment, I finished another poem.

GREETINGS FROM HOME

"Ésta es su casa"
they say in Mexico to let a guest know
that he is welcome in that home.

"Come in and rest your feet a while"
is heard in Montana, and my father tells the guests
as they leave, *"Run both ways and hurry back."*

But what does one hear
when far from that celestial home
and homesickness for Heaven
overwhelms
one
alone?

Marita: Missing in Mexico

Here in Mexico there still is no temple
with the golden letters, *Holiness to the Lord*
where I can go and hear them tell me,
"Welcome to the House of the Lord this day."

My Father knows I am far from Home.
My friends know also and remember Marita and me.
Power from the prayer circle
reaches through time and space with comforting hand
to guide, protect, and bless us
until that Day comes when I can finally
put my arms around Marita and say,
"Come home with me, come home."

And after that Day
we will walk together
toward our only Home
until that Bright Morning
when Elohim and Heavenly Mother
greet us with open arms, saying,
"Well done,
You good and faithful servants.
Enter into thy rest
To go no more out."

Chapter Sixteen

Tuesday, September 21, 1976
Polanco

THE PESO EXCHANGE INCREASED to 19.90 on the dollar, and that made the peso about equal to a nickel. I only had three pesos left in my purse. All my clothes were dirty, for I had no money to wash them, and I had been eating only oatmeal and milk for more than a week. I picked up the letter and the check from my folks at the law office when I went in for my appointment. Lic. Rivera had spent his vacation in fun and sun. He had a rich new tan and he seemed exuberant—eager to get back to work on my case.

"The judge is on the Cruzes' side so far," he explained from his comfortable leather chair, "but we will surprise him when we go to court on Thursday. He isn't expecting us to show up."

"Why not?"

"He put the file on your case in his desk drawer and didn't publish the date and time of the next hearing as he was supposed to do. That's a way of keeping you out of court."

"That's outrageous! How did you find out about it?"

"Well, I looked around, but there wasn't anything about your case. So I had a lawyer from Puebla peek in the judge's desk drawer when no one was looking. The hearing's at 11:00 A.M."

"What a system! Well, did your spy see anything else?"

Mr. Rivera leaned back and smiled. "Antonio has been busy. He introduced his proof to substantiate some of his lies. He showed that you got a driver's license in Puebla in 1973 and taught at the Normal Superior there."

"That's true," I confessed. "But you know how those things are done. I gave my photo and my money to Adriana, and she gave them to a friend in *tránsito* [Department of Transportation]. I did the same in Torreón when I got a driver's license. I don't know anyone who has actually got a license in Mexico by taking the test in person. But just because I got a license there and worked during the summer there doesn't mean I had a permanent residence there. Besides, I have another license I got later in Mexico City."

"I know that," Mr. Rivera agreed. "But Antonio also turned in a newspaper clipping from *Novedades* of Puebla as proof you lived there. It was of your baby shower or something."

"He what?" Astounded, I remembered the weekend before Marita was born. My in-laws had invited me to Puebla for a small baby shower with guests from the family and some Relief Society sisters I had never met before. Newspaper photographers came by, and later, I saw the picture with a caption written by a society editor with no understanding of Mormon ways. It said we had toasted with the finest wines, for instance. "But going to a party one weekend in Puebla isn't proof I lived there!"

"I know it and you know it," Mr. Rivera soothed. "And I'll make sure that the judge knows it, too."

"After this, I wonder what other lies are in store for us."

"I don't know, but we'll fight them. I took your case because you seemed innocent, and I will do all I can to get your daughter back for you. I realize that we'll need the Lord's help, too. Señora, will you pray for me?" he added humbly.

"I pray for you every day," I assured him, "and so do my parents and friends."

With a great sense of relief, I cashed the long-awaited check, bought some food, and washed my clothes. Then I taught a lesson on nouns at the Institute as a student teacher. Although I'd already taught six years, I learned something every night from observing or teaching the Institute classes. It was a blessing to have this tie with the real world of normal people working toward educational goals. They treated me well and built up the self-esteem damaged by Antonio's assaults.

After classes, I called my parents. They had upsetting news. Mr.

Rivera's letter and a page of new fees had arrived in Montana—$4,200.00. And he wanted fifty percent of it soon. We had hoped that his new fees to cover the next six months would have been less. I gulped, "That's so much money! I'm so sorry to bring this burden to your lives. It's a nightmare!"

My father asked, "Did Mr. Rivera ever ask you what kind of living I make?"

"No, I don't think he asked right out, but I had mentioned that you had been a State Representative."

My had father served three terms in the Montana Legislature, and nobody makes any money at that. In fact, they said about my father, "He arrived with a ten dollar bill in one pocket and the ten commandments in the other and never broke either one." But Mr. Rivera probably assumed that we were a wealthy family if my father had been a *diputado*—Mr. Rivera must have thought that meant a representative on the U.S. Congress level. Plus I had managed to have *him* as my lawyer and he worked only with American companies and airlines and other people who could afford him.

I wondered if we should try to find a lawyer with more reasonable fees. I told my parents about the judge in Puebla hiding my file. Daddy suggested, "Please keep track of all the trips those lawyers make to Puebla or whatever else you know they do on the case. I'd like to see if reality matches the estimates."

Thursday, September 23, 1976

Court day in Puebla. We left Mexico City in Mr. Rivera's car before 8:00 A.M. Both lawyers were in a good mood.

At 9:15 we entered the court and read the five-page *auto* prepared by Antonio's Puebla lawyer. In it, Antonio had sworn that he had never lived in Acueducto with me, nor in the USA, and that he had never worked or gone to school in the States. He maintained that we had always lived in Puebla. We left the court to prepare strategy in a downtown restaurant.

During brunch, while the lawyers drilled me on questions the judge would probably ask me, Mr. Rivera asked several times, "You aren't afraid, are you, Señora?"

"No," I said, but I didn't feel confident either. I prayed silently that

I would be guided and helped in the courtroom.

We entered the courtroom at exactly 11:00 A.M. They had not expected us, just as Mr. Rivera had predicted. We stood around waiting, talking, and waiting some more. At last a middle-aged, well-fed Mexican man emerged from the side office.

Judge [*Juez*] Casco was cold and dismissive to me and seemed disgusted to have to stand by the desk in the middle of the room with a secretary to record our dealings, as in a deposition. He warned me to tell the truth or face penal action for perjury.

After I answered the birthplace-age-profession-address questions, he asked to see my *forma migratoria*. I didn't know what to say. I had no visa status yet. Mr. Rivera jumped right in to explain. The judge hauled out a big navy-blue book and began pointing out paragraphs. Mr. Rivera flipped through the pages to other sections and read some of the paragraphs aloud.

Immediately, the judge recognized my lawyers knew what they were doing, and a friendly smile appeared. Suddenly there were more smiles on everyone's faces. Señor Juez decided to postpone the hearing until noon, 6 October, to give me more time to get an answer from *gobernación*. The hearing was over before it began. I thought we were leaving immediately.

But somehow, Mr. Rivera managed to get the judge to accept a short visit in his office with us alone. He whispered to me as we went in, "It is something like a privilege that the judge would want to talk to us informally. Just tell the judge briefly what has happened this year so he can hear your side of the story."

The judge sat behind his desk, friendly and listening attentively. Occasionally Lic. Rivera interrupted me to add relevant details I had skipped. And the judge interjected comments such as, "You are going to see *La Justicia Mexicana*." The brightest moment came when the judge said, "The family has surprised me with all their lies. The custody of the little girl was hastily arranged."

He pulled down a book and showed me a paragraph reading that a child under seven should be with the mother. He concluded, "The girl should be with you, Señora. You can bring her up better, and you have better means and education to give her more opportunities than your husband can. You really did live in the United States. The house Antonio insists was your *domicilio conjugal* is really his parents' home."

I could tell the judge was angry that the family had tried to deceive him. We assured Señor Juez that we would give him the proof he needed to establish the truth of all I had told him.

Emphatically, the judge praised my choice of lawyers, "You have excellent legal counsel, and I'm going to help you, too. I will begin some paperwork to let Marita be with you while we settle this case," he volunteered.

As we walked outside near the fountain, we were all elated by our victory. I gave Mr. Rivera a little hug and said, "Thank you! Thank you!"

And back in Mexico City, I celebrated by skipping classes and going to bed after a fervent prayer of thanks for softening the judge's heart. I hadn't slept well for nights.

Hours later, I woke up. My headache was gone. I called my parents with the good news of our progress at court. My father told me he had just sent $1,660 dollars. That was 80,000 pesos! I figured I might have to sell my house in Orem to pay for everything, but I was willing to do it.

Saturday, October 2, 1976

Antonio, thinking I was at BYU, sent two letters to Mr. Rivera's office, begging me to come live with him again—saying that he would do whatever I asked. I looked through my other mail. The immigration papers had at last come from Denver with the proper seals, evidence that Antonio had entered the United States as an immigrant in 1974 and not as a tourist as he claimed. The letter from my father included the check for Mr. Rivera and one for me.

After Mr. Rivera read the letters from Antonio, he mused, "Well, it's just as I've always thought: he's using Marita to pressure you to return to him so he can control your life again. These letters show his immaturity. They're a last resort for him."

I agreed totally. "I'm going to ignore them and him."

"Wait a minute, Señora. Don't' tell him *no* definitely. Remember to use his ambivalence. It's obvious from these letters that he's still in love with you," Mr. Rivera pointed out.

"But I'm not in love with him! It's dishonest to string him along when I have no intention of making up with him," I protested.

"I know that," he reassured. "And I certainly know you would never be happy being married to him. But think of Marita. Go see her tomorrow. Soon I'll have the writ ready for court asking the judge to give you custody as he mentioned. And once you have her, I'll take you to the airport myself and arrange everything so you can leave safely."

Sunday, October 3, 1976 — Journal entry

Lupe went with me to Puebla today. My in-laws' ward has just been divided, and there was no more room for all the members to attend at the stake center chapel. So, church services are now held every Sunday at the Cruz home until a new chapel can be built. Marita was sitting on one of Ana Maria's kitchen chairs, attending Junior Sunday School. She slithered down as soon as she saw me, and we climbed up the stairs to the balcony above the patio where the lady missionaries lived. I hugged her and kissed her.

Then she opened the presents I brought: a bag of Twinky Wonder plastic doodads, streamers, a sucker, a balloon, a small broom, two pairs of stockings, a new T-shirt, and a card I made. We traced the outline of my hand next to hers and sang some songs. She kept telling me she wanted to go with me. After fifteen uninterrupted, happy minutes together, Antonio found us.

He read aloud two letters he had written, one to me and one to my parents. He wanted me to live with him, immediately. Marita had been sick all of September—she always got sick after I visited, Antonio complained. She wouldn't eat. They had to give her four shots. She is so very thin. She has hives and sores all over her body, a cough, and a bad cold. The stress is taking its toll.

I don't know what to do. She gets sick when I'm not there because she misses me. She gets sick after I leave because I can't take her with me. She is so young to go through such a trial! I hope she can hang on a bit longer. When it was time for Lupe and me to leave, she clung to my neck, sobbing and begging to go with me. I held her tightly, trying to comfort her.

All I could say was, "I will come and see you again . . . and someday you can go with me on the bus and then on the plane."

It broke my heart to say only this much when she had constantly asked me so sweetly every five minutes to go with me, "*Allá . . . muy lejos en el Avión.*"

Antonio growled, "No you can't go with her because your mommy won't bring you back here!"

She screamed and wailed as I stepped to the curb to cross the street. It tore me up inside to hear her cry like that. I went back to comfort her. She clung to me fiercely and then finally quieted down. But once we had said our last good-bye and I had turned the corner and was out of earshot, I cried all the way to Mexico City. I hoped she would somehow know that this was a temporary situation that would pass. Yet, those hours were a repeat of the scene exactly nine months earlier in our Orem home. He refused to let her go with me in January and he refused in October. She begged to go with me both times. I thought I had reached my limits at other times during the year in my quest, but nothing wrenched my heart and insides like today's visit.

Wednesday, October 6, 1976

As we entered the Puebla court, I saw Antonio standing by the judge's door with four of his lawyers and assistants. I didn't recognize any of them. I ignored Antonio's glares, and soon the judge invited us all to go into his small inner office. There was no room for the lawyers to sit down so they stood while another dispute erupted about my migratory status. At last Judge Casco decided to proceed without my FM form, and he opened a sealed envelope with questions that Antonio's lawyers had prepared to ask me.

Mr. Flores read the list and persuaded the judge to eliminate three questions. After an energetic discussion of the interrogatory questions, I was just sitting there as a spectator watching interchanges between

Antonio's lawyers and my lawyers and between the lawyers and the judge, and suddenly the hearing was over. I had no chance to speak. We all signed a document attesting to our presence there, and the judge ordered everyone out of his office but Antonio and me.

Sternly, seriously, the judge talked to Antonio. Then to me. He asked me four times at least, "Will you go back to him?"

Each time I emphatically responded, "No."

Would Antonio take me back? The answer: "Yes, if she would accept me."

Why wouldn't I go back to him? I explained to the judge, "Because he is cruel to me. And he doesn't have a home or a job or anything to offer me. And he wants me to maintain him while he goes to school!"

The judge finally suggested we consider a voluntary divorce and decide what we will do about Marita's custody. We promised to think about it.

Friday, October 8, 1976

Rain pounded the streets hard all day. I took my final exam half-heartedly, then walked into the rain where no one would notice the tears on my face. My course at the Institute was over. I had worked hard and had received a good recommendation, but I still didn't have a current FM form, so I probably wouldn't get a job after all. No FM form, no job, no money. What would happen to me?

The latest letter I received from my folks was very upsetting. They'd sent me Mr. Rivera's fee breakdown, and I called a friend at another law office to see if his prices were reasonable. I found that he listed some fees for services that were normally free in certain government offices. And for some that were only twenty or thirty pesos, Mr. Rivera was charging two hundred dollars. Other charges were also out of line. Were we being taken for a very elegant but expensive ride? Or did he pad the fees for necessary expenses, such as the bribes I knew very well he was paying?

Saturday, October 16, 1976

The long, weary week was nearly over. Between all the worrying, crying, and praying, I worked on the handouts and panels for the

Relief Society Exposition. There were eight panels two meters long for missionary preparation and six for visiting teaching. My roommates criticized me for doing all that work for free, but they didn't understand how important it was for me to donate my time and talents to build the kingdom of God. I had covenanted in the temple to do all I could to prepare a Zion people, and the display was only one effort among many in a lifetime of service. My "pay" came when Sister Eleanor Brown of the Relief Society General Board praised me, "You have done an excellent job. We'd like to use all of this for the exposition in November."

Marilyn beamed, "I knew you'd do a good job, but I never expected anything as fantastic as this! The Board wants to use them for every exposition in the country, five more times at least."

At home I looked back over the distressing week I'd had and wrote in my journal.

Sunday, when I had been asked to serve as the teacher development director at church, I broke down crying in the bishop's office. Concerned, Ruben DeAnda and his wife, María, took me home to eat and spend time with them until I could pull myself together. Ruben was working on ad campaigns for the Mexican government, and I enjoyed examining his art work. Maria agreed to visit Marita with me in Puebla soon, and I went home feeling strengthened.

Then I called Mr. Schofield to ask about Mr. Rivera and his fees. He advised me not to cause any problems since we were coming so close to getting Marita. He also advised me not to discuss the fees with Mr. Rivera since he had sent the letter to my folks, not me. My parents agreed with that advice, too.

On Monday, María DeAnda went with me to Puebla. A positive, gracious person, María was the support of angels for me during the disappointing day. Papa Dan refused to let us in. We waited. Mama Rosita eventually appeared at the gate. She looked tired, subdued, old. Wisps of unruly hair strayed from her wrinkled face, and her eyes were heavy and sad.

I asked simply, "May we come in to see Marita? I told her I would come back."

Without defensiveness, she explained, "Antonio has given us an order not to let you in or he would take off with Marita to Jalapa or somewhere else and not tell anyone where." Her voice shook. "I'm afraid Marita would die if he took off like that. She's been very ill. Each day she gets worse."

Alarmed, I begged, "Could you bring her to the gate if you won't let me come in?"

Mama Rosita shook her head. "If she sees you again, she would only get worse."

"But she's sick because she wants to see me and be with me. No one will let her. Can't you talk to Antonio so we can work something out and end all this suffering?"

Her eyelids flickered. She sighed and confessed, "I am too old to be taking care of children anymore. I am weary of this difficult situation, and I want it to be over with soon, too. I will talk to Antonio."

She had barely left the gate when Antonio drove up for lunch. The next half-hour was bizarre. He told me I could never see Marita again, not to come anymore, that he was looking for a new wife, and that he'd get married in the Catholic Church because he didn't like the strictness of our church anymore. Then, boasting, he also claimed that he'd been ordained a high priest the night before in the LDS church. I knew that was impossible. Even if the question of his worthiness had been resolved, Bishop Morrill was holding his membership records in Utah.

Unwilling to listen to more madness, I began walking down the street. He fired his parting shot, "We'll see who runs out of money first. This could go on for ten years, you know!"

On Tuesday, Ruben DeAnda took a print of my only photo of Marita suitable for passport use and blocked out the background. The next day, the American Embassy put the photos in my passport and cancelled the I.D. card. I was ready to leave the country.

Thursday, I dissolved in tears when we didn't go to Puebla after all, much less leave Mexico, and we couldn't find the judge. After I had called the law office many times, sobbing in desperation, Gloria suggested I call Papa Dan about Marita.

He told me Marita was doing better, then asked, "Mari, is there any chance you can take Antonio back? Please pray about this. Find out what the Lord wants."

After I called Gloria back, to see if the judge had ever shown up (no, he hadn't), I was still upset. Suddenly Mr. Rivera was on the line. "Señora, we are doing all we can," he snapped. "And if you don't like my services, you should get another lawyer!"

I was silent, shocked at his tone. He continued sharply, "I have the feeling that you don't trust me anymore. I can't work this way. I'll return your father's money so you can carry on with some other lawyer. But I have never lied to you. I promise that you will leave Mexico with your daughter," then hung up.

I sat on my bed, numb and bewildered. I began to pray. I wondered if I should get another lawyer who wouldn't charge so much. But who would I get that I could trust? And who could pick up the case without losing ground? I knew Mr. Rivera had made a lot of progress lately in Puebla. I cried and prayed for hours. I felt helpless.

Eventually, I realized that I couldn't stop what I had begun. I had to continue. Late in the day, I called Gloria and apologized. She accepted it and comforted me, "I do understand your reactions to the situation here. You can call me any time and say anything you want and scream if you need to, if that helps."

Then I felt better. I finally realized what could happen if I tried to force things to go faster than they normally can in Mexico. I had to remember BIG FIVE and be patient one more stretch of time.

At our next meeting, on Friday when I signed a new writ, Mr. Rivera was friendly. The petition explained that Marita was sick, asked the judge to name a good pediatrician to examine her, and requested again that the judge place her in my care. While Gloria retyped parts of the writ, Mr. Rivera told me how he had worked with North Americans for twenty years and knew how both sides think. His hardest job was keeping his clients happy while the process continued to drag on and on in Mexico.

He repeated the idea that I could get another lawyer if I didn't trust him and offered some referrals. But I told him I would trust him and left feeling better, after all.

Chapter Seventeen

October 21, 1976 — Journal entry
Polanco

Another court day, another view of Mexican justice. Señor Castro's cold stares, frowns, and curt answers turned the room into a quick-freeze locker. Clearly, he was stalling the case, from pressure from the Cruz family or from holding out for a bribe. Unfortunately, that's the way things are here in Mexico. In a formal, outward sense, bribes are not legal or openly acceptable in many circles. Yet anyone operating a business or trying to get a transaction of any size completed will soon find that if bribes aren't paid, the parts don't come or necessary action is held up for a long time. In an informal, integral sense, a slush fund for bribes is a "must" for negotiations to be paid on the quiet throughout all levels of Mexican society. I even paid a thousand pesos on the side to the doctor who delivered Marita so that I would be assured a quiet, private room and expert care at the Social Security Hospital, La Raza.

So, at court, instead of custody we got excuses. I imagine the judge had received a bribe from the other party and was waiting to see if mine would match it or better it. Whoever paid the most money for their "justice" won. But for now, he wanted my papers from *gobernación* and assurance that I wouldn't leave the country if he gave me custody. Mr. Rivera assured him I would stay.

Monday, October 25, 1976

Finally! I spent the day in Puebla with the lawyers—with results! Before they went into the center of town, the lawyers had dropped me off to take presents to Marita. No one would let me see her, and Mama Rosita was angry because Antonio had recently been served with more papers. With disgust she exploded at me from inside the gate, "Stop wasting your time! Go back to the States and start working again! Forget Marita for now. You can have her when she is older!" She walked away in a huff.

I hung around for another hour or so before I finally took a dirty, dusty bus to the Zocalo where I joined the lawyers. On the way to the Zocalo I thought about Rosita. She had been raised watching her mother and other women learn to be stoic and submissive, accepting orders and defeat with dignity, in the traditional *mujer abnegada* role. I wasn't raised that way, and I determined she wasn't going to get me to give up so easily and resign myself to going home without my daughter—not without examining every option.

My lawyers had located a good pediatrician who promised to give Marita a very thorough examination. Then we went to see the judge. Actually, I only saw him through the window in the wall dividing his office from the steno pool. I could see Mr. Rivera in there with him, making energetic, expressive gestures with his hands, his face animated. At first the judge chewed his gum slowly, but soon picked up speed. Then he chewed less as he laughed and smiled more. Soon, everyone was smiling and laughing. After fifteen minutes, they emerged—the judge acting friendlier than I had ever seen him.

No one told me, but in my mind I knew there had to be a reason for the change of attitude, and knowing the system, I knew that there had to have been a bribe arranged for at some point.

In the courtyard by the fountain, Mr. Rivera smiled, very pleased with himself. He confidentially announced to me, "Everything is just perfect. It's a sure thing that you will have your daughter, but it's just a matter of time. The judge is on your side now. He has allowed the introduction of a new document giving you custody. He's already begun the paperwork to change the custody from Señor Cruz to you!"

Nearly ten months, who knows how much in bribes, and five separate court actions going on in Mexico and Puebla and I had never seen him so pleased. On the way out of the city, Mr. Rivera explained more.

"Now the judge won't stall the case because he realizes that I will give him your FM form once it's ready." Just the night before, I had told my folks to pray for the judge and my papers because on those two things all the rest seemed to depend. I knew the lawyer would deny that he paid the bribe, but it was obvious he did. And when I told my parents about the "Christmas present," they weren't surprised. They had expected it at some point.

Thursday, October 28, 1976

This week, the peso was devaluated again to 26.50 for each dollar—more than double the amount when I arrived in May. Mr. Rivera couldn't go to Puebla with me and my witnesses because his corporate clients had hundreds of promissory notes to be paid in dollars which would soon be worthless. He planned to spend the entire day rescuing other clients. Even without him our day in court went well. Antonio had been ordered to appear at 10:00 but didn't, nor did any of his representatives. That amounted to a sort of confession on his part, and I gained more ground.

My witnesses, Ann and my former bishop, arrived at 11:00. The judge stayed long enough to carefully check Ann's immigration form and status and then left for a long coffee break while his assistant took the depositions.

My friends gave excellent answers, establishing three points for the court record:

- They knew Antonio was still married to Mari Vawn, and he had a daughter named Andrea Marita Cruz Bailey.
- The couple established their home at Acueducto Guadalupe, Andador 4, Conjunto 8, Casa 3 in Mexico 14, D.F. until July 1974. They then went to the United States where they bought a home in Orem, Utah.
- Antonio abandoned Mari Vawn in January 1976 and separated Marita from her mother in Utah.

They also attested that they knew the Cruz family as well as the exact address where they lived in Puebla. For each point of fact, my witnesses explained why they said those things were true. What a blessing that our former bishop at Acueducto Guadalupe had come to our home in Orem exactly one year before on his trip to the United States for general conference. He also attended sacrament meeting in our ward. He was thus one of the few people in Mexico besides my in-laws who had been in our Orem home. And if Ann had not gone with me two months before that to see Marita, she would not have known the exact address where my in-laws lived.

October 31, 1976
On my way to Saltillo, Coahuila

With no court date on the books for a week or so, I accepted the invitation of a good friend, Mireya Castro de Raygoza, to spend a few days in Saltillo, hundreds of miles north of Mexico City. My ticket cost seventy-six pesos, nearly all I had. I packed a small lunch of sandwiches and fruit to save money. Mireya had offered to pay for my return ticket if I would just come.

Although Mexico celebrated its Day of the Dead on November 2 with various sizes of candy skeletons or sugar skulls and a special bread for the dead to eat, the American custom of trick or treat had trickled down to invade the festivities. The children wandered with a tin can punched with patterned holes over a flickering candle, and they approach saying in "Spanished" English, "Halloween! Halloween!" Instead of receiving candy, they expected others to toss in a few coins. This broke the monotony of their regular begging with simply an outstretched hand.

I threw in no coins at the bus station. I needed every one I had. Other passengers looked as poor as I was. The states to the north—Chihuahua, Guanajuato, and Zacatecas, especially—were economically depressed. From them came most of the illegal or undocumented migrants in the United States. Many felt justified in going to Texas or California to make a living on what used to be part of Mexico. And many left for Mexico City.

During the night, our bus made many stops. I couldn't sleep. I was numb from the cold and alert with anticipation of being in Coahuila again. Coahuila means "place of luxurious growth." It must have been named long ago before it became a desert, for it was currently a desolate area of parched earth and towns that looked dirty because of wind and loose soil as well as a lack of water and finances to keep it greener. But legends told of its former beauty, gardens of diverse trees and flowers, and vast commerce.

As the mountains slipped behind me, the emptiness of the region reminded me of the Montana prairies at home, and I felt comforted again as I did in 1969 when I entered the Coahuila desert to begin my teaching career. Somehow, the catharsis of just the earth and sky and God on this mountainless desert worked its magic again within me. I felt freed from my usual self, released from my own culture and language to something more than being an American to being in touch with the universal human family. From the solitude and refining experiences of wilderness areas, many throughout history have emerged with greater understanding and power to shape their dealings with self and others upon their return to civilization. In such a way, my time in the Mexican desert or in the hills of Montana served me the same: I heard the voice of the heavens, of the earth, of my inner self with more intensity.

From such times and places in my life, I gathered a reserve of strength and clearer vision to know more deeply who I was and what was best for me to do. For most of the years of my life, I have had "thinking places." The first was located deep in my father's trees. To get there I used to walk past the old red barn, the corrals, the slough and into the gray-barked cottonwoods, the willows, and sweet-smelling wild rose bushes. I developed a pattern of wandering through the trees and meadows until I found a likely place to meditate, cry, or arrive at conclusions to questions or quandaries. There, on my father's land that became more dear to me than any other, I matured and grew. After making solemn decisions or feeling a peace, I would return to the house. After those years in Valley County, few spots on earth could compare until I walked under starry skies on dusty streets in the *ejidos* around Torreón in northern Mexico.

An affinity with the essence of the forces of life seemed to surround my soul there in a blend of the here and now and all other centuries crammed into one great surge. I felt closer to the heart of life. Somehow Mexico had the ability to lift my soul to other levels of reality. What was a reality in Mexico might be incongruent anywhere else, but in Mexico I felt more prone to a willing suspension of disbelief in order to feel and process what I saw or heard. I could understand how simple prayers of the Mexican Latter-day Saints could be answered with visions, miracles, and healings. No one had told them that the ministering of angels was reserved for the Saints of Christ's day. If they needed certain miracles, they asked and they received.

Anything was possible in Mexico. Where else do grown men fly hanging upside down from ropes tied to their feet? What other capital city has engineers pumping water under the city to keep the skyscrapers floating?

Though anything was possible in Mexico, doing the simplest things in a practical sense was impossible on some days. Like getting mail out of the post office or buying a liter of milk. BIG FIVE entered into everything, and one never knew when serendipity or calamity would strike. Life was intense, felt deeply by a nation of more right-brained thinkers than I was used to finding in my own country where logic and facts prevailed.

So, in this time out of time, under a different sky and in the light dry air, I rejoiced to feel again a tug on my heart from the desert and the eternal sensations of Mexico.

Monday, November 1, 1976
Saltillo, Coahuila

The bus pulled into Saltillo at 4:00 A.M. Mireya didn't know when I would arrive, and she had no phone at home. I didn't have enough money for a taxi, so I waited at the station until 6:00. I entered a battered local bus shrouded by a heavy fog. I sat in the front seat behind the driver's decorated front dash. A red silky fringe hung above the windshield. A medallion from the Shrine of the Virgin of Guadalupe swung back and forth near an altar by the door. On the altar sat pots of wilted flowers and blinking votive candles. The dashboard was covered with a veneer of mother of pearl.

My seat in the front offered the best view of the city's street signs, and I asked people if we were approaching Fraccionmento La Madrid. I had never been to Saltillo before, and I strained to peer through patches of fog to see where the bus was. The mists rolled, featherlike at times, as the city appeared and disappeared. Cold, damp air oozed through the cracks in the bus, chilling me to the bone. When the bus had made the full circuit of the city, I stood numbly at the station I had started from. I was not sure what to do next.

Just as I was about to board another local bus, an old man approached me. Tall, dignified, and worn by hard work and weather, he asked me if I needed help, his voice and eyes kind. I felt safe in explaining my predicament.

He understood. "I know how it feels to be in a strange place and not know how to get somewhere. I was a *bracero* in the United States. I didn't know much English, but kind people helped me."

His gnarled hand reached into his left shirt pocket and pulled out a fifty peso bill. He put it into my hand, took me to find a taxi, and slid in beside me so the driver wouldn't take advantage of me. For a few minutes he chatted with the driver and before long, we stopped in front of a new, light-brown brick home not far from the bus station. Amazing. Everyone I had talked to had told me it was very far away.

I knew that most Mexicans desire to be polite and sensitive so you won't think they don't want to help you. Even if they don't know where a place is, they invent directions in an effort to help. I thanked the old man and the Lord for saving me from an unpleasant situation. I rang Mireya's doorbell at 8:00 A.M.

Johnny let me in. Fair-complected, thin and wiry, and about my height, Johnny hadn't changed from the first time I met him in 1969. We were both twenty-one then, but he was already the district president at church. For nine months I was engaged to Johnny's best friend. The next year, I played matchmaker and introduced him to Mireya Castro, one of my students from the American School. I had also introduced her to the gospel, and she and her family joined the Church. Johnny and Mireya were married in the Arizona Temple not long after Antonio and I were. Through the years Mireya was the only former student who continued to write to me. She had called regularly to follow the progress of my case; knowing she prayed for me always made me feel loved.

Johnny gave me a big *abrazo* and led me to the bedroom where Mireya was just waking up. Dark brown curls fell around her plump round face as she raised up on one arm.

"Mari! You really came!" I hugged her.

We spent the first two days of my visit catching up and laughing about old times.

Mari Vawn Bailey

Thursday, November 4, 1976 — Journal entry
Saltillo, Mexico

After four days in the desert, I experienced refreshment to soul, relief from my suffering, and renewed closeness to Father in Heaven and to the feelings I felt six years ago. I had forgotten how beautiful, how peaceful and secure, and how real those feelings were. On this trip I have felt less a part of earth and more a part of eternity, as though Father's loving arms are around me in peace, adding strength for the challenges ahead.

Mireya, as the District Young Women's President, began inviting people to come to her home last night to listen to me give a presentation on her favorite theme.

"You're famous," she told me. "I've told so many people about you for years. Now that they know you're here, they want to meet you."

Everyone came—friends, relatives, and even Saltillo's district president. I talked for over an hour on "Preparing for the Eternities." In spite of its spontaneity, it seemed as though we had planned it for a month. It was a real highlight for us.

In fact, all went well on my visit, and the only thing I don't like about being here is the cold. I haven't taken my coat off once since I arrived, and I sleep in my clothes every night. With no central heating in most Mexican homes or buildings, the only warm place in winter is in bed. During the day people simply add another layer of clothes to achieve a comfortable body temperature. I add the layers, but just knowing there is nowhere to go to get warmer, I psychologically shiver.

Just before I boarded the bus for Mexico, the district president and his wife discussed my situation with me. "But why," they asked, "does no one in the Church in Mexico City or Puebla help you?"

I said I didn't know, but I have thought about this issue a lot. I realize that we are all human and that some local Church leaders are just as human as anyone else and subject to their free agency, personal preferences, and prejudices in how they implement policies and procedures of the worldwide Church. Of course, the leaders are supposed to be living close to the Spirit in order to receive revelation as to what they should do and advise others to do. Some leaders are wiser and more in tune than others. Since they are are all lay leaders and have families and professions as well, they have to juggle their time and priorities in order to watch over the sheep in their flock *and* do what it takes to be in tune with the Spirit.

I have a firm belief our restored Church itself is true and perfect as far as having the same priesthood authority, organization, and goals as the church during Christ's earthly ministry. I also believe that the prophet receives direct revelation from Christ himself. But at the same time, I realize that as much as the leaders under the prophet also receive inspiration and for the most part sincerely lead the Church well, there are some leaders who make mistakes.

But the principle of repentance exists, and most lay leaders learn from their mistakes enough to improve their work. For those leaders who for some reason continue in some errors, I know they will eventually be found out and corrected. In the meantime, the Church members who might suffer because of human error or human nature will be blessed if they are patient, forgiving, and do the best they can until the situation improves. Since I find myself in the latter position, I hope the Church leaders will soon agree on how to proceed in our situation.

Sometimes people get confused and think the "Church" has let them down when parts of the system and parts of the "program" do not help them in their hour of need. But there is more to the Church than just the people or the programs. Some people are in the Church, but the Church (the gospel of Christ) is not functioning well in their daily lives.

I am learning there are different levels of action, expectation, faith, purity, and understanding. At times

Church leaders want to help one person, but they are limited in what they can do because some actions will have far-reaching effects on too many other people.

I realize that as the Church leaders find themselves limited in what they can do to help me, I still have access through prayer and faith to the number one leader of the Church—Jesus Christ. As the creator of this earth, the Great I AM and the resurrected Messiah, he is not limited except by eternal laws. I know he has the power to bring about many miracles if a person has enough faith and pays the price. There is no other way but to rely upon him.

I am on the bus now, on the way back to Mexico City, and I remember other mothers out in the desert, concerned about their children. The words to the poem I wrote recently play themselves out in my mind as the miles slip behind me as I cross the desert.

TESTS OF SARAH

I find another Sarah in me, and
I find types and shadows in His hand
moving through the moments of this year.
My Lord, my Father, there has been no ram
in the thicket yet for my daughter,
nor has she been delivered from the hands
of her abductors, as was Sariah's son, Nephi.
Those other mothers had words from on high
promising the glory that would be revealed later
in their posterity.

With these words of promise,
how could it be that those children would perish in
    the desert?
The fire of faith purifying is felt the hottest
when logical, human reason cannot easily comfort
the ache in a mother's soul
until she knows that her child is safe,
those prayers are answered and Father did indeed

fulfill his words and promises in his own due time
so the mother's offering and sacrifices
are accepted and answered
with blessings on her head.

For those other Sarahs,
their hour of rejoicing is known
to all the children of Israel who read
and remember.
For the Sarah I am this year,
there is no page written yet
to tell the hour or the manner
in which my child
will be returned to me.

My Sarah's test
is not over yet.

My Lord, I wait.

Tuesday, November 9, 1976 — Journal entry

 This is the last page of this journal I started when I first turned toward Mexico six months ago. It is November now, and the dreariness of winter days is settling into the city, adding a deeper shade of gray to the already smoggy skies. The hours seem interminable. I have little to do except teach my roommates English two hours every night. A friend joins us, and he pays eighty pesos a lesson. The other hours of the day I wonder when my empty arms and aching heart will be filled.
 Yesterday I took my passport to *gobernación* for a new visa. For the first time since my visa was stolen, the paperwork has been completed and signed. It states I have permission to be in the country for six months for the express purpose of getting my daughter. I celebrated with relief and joy to hold a copy of the *oficio* in my hands! It will still take a few weeks to get the FM3 form so I can

show my papers to the judge in Puebla. Without it, I can't leave the country, the judge can't give the final decision, I can't work, and I still do not exist in the eyes of the Mexican government.

Marilyn invited me to Cuernavaca for the day, and feeling more cheerful than I'd been for weeks, I boarded the bus. Marilyn and I talked every minute I was at her house, at the restaurant for lunch, in the car, and at the bus station before I left. We raced our words and emotions, trying to squeeze them all in. Our laughter and tears were a comfort to our souls.

Before I left, she handed me a copy of Elder Neal A. Maxwell's BYU talk "But for a Small Moment" that I read in the solitude of the bus ride back. It was a turning point for me and gave me a needed perspective on trials, testing, endurance, and not letting the pressures of time and tests cloud my eternal perspective.

I promise myself more fervently than ever before that I will not allow anything to drive me away from here until I can safely leave Mexico with Marita. So many moments this week have brought me to the brink of giving up and leaving without her. Not anymore. I vow to ponder this talk if I ever waver again.

Chapter Eighteen

Monday, November 15, 1976 — Journal entry

Today at *gobernación* I signed the FM3 documents, gave them my photos, and let them take my thumbprints. However, they said I still wouldn't receive the form to use until "next week." Mañana, always mañana.

Tuesday, November 16, 1976
Polanco

Two months earlier I told Marilyn I wouldn't be in Mexico for the exhibition in Churubusco. But there I was, standing by my walls of panels once again, as Regional Representatives, stake presidents, and stake Relief Society leaders moved through the hall. I had known many of them for years. Some ignored me. Others greeted and encouraged me, saying they knew the Lord would answer my prayers soon. Most of them just looked at me, saying nothing. Few people expected I would still be in Mexico after all this time.

The evening drained me emotionally. If it hadn't been for Marilyn a few feet away with her food storage display of dried slices of tomatoes, dehydrated pineapple, and new bean sprouts, I would have felt very alone.

Through conversations with various people at the exhibition, I gathered disturbing news—scary rumors of another peso devaluation and a military takeover before 1 December when Mexico's new president,

Jose Lopez Portillo, would take office. The people of Mexico were weary of widespread corruption, and I knew a takeover was possible. Fear gripped me. I had no food supply, no job, no protection, no papers to leave Mexico. Getting to the border and out of the country under martial law was a terrifying prospect. The feeling of anxious desperation returned. By the time I reached my apartment, I felt alone and *desamparada* [forsaken].

As I read through the book *Winning through Intimidation*, I recognized tricks Antonio was using against me and methods I might have to employ to win in the long run. I loved the image of the turtle winning the race in spite of the hare's devious methods along the way. I understood better how Hare Antonio could sleep at night untroubled by conscience after I read that "honesty" is a subjective, relative thing because everyone tailors his definition of honesty to conveniently fit his own actions and the givens of life's situations.

The Fiddle Theory also made sense: "The longer a person fiddles around with something, the greater the odds that the result will be something negative." Right. I knew that if something didn't happen soon, the mess in court would be so tangled that only the next decade would give us time to straighten it out. If I survived a possible military takeover and was still able to fight Antonio at court and in his home, I planned to use some of the advice I found in the book: Accept the reality or don't play the game. Be prepared and confident. Be cool and gutsy. And come through at the moment of truth.

Friday, November 19, 1976

On the way down Insurgentes Sur, tears came to my eyes as I read on a billboard:

*El esperado amor desesperado
si no le ha llegadono se desespere.*

[Don't give up hope if the love you've been waiting for so desperately hasn't come your way yet.]

It was poetic justice that on this six months' anniversary of my arrival to Mexico, Lic. Rivera told me during my visit to his office that he would help the judge write the custody decree on Friday. Papasito, Antonio, and Marita would probably be summoned into court in December. It was possible I could take her home with me after court that day. The judge's assistant, a woman, had read my file and openly favored this action. She insisted that Marita must be with her mother.

Meanwhile, I learned that Antonio fired his lawyer and hired another. The first lawyer was an LDS bishop I'd never met or heard of before. He obviously knew nothing about my good character or life. This lawyer/bishop had sworn in court that he knew me and that I was a prostitute. Such blatant libel was the worst perjury, but typical of the concoctions in all the court records of Antonio's legal actions that I read in August. The lawyer probably assumed he was safe in his perjury because no one thought I would ever arrive in Mexico to challenge his lies. The stories they made up had to be horrible enough to convince the judge in January that I was an unfit mother, so he said whatever it took to start divorce proceedings.

Of course I was glad to hear Antonio no longer retained him as a lawyer, and I felt doubly glad I didn't have that man for a bishop. He was the worst case I knew of someone who compartmentalized his workaday life to comply with Mexican tradition and yet somehow could function as a bishop on weekends. Of the attacks against me during the year, this one was the most difficult for me to understand and to forgive.

As the weeks passed, I had waited for the Puebla doctor to examine Marita. Although I had gone to visit her several times, they never let me see her. I didn't know if her health had improved, and the opposing lawyers kept stalling on a doctor everyone could agree on. The judge didn't sign the order until the middle of November, and they had to give Antonio time to ask his own doctor to examine her. Marita's health was constantly on my mind. Why didn't they do something?

Mr. Rivera said, "I've done everything by now that I have to do for the case. It is a matter of timing. We are waiting and watching to make sure that what is left to happen happens with precise timing."

I knew I had to see Marita again soon, but I was weary of the refusals at the gate after I had given all my time, money, and effort to go see her. Mr. Rivera encouraged me, "You have a right to see her, no matter what they say to keep you away from her. It is critical for her to see you this week so that she will remember you when she sees you in court. She needs to respond well to you."

I had not seen her or held her for two months—a long time in the life of a three-year-old. We both suffered for want of contact with each other.

Before I left the office, Mr. Rivera confided, "The main problem in cases such as yours is that most American women lose patience, give up, and return to the States before any results can come. Most cases require at least six months."

I looked at him, astonished that he would think I could give up now. "I have to wait. Marita is the most important thing in the world to me," I stated firmly.

Sunday, November 21, 1976

Betty, a fifteen-year-old girl from our ward, met me at the Estrella Roja Bus Station at 7:40 A.M. to go with me to Puebla. After we got off the bus, we stopped in front of a shop to pray. Then we walked down the street to the house and straight through the gate behind two LDS women going in for church, and no one stopped us from entering. But we didn't attend church there. We had more important business. Marita had to know I was there to see her.

The Spirit had prompted me strongly before we had left Mexico City that Betty should wait outside and watch the *despacho* door so no one could take Marita out. Betty told me later that Papa Dan stood on the roof and looked down at her for a long time, so I appreciated her standing guard while I was inside trying to see Marita.

Mama Rosita came to the patio and invited me to the services. I simply stated, "I've come to see Marita."

Exasperated, she glared at me and demanded, *¿Por qué te expones?* I looked back blankly, not understanding fully.

She went on, "You put yourself and Marita in great danger when you come here while the court case is still going on. We can call the police to come get you, you know."

I snapped back, "That's a lie! I have a right to see her!"

She backed into the doorway to Ana Maria's living room where they waited for her to start Relief Society. She sputtered, "You can *not* see Marita."

I walked a few feet to the west and tried to enter the other part of the house, but they were holding priesthood meeting in Rosita's living room. I returned to the patio and looked up to the windows on the second story, searching for a glimpse of Marita. Only Teresa looked back at me. Then Antonio came out, and he never left my side for the next two hours.

I searched every room I could, looking for her. I shouted her name, hoping she would respond. I pushed hard on the door to the new bedroom adjacent to the kitchen, but couldn't open it. I decided Teresa must have been keeping her in there. I hoped she heard me calling her. After awhile, I returned to the patio and Antonio stood there with me, trying to pump me for information.

I wouldn't answer many of his questions and gave curt answers to the rest. I moved to the attack: "Marita is in her formative years. If she is to become an effective mother someday herself, she needs to be with me now."

"But I don't want to let her go, and I don't want to cause a trauma in her life." He admitted, "I know that if I lose this court case, I will be excommunicated from the Church."

"Does that matter to you?"

"Yes, it's still important to be LDS."

I puzzled, "Why haven't you repented at all this year for the pain you have caused us?"

Boldly he confessed, "If I did, I'd have to give Marita back to you. I have her because of my astuteness, and I'm going to keep her."

I was stunned. He clearly knew that he would lose Marita if he was sincerely repentant. He also knew repentance meant being able to feel pain for the wrong done to others and making a promise not to hurt them again. The restitution step would be so easy in our case. Return Marita. Let her go with me. But no. We haggled about other details, and by noon, it was obvious we were getting nowhere.

I began reading key scriptures to him about the Lord's view of lying and other offenses Antonio had committed. After I read several references, he admitted, "Well, I have lied some." But no words of repentance came.

I read other verses and stopped occasionally to ask, "Don't you want to repent or ask forgiveness yet?"

He answered "No" every time.

I opened my Spanish scriptures of the Doctrine and Covenants to

Section 98 and began reading verses 23-25 aloud to him.

> Now, I speak unto you concerning your families—if men will smite you, or your families, once, and ye bear it patiently and revile not against them, neither seek revenge, ye shall be rewarded;
>
> But if ye bear it not patiently, it shall be accounted unto you as being meted out as a just measure unto you.
>
> And again, if your enemy shall smite you the second time, and you revile not against your enemy, and bear it patiently, your reward shall be an hundredfold.

By verse 28, he became more uncomfortable as I read,

> And now, verily I say unto you, if that enemy shall escape my vengeance, that he be not brought into judgment before me, then ye shall see to it that ye warn him in my name, that he come no more upon you, neither upon your family, even your children's children unto the third and fourth generation.

But he still did not humble himself outwardly or ask forgiveness. Then with greater intensity, I read verse 40 and beyond.

> And so on unto the second and third time; and as oft as thine enemy repenteth of the trespass wherewith he has trespassed against thee, thou shalt forgive him, until seventy times seven . . .

He stood there with his back against the rust-colored patio wall, taking it all in. Before I went on to the next page, I gave him one last invitation to repent or let me see Marita. He refused to repent, but he asked, "Have you really forgiven me?"

Humbly and sincerely I emphasized, "Yes I have. And I told you that in July, too. But forgiving you doesn't mean I can take you back. It means I understand you pretty well. And I pity you. I don't hate you. I just can't tolerate what you do and say anymore. And even though I forgive you, I won't be around for you to abuse any more! I've had it!"

In my most deliberate forceful speaking voice, I read the verses that

I had waited a year to bring to his attention, 44-46:

> But if he trespass against thee the fourth time thou shalt not forgive him, but shalt bring these testimonies before the Lord; and they shall not be blotted out until he repent and reward thee four-fold in all things wherewith he has trespassed against thee.
>
> And if he do this, thou shalt forgive him with all thine heart; and if he do not this, I, the Lord, will avenge thee of thine enemy an hundred-fold;
>
> And upon his children, and upon his children's children of all them that hate me, unto the third and fourth generation.

I looked up at him occasionally as I spoke. He seemed amused and not at all affected by my furor and seriousness. With a semi-smirk he acted as if this were all a big joke. How could I judge this stranger who was my husband? It was impossible. I felt relief in knowing I could leave the avenging to the Lord and wash my hands of him. The law of the harvest would bring what he deserved in natural consequence to his poor choices, both on earth and in eternity.

As instructed in a priesthood blessing more than a year earlier, the Lord told me that he would fight my battles for me as outlined in Section 98 if I found it to be necessary. I knew it was time to let Antonio know this formally. Since I had never done such a thing before, I wasn't sure if I should bring my arm to the square or not to formally charge him. But I knew he would pay attention to me and remember it if I did.

I put on my red nylon jacket and asked him to give Marita the presents I had brought for her. A surge of energy filled me. I looked Antonio in the eye as I raised my right arm to the square and declared, "I testify against you. I bring against you my testimony of all you have done this year and other years to hurt me, Marita, and my family. I am asking the Lord to fight my battles for me as he has said in Section 98. I will do no more. I say this in the name of Jesus Christ, Amen."

"Amen," echoed Antonio, visibly shaken and finally affected by it all.

I turned and walked away from him to the gate. As I stepped out the front gate, Betty put her arm around me and we stumbled down the street, crying openly. I sobbed uncontrollably. I couldn't bear leaving the house again, the fourth time in a row, without seeing Marita and comforting her. Yet, I had done all I could.

Back in Mexico City, I wrote in my journal for solace. I had nothing to show for my trip or many of my efforts all year, but I counted the blessings, not obvious to others:

> Tonight I thank the Lord for his watchful care over me. There were a few times today that Antonio grabbed me much too roughly and could have hurt me, but he stopped. Yesterday a car that I didn't see stopped just before it ran over me. Almost every day I go out into a city of twelve million people—alone. I don't know how many times I've been innocently standing in a dangerous situation or have been prevented from entering one, but I know the Lord watches over the single mothers who are valiantly trying to keep their families together. One day, I will stand safe in my parents' arms and Marita will be with me.
>
> Never in my life do I remember speaking with such force as I did today when the Spirit moved me to testify against Antonio. In spite of my pain now, I love the Lord, and I know he will not fail me.
>
> *But for a small moment* says the Lord in Doctrine and Covenants section 122, and in our small moments of this earth life hang the outcome of how we spend eternity. What a difference our small moments and decisions make as to the glories we accumulate from earth life. So much can be lost so quickly here, and so much is bought with such a high price in this life. I am willing to pay the price. I pray I can do it and see clearly enough for the "small moments" ahead.

After all, if I looked at what was happening to me from the Lord's perspective, those eleven months Marita had been separated from me so far was only one "minute" in Kolob time. Since modern revelation informs us that a thousand years is but a day with the Lord, 41.6 years is an hour on Kolob near where he resides, and 8.3 months of earth time is a minute to him. So, as I prayed, it helped to remember that if I got the answer of *Soon*, it was relative. I just hoped a few Kolob seconds would be enough to see him fight my battles and bring us home.

Wednesday, December 1, 1976 — Journal entry

>In the middle of the night, Lupe flipped on the light switch, waking me. I asked as calmly as I could, "Why did you do that?"
>
>She sneered, *"¡Ni modo que voy a acostar tan temprano como tu!"* [No way am I going to bed as soon as you do!]
>
>After rummaging in a drawer, she left the room. I got up and turned out the light. She came back in and turned on the light again. Pressures boiled inside me—from so many circumstances that had worked against me all year, from failed promises, from living in the limbo of not knowing, from people intimidating me and acting as though I didn't matter. Pure rage mounted inside as I lay there. Eventually Lupe turned off the light and got into her bed.
>
>By then I was sitting upright, my fists clenched at my temples, screaming out my agony, my rage, and my helplessness in one long loud "AAUUGGHH!"
>
>Poor Lupe shot out of her bed, scrambling and stumbling into the next bedroom. When I poked my head into the hall to see how she was, I saw Dora and Coco giving her water with sugar in it to help reduce the shock and keep her from fainting. They refused to speak to me, and I didn't go back to sleep again.
>
>Today was a holiday to give workers a chance to attend or to celebrate the changeover from Echeverria to Lopez Portillo. But only paid commoners filled certain buses that made their way to the ceremony, *para hacer bulto* [to make a crowd]. My roommates stayed home because, like almost everyone else, they feared bombs or a military takeover. I left at 9:00 and walked through the almost deserted streets. I was so agitated I didn't care about bombs. Almost no buses were running, but eventually I made my way to Acueducto, hoping Ann would be

home.

She was, and I wept out my frustration and anger until my overburdened heart had emptied enough to talk. Ann was a good therapist. She listened to me and busied me in making salt-dough Christmas ornaments and beads to string into a necklace for Marita. Later we went out to lunch, window-shopped, and saw a movie. I returned to my apartment after dark, apologized to my roommates, and resolutely picked up the frayed threads of my life again. Where would I find the patience?

Friday, December 3, 1976 — Journal entry

My mother has been experiencing a similar fretting and frantic waiting. It wears on me to get her phone calls and have no progress to report. Most of our desperation lately stems from looking at the calendar. There is nothing else to do in court right now, except wait. There are two more working weeks left before everyone takes off for Christmas vacation. Parties start on December 12 for the celebration of the Virgin Guadalupe, and they don't end until January 6 when the Three Kings come to put gifts in the children's shoes. Even if we don't have any extra delays during those next two weeks, it will take a miracle to produce my FM form, a final decision in the Puebla court, and custody of Marita by Christmas. How could these things happen in two more weeks if they couldn't happen in the last seven months?

I had little to tell my parents when they called in desperation every night that week, hoping for some change. They want us to be home for Christmas, but the reality of the situation had reached them, I knew, when my mother told me that if I didn't make it by then, they would leave the tree up until we DID come home.

I left the apartment at 10:00 A.M. and walked for seven hours along Reforma, Insurgentes, and Independencia while I looked for some oil paints, brushes, and enough supplies to keep my mind busy during the long wait of

December. I knew the president of Mexico has installed his new cabinet and is making personnel changes in *gobernación*, more excuses for holding up getting my FM form ready.

But mostly as I walked, I was thinking and trying to accept the reality that I might have to stay in Mexico all month and maybe into 1977. Before today, I had not allowed myself to consider the possibility of not being with Marita for Christmas. What could I give her for Christmas if I can't be with her?

After I bought the painting supplies and held them in my arms, the heaviness began to lift. The prospect of creating something beautiful focused my thoughts more positively. As I plan the design of the new paintings, excitement is replacing despondency. Years ago Linda and I had made a pact: that if we weren't able to get to it sooner, that at age sixty we definitely would take an oil painting class together. Now I had the time, the place, the need and the solitude without interruptions. Painting will fill much of the void around me and in me.

By late afternoon I arrived at Nancy's apartment to give her a Spanish lesson. She is learning Spanish quickly, and I had fun tutoring her and taking trips into the city with her. She and her husband live in Lomas within walking distance of my apartment, and I ate supper with them before they walked back with me to Polanco.

I arrived in time for our favorite soap opera, *Mañana Será Otro Día*. My roommates were eating their supper from their laps, watching Marianna explain one more time how she was searching for her lost son who had been taken from her at birth. I wonder how she could be so cheerful after so many years of looking for him. I thought bitterly, *Sure tomorrow is another day, another day to hope and look for your child, but how do you handle it so well when a whole year of "other days" has passed and not much has changed? How can you accept it and go on? How will I be able to bear it if I have to endure all this into 1977 or beyond?*

When I talked to my parents tonight, my father was

pleased I have paints again and could find a creative release for my stress. I didn't want to explode again. Lupe refused to sleep in the same room with me for several nights, preferring the couch to my company. Although I haven't oil painted for fifteen years, my father suggested I paint something for Mr. Rivera. Mireya had asked me to paint one depicting the missions of our lives together, and I'm planning one of the Savior for Marilyn. I have plenty to keep me busy during the holidays.

Tuesday, December 7, 1976 — Journal entry

Nancy and I attended the English-speaking ward's Spiritual Living lesson at Eleanor Brown's home this morning. Before Sister Brown began the lesson, she passed around Christmas candy canes she had bought in the States as a surprise. I enjoyed mine, but I began feeling homesick. I knew the candy cane would be the only familiar touch of Christmas I would experience this year. She prefaced the lesson with moments from history of the Church in Mexico.

When they divided the first stake here in Mexico City seven years ago, President Marion G. Romney attended from Salt Lake. He told the congregation that the Day of the Lamanite had commenced. When I heard that, I realized that the 1845 prophecy of the Twelve Apostles was being fulfilled. He also said that Father Lehi and many other Book of Mormon prophets were present there that day when the first stake of ALL Lamanite leaders was formed. And they were also present at the 1972 Area Conference in Mexico City. Since I had also attended the conference, I loved knowing that I had been there with them.

As Sister Brown related these details, tears wet my face because I felt closer to those prophets and also to those angels, whoever they are, who are protecting me so well this year. Then, she began the lesson on Joseph Smith's trials in Liberty Jail. I told myself I would stay and listen just as I did last spring in Orem when the lesson was on understanding the bereaved. But I wasn't strong enough today.

I heard a voice from a tape recorder repeat parts of the scripture in the Doctrine and Covenants that the Prophet wrote while in jail:

> O God, where art thou? And where is the pavilion that covereth thy hiding place? How long shall thy hand be stayed, and thine eye, yea thy pure eye, behold from the eternal heavens the wrongs of thy people and of thy servants . . . how long shall they suffer these wrongs and unlawful oppressions, before thine heart shall be softened toward them . . .

The flood of tears was released. I ran out of the room, sobbing.

I met with Brother and Sister Schofield in their home tonight for some counsel on handling things better in the future if I start feeling so desperate as I have this past week. They suggested that:

1. I can't force the Lord, the lawyer, or the judge. It must all happen in its own time . . . not the time I hope for.

2. I must accept being here for as long as it takes. If I decide to stay for the long haul, and it takes less time, I will be pleasantly surprised and blessed.

3. I will survive being alone for Christmas. I survived other Christmases alone here in Mexico before, and I can do it again if I have to. I must remember eternal perspectives.

4. Since I am so close to results in court, I can't give up now and go back home. I must live in "day-tight" compartments just living hour by hour, day by day. If I can manage that and not permit myself to consider the future, then I'll remain calmer and survive better. It is thinking about the future that causes my desperation to set in. I must avoid doing that.

5. I must continue keeping my mind busy by painting, reading, writing, teaching, visiting people, etc. I must exercise my body in order to release frustrations. Brother

Schofield suggested I walk as fast as I can for forty-five minutes a day. I agreed to do that.

6. I'll continue to live the gospel the best I can so the Lord can bless me when the time is right.

For Marita I will live, love, and triumph. I can see quite clearly now that the desperation of the last week or so has come chiefly from the pressure of time. I suppose that somehow during all these months of waiting, the idea of *one year* or *this year* always lurked in the background. A need for closure is natural, and I had thought it surely would be over by the end of this year! And suddenly the end of the year is only three weeks away!

Saturday, December 11, 1976 — Journal entry

This morning I received a Christmas card at the law office. My friend Denise Lindberg had written on the top: *Remember the blessing which Moses pronounced upon the children of Israel: 'The Lord bless thee and keep thee; the Lord make his face to shine upon thee and be gracious unto thee, the Lord lift up His countenance upon thee and give thee peace.'* I cried every time I have read it today. How I needed the blessing of peace, especially after I received more legal news at the law office.

Now there is no more wondering. Today I know for sure that I will have to wait until 1977 for the end of this nightmare. All it took was a report from Mr. Flores after his most recent trip to Puebla to confirm what I had expected to hear. The doctor won't examine Marita until the middle of January, and the judge won't make a decision without my FM form. The judge wasn't in his office much this week and didn't do anything on my case. But Antonio has been busy trying to stall the case and get a writ of habeas corpus. However, the judge won't make an interlocutory decision about it until next week.

I decided to make Marita a Christmas stocking and fill it with fun gifts. I was fine until I glanced through the toy section at Woolworth's on Insurgentes Sur. Then I got sick, realizing that I would not be with her on Christmas. I had so very little money to buy her anything nice, and her cousins would wreck whatever I gave her as they had the other gifts I had brought her. What could I give her, then?

After some deliberation, I bought some cups and dishes, a comb, mirror, and bracelets. It hurt me more than anything to have such meager gifts. She had suffered so much. I wanted to give her something magnificent to make up for it.

My roommates left for Acapulco, leaving me an empty apartment to set up my canvases and blend colors in peace.

Wednesday, December 15, 1976

Mr. Rivera and Mr. Flores took me to Puebla to see the doctor, but after waiting a while we left because he was "too busy" to go to court with us as planned. Then they took me to see the judge who, smiling and cooperative, agreed to give me a court order to see Marita more often and to call the Cruz family to court in January. I signed both writs and read one that Antonio recently introduced asking the magistrate to read our main file and comment on it, an obvious stall. I met the President of the Supreme Court of Puebla informally, and my judge told him about our case. Apparently he had asked about me before and had wondered if I had ever gone to court there. Once the higher court judge knew for himself what sort of person I was, and if he ever read our case, I hoped he would realize that Antonio had already lost. I assumed Antonio knew it also and was stalling the case with the writs.

When I told Mr. Rivera what Linda wrote in her last letter ("Antonio has just about hung himself"), he nodded and hooted, "He *has* hung himself! I'm not too worried about the measures Antonio uses to weary us. Once the judge makes the decision, the situation will be the same as it was before he took Marita out of Utah. You will both have equal custody before the law." We left Puebla feeling good about our accomplishments.

When I called my folks with my progress report, they were pleased. They told me to buy Marita a gift from them. I bought two books of figures we could cut out, a Japanese goldfish with three tails, a fishbowl, and some food.

I wrapped the other presents and slipped them into the bright-yellow felt Christmas stocking I had made in Relief Society. I glued a Snoopy and an angel made of felt onto the stocking for her. Little by little, Christmas spirit replaced the desperation in my heart.

Saturday, December 18, 1976

Gloria handed me the miracle court order that Mr. Rivera determinedly got for me just hours before. The judge, on his last working day, signed the court order giving me the right to visit Marita at the Cruz home on Saturdays and Sundays during mornings or afternoons. The order also called Antonio and me into court on January 12. Oh, he did it! He did it! He got the court order I needed! They must have had an outstanding lunch together. This was quite a Christmas present!

Gloria and I were beaming. We stood together by her desk looking at the court order. Her brown eyes dancing, she said, "Señora, you are so very lucky to have that order. Mr. Flores was absolutely amazed to see a judge actually sign such an order. He had never seen it done before in his life! And besides that, the judge waived the three-day waiting period and let Mr. Rivera bring it here for you to use immediately!"

I left for Puebla at once.

Antonio read the order, shrugged, and opened the heavy metal gate. When Marita saw me in the living room, she ran straight to me and shouted, *"¡Momi, Momi, Ya veniste!"* [Mommy, you finally came!] I was thrilled to hold my little girl again after three months and to stroke her fine brown hair. I gave her the fish and the stocking. She was enchanted. She asked me to help her make a piñata.

With a flour and water *engrudo* paste, we started gluing tissue paper strips to a small clay pot. In spite of our plan to make a fish, the piñata turned into a parrot and nearly all her purplish blue paper strips encased her hands as she pasted layer after layer in little rolls around her fingers. I helped her wash the papers off in time for supper. She ate some corn and sucked the contents from a raw egg. That's all she wanted.

I told her I had to leave when the sun went down. She accepted that, and I walked through the patio gate where Antonio stood. As I passed under the stone archway, I said, "Thank you for letting me see her."

He glared, scowling but a little astonished, "Don't thank me. Thank the Lord. That's the only way I can figure out you got in today."

The gate clanged shut behind me, but I rejoiced for a peaceful afternoon with Marita, compared to what I remembered three months ago. She had grown taller, was more independent, tougher, even bossy, *mandona*. Had she been away from me too long for us to be mother and daughter again? She acted more like the perfect little hostess intent on entertaining her guest. She hugged and kissed me, but she did that to everyone.

Her speech was changing and sounded so charming. For a three-year-old, her Spanish was nearly perfect, but she did say *pos sí* in the cutest way and *pongue* instead of *puse*. However, she called me "Bailey" sometimes instead of "Momi," and Antonio called her Andrea, not Marita. While we were working on the pinata, she asked me, "Do you love Papa?" I didn't want her to feel that she shouldn't love her father just because I didn't, but I wondered if Antonio was telling her that because I didn't love him, I didn't love her either.

One thing was sure: My determination to spend every possible hour with her. That bond had to grow between us again. Since I had seen her only a handful of times, I had been a near stranger to her during the year. Of course she wasn't as close to me emotionally anymore. Nevertheless, this last visit pointed out to me the great need Marita had to know me again—as a person, as her mother, and as someone she needed in her life. I had to be with her much more. I was thankful for my Christmas present that year: a court order that would allow me to tease her, hold her, and share my love with her more often.

Chapter Nineteen

Monday, December 20, 1976

EVEN WITHOUT SNOW ON THE GROUND the Spirit of Christmas transforms the heart in Mexico City as elsewhere. Panels of colored lights make mosaics of holiday scenes along the principal streets and around the Zocalo. Parents and children drive along Avenida Juarez and buy helium balloons shaped into animals from vendors at the Alameda Park. *Posadas*, parties, decorations, and Christmas music add gaiety. I could spend Christmas with Marita because that day fell on a Saturday. Ann invited me to stay overnight with them on Christmas Eve and go on to Puebla in the morning.

Tuesday, December 21, 1976

My report to Mr. Rivera about my visit with Marita lasted more than an hour. He had wondered if I would get in to see Marita, even with an order from the judge. I thanked him, over and over, for the miracle. Humbly, he explained,

"Señora, I can still hardly believe it myself. That sort of thing is *not* done here in Mexico. I mean, the judge signing it just before vacation and waiving the waiting period and so forth. Although I haven't seen it happen before, I was determined not to leave Puebla empty handed."

Lic. Rivera, optimistic though he was about the case, pointed out that I didn't yet have physical possession of Marita. He warned me, "In these custody cases, the family usually does what it can to turn the child against the other parent. If you don't get closer to her right now, then she will change so much in even a few more months that you'll be complete strangers by next year."

I agreed with him, and he went on. "We have come a long way in this case. In essence, you have won it, and I could give you a pile of papers showing you that. But I want more than a stack of papers for you—I want practical results. And that is for you to actually have physical possession of Marita."

I hadn't considered that I might have custody on paper only. "In the courtroom, will she want to be with you more than with Antonio?" he asked insistently. I had the same question; I didn't want a violent scene when the time came for her to go with me.

He continued, "If you want custody and possession, then you have an important part to play in our 'masterpiece.' I can only do so much in court. I need your help in getting the family to change their ideas and fears concerning you. You have got to get closer to all of them. It is *imperative* that you deceive them. Lie if you must. You must make them believe you are going to stay in Mexico to live. And it will work better if you would give Antonio hope by dropping the matter of divorce."

I was shaking my head in protest.

He was ready for my reaction. "I know you aren't a hypocrite. You are very straight arrow and honest, sometimes too much so for your own good. Antonio knows your mind, your character. He knows you have never lied to him or tricked him. That's why he'll believe anything you say."

"No," I whispered. "I can't."

"Think about your daughter," Mr. Rivera's voice cut across mine. "You must save your little girl from that family. Antonio doesn't care about her. He's just using her. They aren't going to give her a good education or take care of her. Fight for her! Let this one religious principle go in order to save her!"

I stiffened. To save Marita? Could I?

Mr. Rivera was pacing the room but his eyes never left me. "Señora, you absolutely *must* make friends with your mother-in-law again. She runs the family."

I nodded.

Then he was standing in front of me, eyes holding mine. "You will take her a Christmas present."

I gasped.

He added, "And take one to Antonio, too." He leaned closer, only inches away. "Give him a Christmas *abrazo* while you're at it."

I shuddered. The thought of his kiss a few months ago set my stomach churning. How could I hug him? Why must I?

Mr. Rivera straightened up, nodding thoughtfully and interrupted my memories, "You need to do things that Antonio doesn't expect. Make him a Christmas card, too. Make everyone there a card. And speak to him in Spanish more. It will affect how he feels about you. Speaking English makes you seem more distant. I realize that it's a conflict for you to decide to lie and deceive them, but I don't see any other solution."

He let me absorb that for a moment and then concluded with, "Have you ever cut open a sea urchin? On the outside there is a hard shell and poisonous spines. But on the inside, it is very soft and unprotected. Vulnerable. I will do all I can to help you, Señora, but you must help me too."

I still said little, and he left the room saying, "You think about it the next few days and call me Friday with your plan."

Wednesday, December 22, 1976

I began a fast and talked to Bishop Ruiz, who still wanted me to train new teachers on Sunday evenings when I returned from Puebla. Although he still wanted to do something to help me, he said, "I don't know what to do after talking to President Lozano about your situation. He says that Antonio seems to be telling the truth, too. Who are we to believe?"

Protesting with all the conviction I could express, I replied, "I've never lied! I've never consciously tricked anyone!" But Antonio had. After I had told him about how Antonio's bishop had conspired against me and lied in court, I asked, "What does President Lozano say about bishops who perjure themselves in court? Are they to be believed over the word of a foreigner? I don't understand it. I have proof that bishop lied. How does Antonio get away with it? And how can it be that Antonio is the elders quorum president in his ward now? He's not worthy. He's a warm body who is there every Sunday. That's all."

I thought other things, *Why do so many people in the Church here seem to give him the benefit of the doubt? Because he's a man and a Mexican? Why won't they believe I am speaking the truth? Because I am a woman and an American?* But I didn't say those words.

Bishop Ruiz didn't understand either, and he offered to go to court with me in January so he could make his own evaluation of Antonio. After supper I took a bus over to Lomas and walked a few blocks to Bishop Schilling's house. He was the bishop of the English-speaking ward. I hadn't worked out in my mind yet how to resolve my dilemma, and I pondered his advice for hours afterwards.

The bishop reminded me to think of the eternal perspective when I thought of the time I'd spent trying to get Marita back. He suggested I imagine myself fifteen or twenty years into the future, looking back on 1976, as my daughter walked with me happily beside a young man to get married in the temple. How could Antonio raise her well enough? Her eternal progress was in jeopardy. What was one year (or two) in eternity? It was relatively nothing if I could save her soul by doing some difficult things now.

Before I left his house, he told me about some couples he knew in Mexico who, childless, paid bribes and had false birth certificates made so they could adopt children. He left me with the standard counsel: make a decision one way or the other and wait for the Lord to confirm it.

So, for an hour or more I was thinking and praying and reading Linda's last letter. She reminded me of Abraham's experiences. He said Sarah was his sister (she was by adoption, but that was not the implication the king took). And I thought of Nephi who committed murder under the Spirit's direction to get the records of his people. I wondered how they heard the Spirit clearly enough to take those vital steps.

To every rule there seems to be an exception. Linda wrote,

> *The similarity between the two men is this—both had faith in the Lord, not man. Both loved and feared the Lord, and not man. Both were willing to do whatever the Lord said, regardless of their feelings, supposed outcomes, their limited understandings or anything else . . . Would you lie because you are afraid of what man (courts) will do in not awarding you Marita? That would make you as Antonio, which is self-defeating in all you have done.*
>
> *Will you continue to pledge yourself to the kindness of the Lord, trusting him to work out your eternal welfare? I know you want to choose the latter, but there are pressures to do otherwise. I suggest you*

put yourself in the frame of mind to do whatever the Lord counsels you—no one else. If he says to you, "Tell the truth and all will be well," do so without hesitation. If he tells you to stretch the truth, then do so in good conscience. Fast before you go to court, and follow the Spirit.

I prayed and prayed and didn't make my decision lightly or hastily. I decided to try hedging a little as Mr. Rivera suggested, just for Christmas weekend—to see if I could, if the Spirit would countenance it, if it would help Marita. This decision gave me peace as I planned to trust in the Lord for each situation to see what I should say or do.

In making all those Christmas cards for Puebla, I decided to use quotes from my roommate's book, *El Profeta,* by Khalil Gibran, and illustrate the author's thoughts on the cards. I hoped it would work out like Mr. Rivera envisioned.

Christmas Weekend in Puebla, 1976

On Christmas Eve I joined Ann's family and their friends for games, dinner, and ping-pong until 1:00 A.M. I slept little. In Mexico most people stay up after midnight mass for Christmas dinner, opening presents, and visiting. Teenagers were huddled in serapes around foul smoking fires of automobile tires, and they were setting off cherry bombs and firecrackers most of the night. They were still at it when we left Acueducto at 5:15 A.M. As the car moved through the streets toward Pino Suarez, thick, foggy black clouds of fumes pressed low into the city from other burning bonfires. I was gagging from the smoke.

Because the bus tickets to Puebla were already sold out at 5:50 A.M., I stood around at the bus station, praying and searching for an hour until I found a ticket that someone had brought back. I knew I wouldn't spend Christmas with Marita unless I arrived in time before the family left for their picnic. At last I boarded the battered old bus that took me to Puebla.

I arrived at the Cruz house about 9:00 Christmas morning. Tall, fair-skinned Julio, my brother-in-law, unlocked the gate, and I gave him the present and cards for his family. He was visibly pleased and I found it easy to respond with affection and happiness. More Christmas miracles besides the court order began working from that moment on.

The family might have attributed my change of feelings to the Christmas Spirit, but the spirit of true charity also entered their home with me, surprising me too. During the next two days I did and said things I had never dreamed of a few days before.

As I waited in the living room, Antonio walked down the stairs. I complimented his new clothes; he blushed. When I gave him a present, he stammered over and over, "I don't deserve it," and he gave the gift to Marita. The only toy I could see that she got for Christmas was a tub-shaped car she could pedal.

During the *abrazo* I gave my father-in-law, I told him sincerely, "You are the only family I have here in Mexico." I gave him a card and one to Mama Rosita, too, plus a present. They responded warmly and invited me to go on their picnic in the country.

At Xacachimalpa, Julio and Ana Maria were building a country home with a huge swimming pool. We ate on tables inside the nearly finished house. We enjoyed traditional food: *picadillo*, *bacalao*, avocados, *sopa*, and some nut cake. As I sat at the table along with twenty other family members, they passed the food to me cheerfully. We all ate and laughed together. They began treating me as part of the family again, and I thanked the Lord for softening their hearts—and mine—to feel the true spirit of Christmas.

Outside, it didn't seem like Christmas. The children waded in the swimming pool, and we hiked in the surrounding hills and showed Marita some water beetles in a pond at the bottom of a gully. The cousins broke two piñatas and Marita scrambled for the fruit and candy. Mostly we sat around on the grass talking with the family, and I played with her. As I observed everyone interacting, I realized again that in their way, they loved Marita and tried to take good care of her.

By evening, we returned to Puebla and it was time for me to go back to Mexico. I put Marita in bed and rubbed Vicks on her chest and back. She was quiet and sad. Antonio stood by the bed watching. Smiling at her I asked, "Do you want me to give Papa an *abrazo*?" He stood rigid, his arms at his sides. I had to lift his arms to give him a hug. Marita smiled but refused to kiss me or say good-bye.

Antonio walked with me to the corner and stayed to talk until a bus came. He was warming up to me. During the day, I had said positive encouraging things, and Antonio responded. His vulnerability frightened me. He had always fought it by dominating me, hurting me. Yet, on Christmas his parting words were, "This year's suffering has changed you. You're more mature—only a mature person could give presents and cards to people who have done so much to hurt her."

I slept on the bus the entire trip to Mexico City. When I got home to Polanco, it was eleven and the buses were still full of people celebrating Christmas. Exhausted from the long day and from so little sleep, I prayed only long enough to thank the Lord for the Christmas miracles of being with Marita after all in a peaceful atmosphere, of watching her open her presents, and playing with her all day. Before I went to bed, I called my parents to wish them a Merry Christmas.

The next morning I numbly dragged myself out of bed to begin the pilgrimage to Puebla again, and I arrived in time to sit with Marita through Sunday School in Ana Maria's living room. She hadn't eaten breakfast, so we went upstairs to Rosita's kitchen to find some food. Antonio followed us. While Marita ate, he told me he had taken the Christmas card I had made for him with a quotation on love from Khalil Gibran and had asked all the adults in the house what they thought it could mean. Everyone had given him a different interpretation. "I didn't sleep all night," he declared. "I want to understand—about love, about me and you." He came nearer. "I want to kiss you."

Somehow I was prepared. I smiled, raised my face, and closed my eyes, holding behind my eyelids the image, not of his face, but of Marita, smiling with happiness in Montana. Antonio took me by the shoulders and kissed me, his lips tentative on mine. He raised his head and, still holding me by the shoulders, asked softly, "Is there any possibility we could ever get together again?"

"Anything's possible."

"Who told you to act like this?" he snapped, in a quick return of suspicion.

My mind went blank. The smile felt frozen on my face. He immediately answered his own question, "Christmas. Christmas did it. Yes. A new year's coming. Why should we go on as we have all of 1976?"

I put my hand on his arms and said, "I will always be Marita's mother and you will always be her father. Nothing can change that. Why shouldn't we be decent about it? True Christian principles of love and forgiveness have done wonders for all of us this weekend."

After church, Marita and I broke the piñata and attended her cousin's birthday party. All too soon evening came, and I boarded another bus back to Mexico City. All the way back, I marveled at the gift I had received—the gift of true charity, of loving one's enemy and returning good for evil, the gift of peace. And a sureness that although I had gone prepared to lie little white lies if I found it necessary, a greater truth had transformed it. As it had turned out, I didn't receive a single present on Christmas Day that I could hold in my hands. But it didn't matter because I had been given so much more.

Friday, December 31, 1976 — Journal entry

No more entries for 1976! There will never be another year like it. Thank God. A year ago I cried and cried on New Year's Eve, anticipating the divorce. I knew it would be a nasty year, but it's a good thing I only had to live one day at a time or I would have been crushed by anticipation, this year was so hellacious. But now that I've lived through it, and my soul has been stretched, I've emerged from twelve months of refining a better, stronger, wiser person.

Mireya just called me from Saltillo to wish me a better 1977. But I had no answer for her when she asked what my goals were for the new year. Besides the obvious one, I have no foundation to plan my life around and not one idea of what to expect in 1977. Nothing. Yet I welcome 1977 as I have never before welcomed a new year, and I walk on in faith into the blank before me. O welcome, New Year! May I be more in control in 1977!

As a pleasant break from so many weeks of heavy duty stress, I accepted an invitation to go swimming today near Cuernavaca with my roommate's cousin and a friend. The day was a classic beauty, the water in Oaxestepec was warm. The sun burned my back and brought out more freckles on my face. Sitting by the pool we ate a picnic lunch of pork meat, roasted chicken, rice, chile, and potato chips. I felt at peace and happy for a change, more relaxed than I had been in months.

Chapter Twenty

January 3, 1977 — Journal entry

It's an anniversary of sorts. A year ago I decided I wouldn't live with Antonio any longer. I didn't have to, but I no longer had Marita either. I returned from Puebla last night after visiting them for two days. Unlike the Christmas experience, this one left me drained physically and emotionally. Antonio kissed me every chance he got, we went dancing, he told me he loved me, and he even asked for forgiveness—the first time all year. I found out that he teaches English somewhere and that he gave Marita a father's blessing for the new year, blessing her to have what the Lord wants for her this year—to go with whichever parent is best for her. Would he give her up? He mentioned once, "I hope you'll let me come visit her."

I have to force myself to face him each trip, I pressure myself to smile when he asks if I love him, and I tell him I do, but in my mind I tell myself that I love him as a human being, as my brother, but not as a wife loves her husband. He doesn't ask me specifically what kind of love I feel, so I get by. My strength comes from the truth in this quote by Elder Dean L. Larsen: "Our moods, our attitudes toward daily living and toward each other are in large measure regulated by our thoughts." And my thoughts control my actions until I leave Puebla. Then my body takes over, and my stomach hurts so badly I can't eat for hours after the stress of being in Puebla.

Marita: Missing in Mexico

January 6, 1977 The Three King's Day — Journal entry

Today was the last of the month-long Christmas festivities. Children nowadays receive gifts from Santa and from the Three Kings, too. I've seen men dressed up as kings at the Alameda Park standing around to receive gift suggestions from children after they finished telling Santa something a few feet away. I received a surprise myself today while visiting Marilyn in Cuernavaca. Elder and Sister Fyans came by for a visit.

Not long after they arrived, Sister Fyans said to me, "You're famous."

I didn't understand, so I asked, "What for?"

She smiled and described the words in the latest *Ensign* that told of my separation from Marita. When I saw Marilyn's copy of the magazine, I knew Lavina Fielding had passed the information along, but it was only partly true to me. The writing was in the past tense, as though everything was all over, and it wasn't yet. I intended to show the piece to Antonio in hopes it would persuade him to let Marita go.

Before the Fyanses left today, Elder Fyans talked to me while I stood on the curb, and he asked me how things were going.

I squinted up at him and answered, "Oh, it's better now. I can go see Marita on weekends, and I'm following your advice to see her as often as I can."

He smiled and was pleased. He said, "You have been a brick through all this."

After I told him that I was being nice to everyone there and they were treating me well also, he hit the ends of his fingers together and said, "So you're not like this anymore, huh. But like this—" and he clasped his fingers together as if they were in Protestant prayer.

I said, "Yes. Ever since Christmas I have felt more peace there while I have visited. Their hearts are finally softening."

He glanced at the eucalyptus trees behind me and

back to my face. "Maybe it had to take longer for it all to happen this way." He patted me on the arm, wished me good luck, and left. He did not offer to help or give me any advice on what else I could do, so I decided I would continue with my "campaign."

Monday, January 10, 1977 — Journal entry

    I am back from Puebla again. A technique Marilyn had suggested—pretending to be an actress in a movie—has been successful in giving me some emotional distance, but I am still worried. The hearing is in two days. Antonio said we can take advantage of this hearing to agree, set down our terms, and get divorced.

    If we don't agree, he thinks it could go on for four more years. He claims to have spent thirty thousand pesos on lawyers this year and says it's up to me to end this unnecessary expense on both sides. He admitted that he had a crooked lawyer at first, but now he has a better one. And he goes along with what the new lawyer says because if he doesn't, he'll lose the case.

    I can understand that point of view because I'm in the same position myself. However, with free agency, one can still decide to lie or not. Do we suspend the principle of honesty just because we are in Mexico? Do we say it doesn't count here and we can pick and choose which commandments we wish to obey? How much do we give in to the Mexican system and go along with it? It is a constant battle in Mexico to be honest.

    Antonio said his lawyers had submitted a counterpetition to limit my future visits with Marita to a few hours on one day of the weekend, only. "Why don't you just get a job and live in Puebla, closer to her?" he asked. "The Spirit tells me this is what the Lord wants."

    Then he gave me a keychain that says, "*You are my love.*" Maybe *his* lawyer told him to do that. How much does he think he loves me? How much is he playing a game with our lives? How much longer, Lord?

One thing is certain: Antonio's parents are praying for the same thing my parents are praying for. Which prayers will be answered and which parent will have custody of Marita? There is a chance I could leave court with Marita in two more days.

Wednesday, January 12, 1977

Before I entered the courtroom, Mr. Rivera drilled me on the five points I had to stress in court:

(1) I don't want a divorce.
(2) I *am* the mother. I have a right to Marita and I want her.
(3) I'm not using Marita as a weapon. Antonio is and she is the one being hurt.
(4) I can have money from my parents to live on (so I won't have to work while she is small) once I have her custody.
(5) I can give Antonio a chance to prove himself able to take care of us and be head of the household again.

Mr. Rivera wanted me to weep, plead, promise, and show plenty of emotion when the time came in court to make my case before the judge. I just couldn't ham it up. Mr. Rivera reprimanded me later for acting like an American, but I thought he should have been thankful I managed to state I didn't want a divorce when I knew I needed one. And he said that if I had insisted more, the judge would have probably given her to me that very day. As it turned out, I still didn't have custody of Marita even though Mr. Flores and my bishop said I did a good job of expressing myself.

Antonio wasn't prepared for my declaration of not wanting a divorce and didn't put up much of a fight when the judge attacked and belittled him. But he made a telling point with his fear I would disappear with Marita the first chance I got. *By the end of the hearing, the judge decided that I could see Marita any day, anytime,* and that we should try to behave like a family for the next few weeks to see if we could effect a reconciliation. The next hearing was set for Friday, February 4.

While Bishop Ruiz traveled with us to Puebla and back, I had several hours to talk to him and tell him more of my side of the story. He had just read part of the court files and realized I had been telling the truth. He was not impressed with Antonio when he met him. He hypothesized, "The reason no one in the Church will put pressure on Antonio is because you started the divorce."

"But Antonio started one in Mexico, too, only a week after I did. Doesn't anyone remember that? Antonio changes his stance every few weeks, it seems, according to what is expedient."

"Even so, we are counseled to tell our families to stay together. Divorce is wrong."

"I agree that it is not good. And keeping families together is an admirable goal in general. But what about all the people who don't fit the general pattern? My heart aches for so many women who endure husbands who mistakenly think their right to exercise the priesthood includes coercion and abuse. It doesn't seem to matter to those guys that Church leaders tell them to behave otherwise. They don't get it. They must not think it applies to them personally."

"Well, Antonio says he wants to keep the family together and that he tried hard."

"Yes, and he thinks he has it made just because of the sealing ceremony. It was simply the first step. Even a temple sealing can't unite gross incapability and sin. If there is not unity on emotional, spiritual and physical levels in this life, there won't be much after this life. After all the years I have lived with him, I don't think he has learned the first law of heaven—obedience. He has not been able to live on a higher level, and it is so hard for me to live with him. He will have to change a lot if he wants me back."

By the time we had reached Mexico City, I had not changed my position one inch after talking to the judge and the bishop. Our marriage was dead. Why not get it over with ASAP? My bishop in Acueducto had offered to help me divorce Antonio back in 1974 and so did Bishop Morrill. They were part of the Church too. Even if the different leaders in Mexico couldn't agree on what needed to be done, I knew we'd get a divorce anyway.

After Bishop Ruiz left the car when Mr. Rivera let him off near a Metro stop, Mr. Rivera said, "Your bishop is different than I thought he would be. I thought he would be a lot more powerful and do something in Puebla. Do you think it helped to bring him along?"

I explained that many people might think Mormon bishops would be like Catholic bishops, with special clothing and a strong personal presence and air of authority. But LDS bishops are on a similar level as a parish priest, and they lead a congregation of a defined geographical area. They are lay leaders who look just like anyone else in their congregation. I explained that stake presidents are on a level similar to a diocesan with about five or six bishops under them.

Our ways require leaders who lead more powerfully by being humble and using their power in the priesthood through persuasion and love. If a Mormon priesthood holder began to exercise his authority in too forceful a manner, he would not have the support of the Lord with him, and people would be reluctant to follow him. I concluded by explaining that it helped to have Bishop Ruiz in Puebla because he could pass his impressions on to Church leaders on higher levels. Perhaps one of them would then take the necessary ecclesiastical action that Bishop Morrill had asked for a year earlier.

I taught my last teacher development class and turned in my materials so I could stay in Puebla with Marita if I wanted to on Sunday nights. I needed to leave Polanco. My roommates weren't any emotional support and constantly criticized me for being so patient and trusting my lawyer. It would be easier to live alone.

I was back where I had been so many times before: facing an uncertain future, knowing I would have to do things I didn't want to do or know how to do. For comfort I reread a poem by John Burroughs:

> What matter if I stand alone?
> I wait with joy the coming years;
> My heart shall reap where it has sown,
> And garner up its fruit of tears.
> The stars come nightly to the sky;
> The tidal wave unto the sea;
> Nor time, nor space, nor deep, nor high,
> Can keep my own away from me.

Monday, January 17, 1977

Yesterday Antonio told me that his mother would let me move into the missionaries' apartment over the *zaguan*. Being that close to Marita should have been appealing, but the threat of being trapped turned my stomach. A wave of weakness and depression forced me to sit down and I had to return to Mexico City earlier, afraid and worn out. The real nightmare was the possibility that I could be trapped by the Cruz family, unable to resist them or resist Antonio. I only survived as it was because I could leave them whenever I decided to. I wrote in my journal about my confusing situation:

> I wonder a lot about the things I am doing, and I don't want to go to Puebla anymore. But I feel I must take advantage of this three-week waiting period and try to soften hearts, to prepare the way, and give the Lord a way to deliver Marita to my hands. Lately I have learned forcibly: **we cannot judge**.
>
> Only the Lord can look upon our souls and know the intent of our hearts and judge our thoughts and actions. I know he has given me strength to do things in Puebla lately that were impossible earlier under my own power. Maybe it has taken more than a year for me to prepare for what I am doing now. I wasn't strong enough to accept it before and the Cruz family and the legal situation were not as open as they were to my earlier visits, either.
>
> In the past few weeks whenever I felt myself wavering and wondering how far to go in Puebla, I turned to Elder Maxwell's BYU talk "But a Small Moment" and studied it. The talk has been a source of hope and renews my strength each time I read it. Tonight I reread the section called "Traps to Avoid in Meeting These Challenges," and I am writing my response as to how well I meet each trap—
>
> •The Jonah Response—that we can somehow run away from the realities that will press upon us. The Lord will insist that we go to Ninevah, and we must pay "the fare thereof." [*First Mexico, now Puebla—these are my own Ninevahs. I didn't want to be required to go to these places, but it has been necessary. I must go to Puebla now two or three times a week. My Ninevah isn't over with just one trip, with just one time.*]
>
> • However rigorous the circumstances are, we must be

willing to go, to trust, and to surrender ourselves to our Father in Heaven, who knows WHY in his divine plans it must be so. [*What I am afraid of now is being asked to go LIVE at the Cruz home after Feb. 4. I would feel utterly trapped. At least, now, I am able to go to Puebla because I know I don't have to stay there if I don't want to. If I am required to live there—how will I remain sane?*]

• The adversary will press particularly in the areas of vulnerabilities. The things that we would most like to avoid, therefore, will often be the things that confront us most directly and most sharply. [*My fears and weaknesses include: (1) Fear—Antonio. (2) Weakness—My voice—it doesn't portray the strength I think and feel. It has been a challenge all my life to use my voice well. Therefore, I must practice my speech that I will deliver before the judge on Feb. fourth to convince him better. (3) My self-image in Mexico—this hurts me because I've always been a forgiver, a peacemaker, not a revengeful person or a fighter. I'm not used to defending myself verbally, and now I must, in Spanish.*]

• Pride, ego. The cure is humility. [*I must humble myself before the Lord and follow the Spirit, not my own mind.*]

• We may assume that we are required only to endure and survive, when, in fact, it is required of us not only to endure, but that we endure well, that we exhibit "grace under pressure." This is necessary, not only that our passages through the trial can be a growth experience, but also because there are people watching us to see if we can cope. [*So far, the Lord has strengthened me so I haven't fallen into this trap. Almost everyone tells me that they don't know HOW I've been able to endure this, that they don't think they could do it if they were in my place.*]

• Another trap occurs when we sense something special is happening in our lives but are not able to sort it out with sufficient precision and clarity so that we can articulate it to someone else.... There are moments of mute comprehension and of mute certitude. We need to pay attention to these moments because God often gives us the assurance we need but not necessarily the capacity to transmit these assurances to someone else. *[I know this is true! It has happened to me so many times. I get the assurance I need to go on. For one example, my roommates think I am a fool to keep trying. They don't know what I know.]*

• The tendency we have—rather humanly, rather understandably—to get ourselves caught in peering through the prism of the present and then distorting our perspective about things. Time is of this world; it is not of eternity. We can, if we are not careful, feel the pressures of time and see things in a distorted way.... It is very important that we not assume the perspectives of mortality in making the decisions that bear on eternity. *[Understanding this principle helps me this month to maintain my sanity in every trip I make to Puebla.]*

...Whatever form the test takes, we must be willing to pass it. We must reach breaking points without breaking. *[I am willing and I have promised the Lord I would do what he asked of me. Yesterday so many times I reached a breaking point. I almost began crying when Antonio was telling me how happy he was that SOMEONE loved him (he meant me) and he didn't feel so much like a NO ONE anymore.]*

The heat of the refiner's fire increases each day. I find myself in more ironic situations that add stress. It must seem that I am doing the same thing to Antonio that he did to me. I didn't plan to do it this way at all, but will I have to indicate at some point that I will stay here, live here, and work here, as Antonio promised Bishop Morrill during our standoff? Will I say I'll stay when I know I must leave with her? I trusted Antonio in Orem. By now, the Cruz family trusts me.

It's ironic that the best way to fight Antonio for my daughter is by "loving" him because kindness builds trust. But I absolutely cannot go on showing so much kindness much longer. I can't stand the hypocrisy. Many wives or husbands stay in a marriage out of duty, not love, enduring it for their children's sakes. I lived in that situation too long with Antonio to consider doing it again.

I've got to get Marita and get out. I've got to go

before any restraining order is given. I've just got to!

Thursday, January 20, 1977 — Journal entry

Parangaricutirimcuaro. Try to say it. My students loved to see if the American teachers could say this place name/tongue twister. I finally learned how to pronounce it as a fun way to pass time in the halls. Now, after living through some extremely difficult days in Puebla, I wish I had some fun distractions or people to lighten up the seriousness of my days. Almost every hour has been a nightmare of confusion, tests of will, and of trying to reconcile myself to the changes of reality that keep coming. My feelings are on a roller coaster ride, but mostly from one numbing level of depression to another.

All the way to Puebla on the bus last night I struggled with how to handle the decision of living with the Cruzes. I was terrified of being trapped—not being able to make phone calls, leave my journals without wondering if someone would read them, come and go when I wanted to, or be near people who could help me. I finally decided, just as the bus was reaching Puebla, that I could make even that sacrifice, if necessary. I just hoped I wouldn't have to.

I rang the doorbell at 9:00 P.M. Antonio couldn't believe I had come so late. Marita, thrilled, ran to each apartment, excitedly showing everyone what I had brought for her. We walked upstairs to Marita's bedroom, and I sat down to talk to her and to hem some slacks I had bought at Sears. Antonio sat down on the twin bed across from me, smiled, and began an hour-long monologue. I mostly listened and encouraged an atmosphere of peace and understanding.

I think he was on a fishing expedition, trying to discover what I planned to do in court on February fourth. I wouldn't say, so he told me he plans to ask for a divorce and demand that Marita remain with him. He said that if I am indeed serious about living with him again, we can remarry when we are both sure, without any of the pressures we have now. He thinks Marita is the pressure now for us to stay together. However, if all I want is my own child, he said that he would be happy to help me out so I could have another baby. Then he could have Marita. [Outrageous!]

He thinks we really are not good for each other, that we'll just make each other miserable if we live as a family again, and that I just say I don't want a divorce because I plan to get one in Utah. He doesn't want Marita to live with me because I would want her to clean up after herself. And he wants her to have a happy-go-lucky life and be sloppy like her father, "like a normal people." He wants me to love him as a person, not as a brother or as child of God in general.

A good test of my intentions, he thinks, would be to sleep in the same room with him—though not in the same bed. I declined the invitation and took advantage of an empty bed somewhere else in the house.

I slept well there, and this morning, we drove over to his school so his friends could meet his wife while Papacito took Marita to her school so I couldn't find out where it is. Antonio took me back to the bus station this afternoon when it was time for me to leave. His parting words were, "I suppose I'll just have to continue to lie and fight dirty if you continue to oppose me!"

Later that same day:

I arrived in Mexico City in time for my appointment with Mr. Rivera, and we talked over strategy. Mr. Rivera insisted, "More than anything in court, you must stress that you don't want a divorce. Cry. Beg. It will help you, especially if Antonio keeps insisting on divorce. The judge creates a testing atmosphere to see how you both will react. YOU MUST FIGHT, *como una fiera*."

"Like a mother lion," I repeated, wondering how to be what the judge was looking for.

"You spoke much too passively before. The judge wants to see a

Latin mother in there, fighting for her child. That's why he gave you three more weeks to fight for her. On February fourth, you must convince the judge that you will sacrifice anything for Marita. Get mad. Defend yourself. Be forceful. Make yourself clear. The judge will listen as long as you keep talking."

I committed myself to practice various speeches before a mirror to find a convincing presentation.

He continued, "You've already won ninety-five percent. You're in a strong legal position with every right to win. The main thing is to prevent Antonio from running off with Marita again. Now keep in mind that during this next hearing the judge will return your status to the way it was on January 3, 1976. You both will have equal right to custody."

I sighed with relief.

Mr. Rivera instructed, "Petition the judge instantly for custody, just as Antonio petitioned in February to give the custody to his father. You should be able to get it then."

I looked down at my feet and hesitated. "What if things don't work out and we drive back to Mexico City empty-handed as we have all the other times? I'm more ready now to consider kidnapping Marita back as you mentioned once."

"I suggested it last July. Things have changed somewhat. But if you want her kidnapped, you'll have to go hire your own G-man. I'm here to help you do it legally, as you have always indicated. You'll have to make up your own mind what you want. I have a harder time dealing with you than with Antonio," he concluded.

I had little to say after that, so he escorted me to the door and left me with a parting thought, "Keep up the good work. Remember, nothing you have gone through so far has been as bad as it could be. Other mothers go through worse things to get their babies back."

In my search for a wise course of action, I thought about other mothers and what they might do. My visit with Bishop Schilling's wife an hour after my appointment with Mr. Rivera proved to be a turning point for me. Her perceptive questions helped me examine my situation better. She stated what she would do if she were me: kidnap Marita. She said that for the longest time she thought I was wrong trying to get Marita back legally. Her words jolted my thinking to other levels. I realized that good people would understand it if I had to take drastic measures I would rather avoid. Then Mireya called me from

Saltillo and I talked to her about it. She understood and offered her support. I felt some of the pressure lift as I considered the kidnapping option, so long repressed.

Friday, January 28, 1977 — Journal entry
Lomas de Chapultepec

A few days after Coco told us that we had to find a new place to live by the end of the month, she disconnected the phone to further convince us. I called Nancy in New York City for permission to stay in her apartment while she is gone. I walked over to see the landlady. She is an old woman who lies in bed all day surrounded by plants, sepia-colored photos, and well-polished knickknacks with nothing to do but answer her phone and talk to her cats. She had compassion for my situation, and after Nancy called to authorize it, she let me move in.

This cozy upstairs apartment is in Lomas, and I have a quiet, pleasant one-bedroom apartment to myself at last. I am tired of the bouncy music the girls played on their cassette player, and here the classical music from the FM radio always soothes my nerves after each trip to Puebla. I can't eat very well during and after trips to Puebla. The stress is exhausting me. Sometimes I nearly faint as I walk. I held up, barely, for three days there this week.

Antonio took us downtown and bought Marita a pair of red patent leather shoes and warm kneesocks. Then he took us to a movie about a man who was trying to take care of his five-year-old daughter after his wife died. I cried in the car on the way back to his house. Marita's mother isn't dead. I'm alive. Here. I want her.

Yet, after the movie Antonio sneered, "She can't be with you, Mari Vawn, because she has a very special father. I do feel sort of funny trying to be a mommy, too. But I won't give her up! I got her because I'm smarter than you even if President Lozano told me I have no right to have Marita. Yes, I'm going to follow my plan. You get it all, MV, or you get nothing."

I decided he hadn't changed much in a year; if anything, he was worse. After the last court hearing Bishop Ruiz told me that he could tell that Antonio knew he had done wrong. Who can reach a person who thinks and speaks irrationally, emotionally, and stubbornly?

I spent as much time as I could with Marita, playing with her cousins, walking through the junk in the yard across the street, or helping Papacito in the shop. Whatever we did, Antonio was always nearby, watching us or talking to me. It seems he wants a divorce most of the time until he remembers that once I'm divorced I can't get permission from *gobernación* for a work permit. And he wants me to work to support him through school. So, he usually concludes we may need to stay married.

His parents hope we can work things out. Papacito offered to let me stay there overnight as often as I want so we can have more time to reach a reconciliation. If I were living with the family, they would let Marita stay with me more. They say all I would need is my own refrigerator.

Their suggestions didn't encourage me much because Antonio's latest proposals made the nightmare feeling come back: He thinks we could get divorced in secret and live together without telling anyone. After a while, when he can be sure I won't leave him and that it's going to work out, we can get married again. But we'd have another child as soon as possible.

He seemed to be sincere about his ideas and hopes I'll agree with him. While trying to conceal how I felt, I said simply, "That would be a sin. I couldn't do that."

I have reached the last page of my third journal. Will my next one also end in Mexico?

> To begin my new journal, I quote a paragraph out of our Relief Society manual:
>
> 7 Steps in Making a Decision
> by Marion D. Hanks
> 1. Be clear on the principles involved.
> 2. Take the long look ahead.
> 3. Think objectively.
> 4. Learn from the successes and failures of others.
> 5. Counsel with others.
> 6. Pray for guidance.
> 7. Decide.
>
> Afterwards, pray for a confirmation and help to carry your decision through.

Chapter Twenty-one

Monday, January 31, 1977 — Journal entry
Lomas de Chapultepec

Being alone after each trip to Puebla is heaven. I rest, listen to music, pray, and plan my next steps. Today I've been writing out different versions of what I could say to the judge in four more days. I've read over my journals for facts. Exactly a year ago tonight I was crying in Sister Morrill's arms because I didn't know where Marita was the night of the daddy-daughter party. What a long way I have come since then! As bad as it is now making all these trips to Puebla, I'll take it over a year ago. How little I knew then. This all shouldn't go on much longer.

Each trip to Puebla begins much the same: I dread going. I fight nausea. I leave the quiet Lomas neighborhood for the jangling, jammed passage through the Pino Suarez Metro station on my way to the Estrella Roja Bus Station.

After the two-hour bus ride, I walk to the corner of the street where the Cruzes live, facing another encounter, another "opportunity" to soften their hearts, to learn something that may open the way for our escape, and to spend time with Marita and win more of her love. I pray before I turn the corner to walk down their street—for protection, for inspiration, for power to overcome the dread, agony, fear, disgust, and despair churning inside as I approach the thick stone walls that keep my daughter a prisoner.

However, as soon as I see Papasito standing behind the counter, a smile appears on my face; my voice greets him warmly. Behind the gentle, kindly facade, I keep functioning as the hours pass, reassuring myself, "This, too, shall pass." Someday, I won't have to do this anymore. Someday, Marita will be safe with me.

Not every hour in Puebla is extremely stressful for me. I've started an oil painting class with Mama Rosita, and we enjoy ourselves at the studio. This helps wear down the barriers. And mealtimes are usually pleasant.

Antonio is the problem. Each day he woos me, flatters me, caresses and kisses me when we're alone. When I can't avoid these attempts or slip away, I stay passive, willing my mind blank so that I won't shudder or scream, suppressing my own involuntary reflexes to hit him or throw up. It helps, sometimes, to imagine that he's a stranger. Even if I wanted to accept his love-making, my body wouldn't let me. And I don't want to. Every so often, his mask slips, showing streaks of his vileness. He threatens to run off with Marita again if I'm not more "cooperative."

I left Puebla after my last visit with a knot in my throat. The sun was setting in clouds behind Popocatepetl, luminescent rays a-stream. The sleepy countryside looked like a peaceful dream. But Mexico is like that. A land of many contrasts all within close proximity—the extremely rich and the incredibly poor, the calm exterior and the rage within, a fascination with death and a celebration of life's little joys, the smiles and the stoic resignation.

To the other Mexico City-bound passengers, I might have looked like an American tourist in her blue jeans and red nylon jacket, enjoying the trip. Inside I was living a nightmare I could not easily wake up from. And going to church, always a strength to me, is now part of the nightmare. The meetings are held at the Cruz home. Ana

Maria's husband is the branch president, Antonio is elders quorum president, and his mother is the Relief Society president. I felt yesterday that there was a conspiracy against me.

It seemed to me that Mama Rosita had asked the teacher to prepare the Relief Society lesson just for me. It was about the damage to children of an unstable or separated family. I sat on the second row, and the teacher repeatedly asked me such pointed questions that tears of embarrassment and pain came to my eyes. Most of the sisters there knew of my situation, but I felt no sympathy from them as they waited for my answers.

I'll never understand how I endured it, but I did: no outbursts, no leaving, and I gave straight textbook answers to the questions. In sacrament meeting Papasito kept looking at me throughout his talk on how to get answers to your prayers. Mama Rosita spoke on being humble. What will happen next Sunday after the court hearing?

On the positive side, Antonio let me go with Marita when Ana Maria invited us to go along with her children to Xacachimalpa. I made no effort to spend time away from the group but wandered around the countryside with them and splashed in their pool.

When I returned to Mexico City, I decided to stay away from Puebla until the court hearing Friday. I need the solitude while I decide what to do. Should I stop the campaign completely? Which course should I take? The cruelty Sunday had made it even clearer that a divorce is necessary. I know that for Mexican families, divorce is the ultimate social evil. Long-suffering Mexican women endure beatings, wait for their men to get out of prison, and accept mistresses, but they rarely divorce.

Well, I am different. I know I can never again love Antonio and that attempts to share a household will only damage Marita more. I once hoped Antonio had discarded some of his cultural traditions, but lifelong membership in the Church, attending Church schools, and a temple sealing wasn't enough. I finally have to agree that in most cases, the advice to marry within one's own culture and race and class is wellfounded. The seeds of our failure lay in our hope that we could do it when most do not. Few levels of love could compete with centuries of culture.

A gulf still exists between how we each experience and interpret realities of time, space, rearing children, government, humor, history, suffering, sickness, death, our Mother Earth, or work. I thought I knew what I was doing when I married him, but how much more I know now of the hidden and uncommunicated assumptions we both brought to our marriage—assumptions we can't part with, beliefs about life that all our efforts haven't overcome. I know now that our upbringing and separate ideas of what love means or how one should treat a spouse will probably never mesh enough to save our marriage.

I have listened enthralled as my sister-in-law Adriana related myth after myth of ancient Mexico, its Indian names flowing from her tongue like music from the gods themselves. I have spent many days in the National Anthropology Museum and have read fascinating books about their history. The Mexicans are still intimately oriented to the ancient past and curse Cortez for making them orphans, cut off from their true heritage by becoming mixed blood.

I remember my students' faces when I brought the poster of the black Ugly Duckling into my classroom. At age nineteen or twenty, they still identified with the forgotten orphan, and yearned that their life story would someday mirror the baby swan's when he was recognized for who and what he was, a noble bird with worth and beauty beyond anyone's dreams.

I suppose Antonio feels the same way—his view of reality distorted by false pride because of the underlying fear and self-rejection. What must it do to him to see our marriage ending, leaving him nothing? That's probably why he brought Marita to Mexico and fights so desperately to keep her. He has his good qualities, of course. Somehow, he wants to preserve our family.

It may be as Octavio Paz wrote, "Like all Hispanic peoples—we have two sets of morals: one for the 'señor,' another for women, children, and the poor.... We are insecure, and our responses, like our silences, are unexpected and unpredictable. Treachery, loyalty, crime and love hide out in the depths of our glance. We attract and repel.... To the Mexican, there are only two possibilities in life: either he inflicts the actions implied by *chingar* on others, or else he suffers them himself at the hands of others. This conception of social life as combat fatally divides society into the strong and the weak." (*The Labyrinth of Solitude*, 1961, pp. 199, 65, 78)

So, Antonio thinks he has to be the strong one, no matter what it costs. For all of us.

Tuesday, February 1, 1977 — Journal entry

Another morning is here and breakfast is done. Again, I am sitting at Nancy's small table thinking things over and trying to plan my next course of action and the words to my speech. I have more decisions to make. I won't be convincing if I don't deeply believe what I say, so I must examine how much I can stand for my principles and how much I am willing to sacrifice. I'm learning that the things that matter most can't be bought or sold or even seen most of the time. Some things matter somewhat while others matter profoundly. How can I discern which things matter profoundly enough that I will not waver on them?

Looking at the lives of people around me, I see that many of these people suffer problems and trials that are difficult for each of them to deal with from their own perspective. Whether we are young or old, married or single, childless or overburdened, I think what really matters is learning to overcome and having the hope of receiving promised glory—if we live well enough to become joint heirs with Christ after the sufferings of earth life are behind us. But in the meantime, some seemingly insignificant things matter more than meets the eye.

For example, Mr. Rivera keeps asking me to let the principle of honesty go in order to get Marita more easily. There are so many levels of law: U.S., Mexican, LDS doctrine, and human nature. Which levels can I obey or ignore without violating what I personally stand for? And within our doctrine, I can obey the same laws on a telestial, terrestrial, or a celestial level, depending where my heart, understanding, and abilities lie. The gospel and its doctrine are real to me, as nothing else is real in the same way. I examine these carefully as I plan.

What I do, feel, think, and say matters because it gives me experience to discern light and truth and to *become* as my talents, character, and intellect are being shaped into a better me. And these things matter because I'm learning how the Spirit operates and helps me as I do more. The motivation to go ahead on a certain plan will come from the two reception centers used most by the Spirit: the mind and my thoughts along with the heart and my feelings—the two should agree. I know I am doing the Lord's will when feelings of energy, assurance, peacefulness, confidence, and righteousness surge through me. I re-evaluate when I feel uneasiness, confusion, and doubt.

I don't know how other mothers who have lost their babies keep their faith up to regain their children, but I know I wouldn't still be here after thirteen months if I hadn't received assurances of success through the power of the priesthood and the Holy Ghost. I was told last May in a blessing that I would be tested to the point of the sacrifice of my life. That hasn't happened yet in a physical sense, for my main sacrifices so far have been offering a broken heart, my time, efforts, and all my emotional and mental strength to get Marita back. Mr. Rivera is asking me to sacrifice my principles, and in a spiritual sense, they are my life. If I betray my real self by how I implement a principle such as integrity, then what do I have left of myself, even if I regain my daughter? Integrity will still matter twenty years from now and for all eternity.

Before I left Utah last May, I typed Elder Bruce R. McConkie's entry from *Mormon Doctrine* on "Sacrifice."

I have been studying it today as I make my decisions. The first part reads, "Sacrifice is the crowning test of the gospel. Men are tried and tested in this mortal probation to see if they will put first in their lives the things of the Kingdom of God (Matt. 6:33). To gain eternal life, they must be willing, if called upon, to sacrifice all things for the gospel . . ."

Now it is evening, and after more pondering today, I have been praying. I told the Lord that I didn't think he wanted me to go on with the campaign anymore. I realized that the same act can be viewed either as sin or righteous obedience, depending on the motivation of heart, mind, and soul. I didn't want to deceive anyone anymore, even in little ways. I plan to follow the promptings of the Holy Ghost as best I can in doing the Lord's will, no matter what. I hope to get a confirmation of my decision before I enter the courtroom.

Marilyn is planning to come to Mexico City tomorrow. I need to meet her somewhere and use her as a sounding board to confirm that my decisions today are the best possible under the circumstances. I also need a priesthood blessing if someone in Cuernavaca could give me one.

Wednesday, February 2, 1977
Cuernavaca

I made arrangements to meet Marilyn at noon at the National Cathedral on the side of the street by the Zocalo on her way to the Lagunilla Market. She drove by in her brown station wagon but didn't see me because I was standing on the other side of the street, across several lanes of traffic. I ran after her, trying to get her attention, but the traffic was bumper to bumper, and I failed. I stayed by the cathedral, hoping she would come back looking for me.

As I waited, I watched the traffic and the constant flow of people around me. I contemplated the glory that was once Mexico—Tenochitlan, the Aztec capitol and religious center built on the very spot I stood. The holiest of Aztec temples, the awesome Temple of Huitzilopchtli, had glowed in white and blue paint and in the red blood of sacrificial victims. Next to it had stood the Temple of Tlaloc painted white with a blood-red background. These two temples were destroyed by the Spaniards, and archaeologists believe that the National Cathedral's foundation was made from their debris.

How I would love to travel back in time for one hour to that same spot five hundred years ago! Diaz recorded some of the dazzling sights the Spaniards discovered in 1519 when they entered the city. I'd seen scale models of Tenochtitlan at the Anthropology Museum as well as the statuary, carvings, masks, plumed capes and he addresses, and other artifacts that feed the imagination.

Diaz reported that on or near the main square he saw aviaries, zoos, a sacred ball court where gladiators fought, residences of priests and high ranking military, rooms and racks of skulls from the sacrificial victims, and the *tianguis* marketplace. At one end of the plaza was the huge calendar stone and at the other end, a huge stone sculpture to the god of war.

The National Palace standing across the street from the cathedral was a dark, square government building built on the site where Moctezuma's magnificent two-story palace once stood. But the palace had stood in the midst of constant human sacrifice in the peak times of the Aztec religion. Christ had told the Nephites during his visit to them in the Americas after his resurrection that he no longer would accept their burnt offerings nor shedding of blood. Instead he required a broken heart. It is interesting how doctrine degenerates when passed down by word of mouth.

Centuries later, the Aztecs took that command literally, to offer a broken heart to the goddess Xochiquetzal who represented "self-sacrifice" as the goddess of love, flowers, and beauty. They felt an obligation to keep their tribal war god, Huitzilopochtli, alive by the blood of human sacrifice. Near the block where I stood waiting for Marilyn, twenty thousand victims were sent to paradise on the dedication day of the Great Temple of Tenotchtilan with their hearts torn from them.

There is an old belief that Latin America will fulfill her true destiny only when the plumed serpent learns to fly. And I believe that

Latin America will only fulfill its destiny when it learns who its people are: descendants of royal blood from the House of Israel preserved to build up Zion before and during the Millennium—a Zion more splendid than any Tenotchitlan with a people more advanced and blessed than any civilization in Mexico the past two thousand years. The glory, the pride, the grandeur, and the riches will all return when Christ returns. I hoped to be standing with Marita to welcome him.

From where I stood by the Zocalo, I felt torn in many directions and sensed a greater need for guidance in my path ahead. My choices the next few hours and days would determine if I would regain Marita and freedom or further entrapments in court and by the Cruz family. I wanted to know more of the Lord's will, even if that meant sacrificing my own will and ideas to his. I knew more than ever that I needed a priesthood blessing to help confirm my decisions and give further guidance in my difficult situation. It was worth it to me to wait for Marilyn and hoped I could catch her eye on her return.

I waited for two hours, then gave up and boarded a battered green bus in front of the cathedral. As I inched my way up the steps of the bus, I glanced over my shoulder at the traffic coming down Seminario Street towards Pino Suarez and saw Marilyn's car partially hidden in the traffic.

I backed down off the bus, scrambled out into the street, and stood in her path, waving both my arms and shouting. She stopped to avoid running over me before she recognized who I was. I gratefully stepped into her station wagon for a refreshing afternoon in the southern part of the city. We had supper at Tres Marias: *gorditas* for her and my favorite, cheese and mushroom *quesadillas*, for me, along with chocolate *atole* to drink.

As usual, Marilyn provided help when I needed it. I'd been longing for the comfort of a blessing. Mireya's husband, Johnny, had planned to come from Saltillo to do it, but couldn't. My bishop and Brother Schofield both told me that praying should be enough. Marilyn invited me to ride home with her to Cuernavaca where her friend Roger, a young man from the States who was learning Spanish for his graduate project from BYU, was taking care of her sons. Marilyn described him as spiritual and sensitive. When I spoke to him, he agreed to give me a blessing.

"There's more here at stake than just getting your daughter back," he said after I told him some of my struggles and dilemmas. "Something rotten and evil is going on." His sympathy was comforting.

So was the blessing. In it he reassured me that my experience had a purpose and was part of the design the Lord had for me in my life and that I was to be as righteous as I could—completely honest. No acts. No falsity. He promised that the words in my previous blessings would be fulfilled and that I would have my daughter with me and see my dreams for her fulfilled. He repeated that the Lord loved me.

During the blessing he referred to Doctrine and Covenants section 122 and Joseph Smith in Liberty Jail. In Joseph's time there were those of the twelve apostles who later became wicked and caused great damage to the Church. Likewise there are some men in positions in our Church today who cause damage, and the Lord knows the intents of their hearts. He is allowing them to go on in their present positions until the time when the true evilness of their nature will be brought out. They will be punished.

And most importantly, the blessing emphasized that *I must be cheerful, not disappointed, even though at times it might seem I would lose and there could not be much hope. I must try even just one more time. When times got difficult and I didn't think I could go on, there would be somebody there to help me.*

Through my tears I thanked Roger for the great blessing. It confirmed what I had pondered and prayed about. I knew I wouldn't go on with my campaign any longer nor get Marita through court action soon, but I knew I could outlast this ordeal and eventually find a way to leave Mexico with her.

The words of the blessing reminded me of one line from the patriarchal blessing I received when I was fifteen: *You will be thrilled to see your children grow* . . . How could I see Marita grow if I did not have legal custody and have her living with me? The hope of this sentence became a reality and gave me strength to persevere. I knew it had to be true that things would work out for us to grow up together as promised. I knew it would be possible, but I didn't know the details of what I still had to do to make it a reality.

In the blessing I was told to read Doctrine and Covenants section 122 often. If I were to take implications from it for my life, I knew I must prepare much more for my own "small moment" and cheerfully do all that lay in my power to do. Then I could stand with the utmost assurance that the Lord in his power would open the way for Marita and me to go home together in safety.

Chapter Twenty-two

> *If the heavens gather blackness, and all the elements combine to hedge up the way; and above all, if the very jaws of hell shall gape open the mouth wide after thee, know thou, my son, that all these things shall give thee experience, and shall be for thy good. . . . [F]ear not what man can do, for God shall be with you forever and ever. (D&C 122:7-8)*

Doctrine and Covenants section 122, the Lord's comfort to the Prophet Joseph Smith in Liberty Jail, isn't very long, but reviewing key verses strengthened me during my trip to Mexico City and while reviewing strategy with Mr. Rivera. I knew he'd protest my decision to be honest as possible. I had to convince him I meant it.

As I met with my lawyer on Thursday, February 3, I told him sincerely, "I can't keep up the plan of deceiving the Cruz family in small ways any more. I won't have them think I like Antonio more than I actually do."

I was expecting anger, but Mr. Rivera sat silently for a moment, then said with equal sincerity, "Señora, I truly can't understand this. I don't understand why you can't let this one principle go to save your daughter. You have suffered so much to get her thus far. You are so close now. You could get her tomorrow if you will say the things in court that I advise you tonight. But you can't be totally honest here in Mexico."

I swallowed hard against the tightness in my throat and said in sorrow, "I'm sorry it's working out like this. I'm not saying these things to make your job harder, really I'm not. But I've done a lot of soul searching lately and I must be honest, in spite of Mexico."

Mr. Rivera stared at me. His voice was biting. "Do you want to take the shorter easier road? You can, if you do as I say in court tomorrow. Or, do you want the longer, spiny one? That's what you'll get if you insist on being honest! Señora, I beg you, don't be naive!"

I said evenly, "I'm afraid the long spiny road is the only one I can walk right now."

Exasperated, he pled, "Do you want to be a martyr? Please, don't! You don't have to do things this way! That's why you pay a lawyer—to find loopholes and help you out. Mexicans take honesty as a sign of weakness. It will take longer if Antonio appeals and drags the case to the higher courts."

"Of course I don't want that!" I declared.

"Well, that's what's going to happen if you are too honest. Do you realize that if you tell the judge you want a divorce, the whole thing will be over? We'll lose all we've done up to this point. If that happens, then you must take responsibility for turning the case into a longer procedure. And I'll be forced to raise my fees. So far, I've been operating on that set fee, hoping this will all be over soon."

At last he begged me to find a solution my conscience could handle so we could get this over with soon. His last words as I slowly left were, "I won't try to persuade you one way or the other, but please go home and think about it all. We'll talk about it more in the morning on our way to Puebla."

Before I left the office, I gave him a copy of Elder Maxwell's talk "But for a Small Moment," hoping it would help him understand my position better.

I walked a long ways before I caught a bus down Reforma to Lomas. I had never felt more helpless and trapped. How much easier it would have been to take the short road as Mr. Rivera asked, but I wanted to avoid Satan's lies of "protect yourself" or "a little lie here and there won't matter." I had been taught all my life "to forget self and lose yourself for the sake of something greater." I knew the time for overcoming Satan is in this life, and I knew in this ordeal, I could not give him any extra material to use against me. Not any deception. Not any unworthy word or action.

It seemed the time was very near for entering the realm of fire for the sacrifice I had been warned of in May. I absolutely didn't know what I was going to say or do that would still allow me to obey the Lord and higher laws and yet not jeopardize the case and lose ground. With laws of different levels in conflict, which would I choose? And sacrifice. What was I prepared to sacrifice? My principles or Marita? It would be so much easier to take the short road, but would I be at peace with myself later?

Yet after all, birth and life and progress must be paid for with means beyond money. In normal times, little daily acts of patience, feeding, clothing, loving, staying up late for, and sacrificing self are required to raise a child after the pains of birth are past. But the sacrifice required of me would include more trips to Puebla, more courage and danger, at possible great loss of freedom, money, and health.

I called my parents. They and many others were fasting for the next day's outcome in court. Both of them said to hedge as much as I could and still feel moral. My stomach knotted with tension nearly unparalleled these past thirteen months. Mere stage fright was superseded by conflict, fear, and uncertainty. I felt hollow. My hands and legs were shaking as I stood before the mirror to practice my speech. I was light-headed, almost dizzy.

I could not sleep. So, I read. I prayed. I cried. I analyzed. I only had a few more hours left before I had to decide what to say in court. I read through my journals and recalled the promises of so many priesthood blessings given to guide me through this ordeal. One, a year old, assured me that after praying I should listen to the still, small voice and often the answer to my prayers would come within the hour. Another, from May 16, stated that once I had passed the test on the principle I was to be primarily tried on, that the Lord would answer my prayers immediately. I would not have to wait a week or a month, but the answer would come immediately.

Well, I was in the thick of the test, and I wanted to pass it by somehow remaining true to myself and to my principles, yet finding the way to have Marita with me, too. I just could not find the words or a clear idea of what I could do to reach my righteous desires.

At one point I flipped open my journal where I had stapled Elder McConkie's entry on "Sacrifice." I pondered it for a long time, especially lingering over the following words of the Prophet Joseph Smith:

> *When a man has offered in sacrifice all that he has for the truth's sake, not even withholding his life, and believing before God that he has been called to make this sacrifice because he seeks to do his will, he does know, most assuredly, that God does and will accept his sacrifice and offering, and that he has not, nor will not seek his face in vain. Under these circumstances, then, he can obtain the faith necessary for him to lay hold on eternal life.*

I prayed some more. The guidance I prayed for did not come before I entered a fitful night's sleep.

By the time I had finished dressing Friday morning I still didn't know what to do about my situation. It seemed I was in the middle of my worst recurring nightmare: finding myself in front of a group of students unprepared to teach and having no more time to prepare. Just as I was leaving the apartment, my mother called: They couldn't find much more money from anywhere. I'd have to find a job or come home soon.

While a chauffeur drove us to Puebla, Mr. Rivera sat in the back with me to go over more possibilities of what I could say. Mr. Flores hung over the front seat, taking the parts of the judge and of Antonio in a series of role playing.

Mr. Flores started out by asking as if he were the judge, "Do you, Mrs. Cruz, want to get a divorce?"

I opened my mouth to answer and closed it again. Asking for a divorce would lower the judge's opinion of me. He would expect me to be the *mujer abnegada* in sacrificing for my daughter.

Little by little as we talked and the lawyers reviewed points of law and how they related to my case, I began to feel my mind sharpen as concepts and issues became clearer than they had been all year. I remembered the promise of the May priesthood blessing and felt that it had become a reality as my mind discerned truth from error and I finally knew what I could do in court in one more hour.

By the time we reached Rio Frio, everything fell into place in my mind and I had no doubts about the solution. I told the lawyers with conviction, "I know what I have to do. I have to agree to go live in Puebla with the family and see Marita more often."

They were flabbergasted when I told them. "Señora, are you absolutely sure?"

When I assured them that I was, they were elated. I focused on that, rather than my fear of being trapped in Puebla, but I had to have some protection from Antonio. Both lawyers assured me that a *separación corporal* would prevent Antonio from seeking a resumption of conjugal rights. I wasn't so sure he'd obey a piece of paper when enforcement depended largely on his sense of honor.

And what if Antonio insisted on a divorce? They advised me to agree and coached me in asking for fifty-fifty custody and other advantages. By the time we reached Puebla and entered the judge's small office once again, I was ready at last, calm and at peace. I felt relieved, knowing I was prepared with a way of escape and a course of action—just in time.

The reality was reinforced again: my agency exists no matter what the circumstances are, and I could make an acceptable choice. I could choose the spiny road in spite of Satan's whisperings otherwise. What the Lord required would be scary, hard, stressful, and uncomfortable, but not impossible. With new decisions made, I felt a total, soul-filling peace. My anxiety shrank to a level I could handle in court.

By the time we left the courtroom, the judge had ordered that we had one month—until March 4—to decide peacefully by ourselves whether to live as a family together or to get a divorce. If we decided on divorce, we were to write up our own terms and give them to him. If we couldn't agree, then the legal procedures would continue as before. Besides, the judge was still waiting for my documents to reach him from *gobernación* before he could make a final decision.

Best of all, I wasn't required to start living in Puebla immediately. I could still visit anytime I wanted, spending the night with the family. The main thing that changed as a result of the hearing was that the judge made Antonio and me responsible for our lives. *WE would have to decide what we wanted, not the judge.* I offered silent prayers of thanks all the way back to Mexico City, for I recognized I had received extra help from the prayers and fasting of so many friends and relatives that day.

I felt the way opening before me once I had wrestled with these paradoxes: it seemed that the best way to "save" my life in court was to be willing to "lose" it by agreeing to stay at the Cruz home; that to get my freedom in the long run, I had to say I'd be willing to give it up . . . and I meant it; and the only way (with the givens of the law and our situation) that I could get a divorce sometime was to say in court that I didn't want one.

I returned to Puebla to visit Marita Saturday and Sunday as usual. I was determined to be true to myself yet keep communication open—and not insult, scare off, or anger Antonio. Saturday night after Marita went to sleep, he argued that I should sleep in the same room with him even though we wouldn't touch each other. I refused. We deadlocked.

At 2:00 A.M. we were still talking about that and other matters. I lay on the edge of the bed with my clothes on while he sat stubbornly near the door, refusing to leave the room or let me leave.

"I'm not going to make a scene and rouse the house tonight," I told him, "but if you ever try this again I'll go to a hotel immediately." I must have dozed off because about dawn I woke with a start. Antonio was gone.

I crept quietly down the stairs to the *despacho* and called my parents collect, hoping no one upstairs would pick up the phone and hear our conversation. Although I knew what had to be done, I needed to hear their voices for added strength to carry it out.

As usual, my father had some good advice, too: "Take the offensive by being friendly with the family. Help Antonio by pointing out his talents. Move his thoughts to different goals. Be as helpful as you can in the home. Remember they love Marita dearly, too, so you must show them in some way that she needs her mother."

After church and dinner were over, I settled down to talk with Antonio's father alone. It wasn't long before Antonio found us and sat down to hear what we were saying. Although Antonio's father tried to get me to "forgive" Antonio, he supported me when I insisted that I needed more time than the week he wanted to give me so I would not have to decide under so much pressure.

Finally Antonio agreed I could take all month. Luckily, he was somehow under the impression that I was a poor, confused soul that had no idea what to do. He thought I was all torn up inside. I insisted that I would not do anything physical with him—no kissing, no touching, nothing—while I was making my decision that month on what to tell the judge. That also included being allowed to sleep in a room by myself. With a few threats, he finally accepted that condition too.

His father stayed with us as we wrote down the problems we faced and their possible solutions. After an hour of talking we only wrote down the following points that we could agree on:

- •We can live together as a family, with these two possible results: (1) We can live together and it will work out to be a normal home as most people would expect, or (2) it will return to what it has always been—a mess, a failure.
- •We can get a divorce and let each other make a new life with these possible results: (1) We may marry others, or (2) we could remarry each other without the pressure we feel now to stay together for Marita's sake.

I had my decision before we finished talking, but I said nothing. During the discussion on one of the points, I told Papacito that Antonio had proposed an additional plan. "I want to make it clear that I will not get a divorce and live with him unmarried until I am more sure. Nor will I accept his third proposal—of having another child by him so we could each have one."

Papasito's eyes opened wide. "You proposed this?" he queried Antonio.

"Yes," he admitted.

His father shook his head in disbelief. I told his father that I didn't feel that much love for Antonio anymore, but I wanted the best for us all.

I wrote my parents a long letter when I returned to Lomas explaining I could stay in the apartment until the first week in March. I wouldn't have enough money to rent another place after that. I hoped the money I had would be enough to cover the bus trips I must make to Puebla for a month. *The bottom line: if I didn't get Marita by March 4, I would have to go home for lack of money.*

I had some good news for my folks, too:

> *Sunday night I was allowed to sleep alone in the bedroom just off the kitchen, a few feet from the stairs. Marita wanted to sleep with me, but Antonio wouldn't let her. I regret every second away from her in this race against time.*
>
> *Every day she is more Cruz, more Mexican. I look to each visit as an opportunity to win her back to me, and Antonio sees each as a chance to win me back to him. But Sunday night, I slept through the entire night for the first time since Christmas.*
>
> *The Lord created this world. He has ALL power and sees and*

knows all things. He knows how Antonio will react and how things will probably work out. I know if I'll do my part and also be as honest as he has asked, then he is bound to fulfill his words to me.

I will send a copy of this letter to Bishop Morrill so I don't have to type this all over again. I want to find out if they could do something in the Church in Utah to pressure the brethren here to do something or locate Antonio if he ran away with her again. Or else, if I do get legal custody of Marita on paper but somehow don't get her right away, I will have to leave anyway. It seems the Church leaders here hope we will get back together. Impossible.

On Tuesday, February 8, I met with Mr. Rivera. His nose and eyes were streaming from a bad cold, but he had come in to the office just to find out what had happened over the weekend in Puebla. I brought him up to date and revealed my latest decisions:

- I must divorce Antonio.
- I must get legal custody of Marita as soon as possible—this month.
- I will accept the risk of Antonio's running off with her again. If he left with her in spite of my having the custody papers, I hoped the Church leaders would find him for me and return Marita to me. I couldn't worry about it.

Mr. Rivera slumped in his chair, relieved at my determination. He wiped his nose and smiled. "I'll start putting even more pressure on *gobernación* to get the papers signed in another week or so and take them to the judge immediately. I'll try to see that the judge lets us know first what his decision is before it's posted for all to see. He'll have to make his decision once he has the papers, you know."

I knew. It was a race against time.

As I was leaving the office, Mr. Rivera told me sincerely, "I understand now that you have to be honest, and it's okay. Do what you have to do."

Chapter Twenty-three

BEFORE I BOARDED the Estrella Roja Bus on Wednesday, February 9, I bought a package of pink modeling clay for Marita, some suckers, and *sugus*, her favorite candy. I arrived about 1:00 when Papacito brought her back from her preschool. We ate lunch, washed a few clothes in the washtubs out behind the house, looked at the dogs on the roof, watched TV at Ana Maria's house, and played with the clay, but I kept a chunk of it in my skirt pocket. Marita and I played with the clay most of the afternoon.

Antonio came home from his classes later in the afternoon and invited us to go with him to do some errands downtown. We had all climbed into the car, when he remembered a paper he needed. He asked me to go back into the house and get it for him, casually handing me his full keychain.

Equally casually, I took it, found the right key for the gate, and let myself into the patio. Then I remembered the lump of leftover clay in my pocket and realized it was no accident I had brought it to Puebla after all. In the house, I pressed the key into the piece of modeling clay, hid the clay, then returned to the car. As the car wound through the streets, I felt comforted by the confirmation of the scripture "let us cheerfully do all things that lie in our power; and then may we stand still, with the utmost assurance, to see the salvation of God, and for his arm to be revealed" (D&C 123:17). The small act of a forgotten paper and a lazy Antonio was enough for the Lord to help me turn the situation to my advantage in answer to my prayers.

We finished the errands about dark and returned in time to see

Mama Rosita's pot of boiled raw milk erupt over the side of the pan, singeing the burner on the stove, as usual. She asked us to pick up bread for supper. The bread store was down the street and around the corner. At the *panadería*, Antonio introduced me to a young and pretty woman putting pieces of sweet bread into our plastic mesh bag with her tongs. In the car he told me, "I have a list of possible mothers for Marita. That girl is number two after you."

I smiled. "She looks very nice. Good luck with her." And I thought, *What do I care? I have an impression of the key now and my ticket to freedom with Marita. Things have turned against you, starting today. You will need more than luck now.*

After supper I told him that I needed to return to Mexico City immediately, and he gave me a list of terms for our divorce. I read it on the way to the bus station, and his terms made me so angry that I decided to buy a ticket to Cuernavaca instead. I arrived so late at night that it scared me to be alone in the city, especially when all the phones at the bus station were out of order. After walking for blocks in unlighted streets, I entered a hospital to use the telephone. Marilyn had pneumonia but promptly came to get me.

After breakfast Thursday morning I showed Marilyn the list of voluntary divorce terms. To give me fifty percent custody, he insisted on the following ridiculous terms:

- Half the money from our property in Utah (though he swore in court he had never lived in Utah).
- I had to live at his parents' house, paying my rent and other expenses.
- Marita had to sleep in a separate room but during the day I could wash and fix her clothes, bathe her, feed her, and take care of her when she gets sick.
- I could not take Marita out of the house, the city, or the country without Antonio's permission.
- I could be free to act as I wished—work, go out, etc.
- Antonio would pay for Marita's food, clothing, education.
- I should not shout, hit, or create scenes harmful to Marita's emotional stability. (If I accepted this condition, wouldn't it be an admission that I might be usually abusive?)

- I return all of Marita's identity documents to Antonio.
- If I chose to stop taking care of Marita, I must relinquish custody to him.

I was furious. Marilyn laughed. When she gained control of herself, between coughs and wheezes she said, "No one in their right mind would ever accept any of these terms. What are you going to do, Mari Vawn?"

At this point I was ready to do almost anything to avoid the traps Antonio was setting up for me in court. I had a plan. I wanted to send a copy of Antonio's conditions to Bishop Morrill to see if he could use it to put pressure on somebody. And I had resolved to escape with Marita.

I showed Marilyn the impression of the key in the clay and said, "This is the key to the front gate. I need someone to help me get out of Puebla without getting caught. Not just a bus or a taxi, but someone there to help me, as Roger said in the blessing last week."

Marilyn took me to meet Jose, a bodyguard for Americans living down the street. Although he was taller and stronger than most Mexicans, I could tell he was afraid of the risks, but he said he'd consider it. Returning to Mexico City for an appointment with Mr. Rivera, I gave him Antonio's terms to read, and Gloria handed me a letter from my mother that held a valentine inside.

> *It was a year ago that we were together in Orem. It was so difficult for me to come and see Marita's room so empty and all the emotions it aroused, but I was glad I could be with you. I still have the valentine you gave me, and you expressed your love for Marita and sorrow that she had been taken from you at such a tender age. You concluded that "Perhaps next year on Valentine's Day, I'll once again hold her in my arms!" I PRAY THAT WILL BE THE CASE. You probably won't get this until after Valentine's Day, but we want you to know, honey, we love you dearly, and you and Marita are in our prayers constantly. . .*

Mr. Rivera, though amazed by Antonio's terms, pointed out: "It's *something* that he's agreed to have a voluntary divorce and giving you fifty percent custody."

I showed him the piece of clay, but he shook his head. "This clay is too soft and you should have got an impression of both sides. I don't know if anyone can make a key from just this much."

I put it away carefully, undiscouraged, and replied, "I doubt Antonio will be so careless again."

We spent the next two hours in serious counseling. Many times he repeated, "Legally, I can't advise you to kidnap Marita, but in practicality, in reality, this is the best thing you can do! It is very dangerous. I want you to understand that YOU are the one entirely responsible for any 'kidnapping' that happens. No one should know that you are considering it, and I expect legal confidentially. (He put his hands over his ears to indicate he hadn't heard a word I had said.) Remember, I should not even be talking to you about this, and I know nothing about it!"

"Don't worry. I'll be the one responsible."

"And please calm down before you go to your painting lesson this afternoon. The people in Puebla will notice you are acting different. They'll be suspicious of you if you are acting so happy when you are there."

February 15, 1977 — Journal entry
Lomas

While I visited Marita in Puebla these past few days, my mind tuned to a new awareness and sifted out details I had never noticed before in the families' routines and the structure of the house that contribute to a good plan for getting her out of the city. But time is running out, and I only have two more weeks until the March fourth court date. If I don't leave with her before then, I may never have another chance. Was it any accident that after Jose's reluctance Mr. Rivera had introduced me to his friend Victor this week?

I need someone to help me after I get Marita out of the house, and of the two men, Victor is the best for the job. I never figured I would actually do such a thing, but here I am making plans for it. After all the advances Mr. Rivera has made in court and after we have done everything possible within legal limits, I have few alternatives. I would lose my mind and soul if I agreed to Antonio's terms of voluntary divorce. I probably won't be granted a work permit, and without any money, I'll have to give up and go home anyway, even if the case were escalated to a higher court next month.

That leaves me with the most honorable of the three choices—to escape with her while I still have a legal right to do it and still have as much right to custody as Antonio has. After March fourth, ¿*Quién sabe?* Mothers do what they have to do to help their children.

Visiting with Victor in Mr. Rivera's office today, I knew I wanted him to help me. From what I am learning about Victor, he is unreal—an actor, a former U.S. Secret Service agent, and more importantly, experienced at what I need. He said he knew how to operate with a team of other agents in split-second timing to completely immobilize the government of a large city within five minutes. He had already been hired by other Americans to get their loved ones out of Mexican jails. He likes adventure, even danger, but won't take unnecessary risks.

Later that same day:

Just looking at Victor's carefully capped teeth for the perfect smile, his thick sandy brown hair, or his intense captivating eyes, one would have never guessed his background. A former helicopter pilot, he had found his niche, along with his actress wife, in the glamorous Churubusco Colony of Mexico's celebrities and film stars. Tall, handsome, intelligent, charming, confident, physically fit, and yet totally accessible, he was making a name for himself in movies and plays. Yet he also had time to make money on the side by rescuing Americans who found their way to him.

During our meeting I recounted the highlights of what I had done to get custody, and I showed him the modeling clay. He asked me to get a key made and try it out soon. He probed for more details of my situation to decide if he wanted to get involved. "How do you know she really wants to be with you after all this time?"

Without hesitation I answered, "I'm sure she wants to come with me! Every time I see her she asks to go back on the bus with me to Mexico. She asks when she can go on the airplane with me. And she is very loving and happy with me."

"Is there a restraining order?"

"No, not as things stand right now," I pointed out. "Both Antonio and I have equal rights to custody. It's the same situation, only reversed, as things were in Utah last year when Antonio took her. I had temporary custody then, but he hadn't been served papers, so it was still legal for him to take her because he was the father."

Victor sat up an inch or two and grinned. "In Mexico possession is definitely nine tenths of the law. You wouldn't be doing anything illegal to take her out of the house in Puebla."

I explored the idea of a contract with him. "And once I get her out of there, he must not find us, or we'll never get out of the country. If we tried to fly out of Mexico, the immigration officials would check their lists, find us, and stop us. I don't have the official paper I need giving the father's permission to take a child out of Mexico. I need someone like you to take us to safety. Will you help me?"

"Find out if the key will work. We'll meet again on Saturday at ten and discuss some ideas for an escape. I want you to look for all the possible times and ways you could leave that house unnoticed. I need that information to decide if we can work out a deal," he concluded.

"Could you give me an idea of your fees?"

"Plan on at least five hundred dollars and more than that for the trip to the United States."

February 16, 1977

I found myself in Cuernavaca again. Marilyn was still sick in bed. We'd spent the day talking over my plans while she coughed and coughed with bronchitis-asthma. I left for a while and found a shack by the side of the road with a young boy in it who made copies of keys. It was a good thing the clerk was only a boy. An older person would probably have refused to make a key from clay, but the boy readily accepted the extra ten pesos I offered him to do the job.

I held my breath as he searched for a blank that would match the outline of the key. He found one that was close and began filing and grinding the blank down to fit the grooves. At last it looked as close a fit as he could make it, and I gratefully paid him what he asked, less than two dollars.

Sweat was running down my face after standing out in the sun waiting for the key. But I was thrilled to hold a hot metal key, gold glinting in my hand, instead of the cool lump of pink clay.

Saturday, February 19, 1977

After my meeting with Victor, I knew I could relax and enjoy my trip to Puebla that weekend, at least, because it wasn't time to leave Mexico yet. Here's why.

We met in Mr. Rivera's office again, and we discussed the key. I had tried it out on Thursday, but it didn't turn in the lock. He told me to find someone to file down the rough edges, and for the sake of planning that day, we assumed the key would work. I explained I almost didn't get back to Mexico with the key.

"Somebody must have seen me trying to use it because Antonio haunted me for the rest of the afternoon. At first, I'd had it in my skirt pocket. Then a voice in my mind said to move it quickly, so I put it in my shoe. A few minutes after that Antonio suddenly came up to me, plunged his hands into both my skirt pockets, and fished around. A little later the voice said to move the key again, so I put it inside some Kleenex in my jacket pocket. Moments later Antonio grabbed my feet and jerked my shoes off. I moved the key to my shirt pocket, then to the painting supplies, then rolled it up in some clothes in the bedroom closet. Each time he looked precisely where the key had been minutes before. Chills affirmed how close to the edge I stood to losing our freedom. He never said what he was looking for, even when I demanded angrily to know what he was doing."

Victor looked at the key with new appreciation and instructed, "You will have to leave the key here where it will be safe until we know you'll have to use it for sure. Above all, on your visit this week, you must do everything exactly as you have in the past. Act as though everything is fine. The difference in how you act could trigger Antonio's sixth sense that you are up to something. Now then, what do you know about possible escape routes?"

"There are only two possible ways," I explained. "One, I use the key to the front gate and carry her out at a time when there are the fewest number of people at home. Two, I open the *despacho* door which also opens out to the street. But it rattles and grates as it rolls up. It would be easily heard."

"What about the back of the house or the other walls? What's there?"

I laughed. "A turkey farm! The neighbors keep a flock of turkeys and chickens just behind the Cruz house. Depending on the time of day, they could set up quite a racket. The west wall is cemented to the wall of the adjacent house which is taller than my in-laws'. The east wall has a lawn and trees on the other side of it, but there is the same problem as everywhere else in Mexico—the huge stone walls and iron gates are built high with jagged pieces of glass to discourage thieves. Even if I did get over the wall into the neighbor's yard, I wouldn't be able to get out of that gate without a key either."

"What about the roof? Do you have access to it?"

"Yes," I replied. "A metal stairway winds up from the kitchen area. But there are a lot of dogs up there."

"Maybe that wouldn't matter."

"What do you mean?"

"I could fly over in a helicopter and pick you up off the roof. I've done that before in jail breaks. Then we could land at a private ranch north of Puebla and drive off in a car later."

I didn't doubt it, but I didn't want the expense of a helicopter either. As we discussed more details after that, I grew more fearful. Victor realized I wasn't psychologically ready to try an escape, and he set up another meeting for the next Saturday morning, giving me one more week to prepare.

February 25, 1977 — Journal entry

> I spent the day sorting through clothes and papers, stuffing the few things I definitely want to take out of Mexico into Marilyn's green duffle bag. It wasn't much: some makeup, a pair of black leather dress shoes, my underclothing, one pair of nylons, and one change of clothes for traveling—blue jeans and a striped India cotton gauze shirt. There was still room for some new

clothes I bought for Marita this week, a Logan green knit outfit with a golden yellow sweater, stockings, and underwear.

All day long I have thought of the words of the blessing I received nearly a year ago: *Marita will come back to you, but in the Lord's own due time and when he is ready. He knows when that time will be, and you can know also, ahead of time—when she will come.*

This week I have known it is time, and I have been preparing. I bought a long dark wig for myself, just in case. Because the court hearing is in only six days, I feel that the Lord will surely answer our many, many prayers and open the way to leave with her soon.

Antonio, suspicious that I may try something, has spent the week looking for my key, but since I didn't have it, I remained relatively calm. The family set traps for me to leave with her all this past week so they could catch me at it. Yet I knew the time wasn't right, so I never left or tried to change my routine, although I had many opportunities to do so. One day, for example, Antonio left me alone with Marita in downtown Puebla while he went into a dry cleaners and some stores. We sat quietly in the car until he returned. At other times we strolled down the street outside their home, always turning back at the corner.

Today I packed and cleaned with the idea that tonight is the last night I will sleep here. I packed Rosalyn's little, green flowered, cloth-backed suitcase that I always take with me to Puebla. In went my green hymn book, a blue denim skirt, makeup, my electric rollers, slip, and all my oil painting supplies. I'll have to leave the suitcase and all its contents plus my beige sweater and purse—all as a decoy to buy me time after I leave with Marita. The family will see my things and hope we are still there.

Beginning tomorrow morning, I must walk humbly and do as the prophet Nephi did: *And I was led by the Spirit, not knowing beforehand the things which I should do.* I dread going to Puebla one more time, but it must be the last trip. I don't know when the best time will be to make the escape, but I wonder if the time still won't be right until the last possible moment, when Antonio is so very sure that all is safe and he has won absolutely. Will it have to be that way? And then the Lord's power will be shown at a time when no one thought it possible? From the words of my last blessing, there was a hint it could be that way.

I don't know what will happen, or how, or when. I just know that I desperately need the Lord's intervention during this next week to end this mess.

I didn't try to keep all the letters I received, but I glued some excerpts on the journal pages from letters I received that week.

- *My father, Manson Bailey: "We are aware of the exemplary life you have lived and the many, many second miles you have gone in behalf of the gospel and the Lord's children you have helped in many ways. If they all knew of your plight and would go to Heavenly Father in prayer in your behalf at the same time, it would be overwhelming . . . It seems you are preparing for many different possibilities of events unknown to you at this time. May these prove to fit in with the Lord's plan of events in your life. Your mother and I are with you constantly in our prayers and support that which the Spirit shows you is the way to go."*
- *Ione Jensen (the R.S. president. of the 51st ward): "The Lord will bless you and help you so you can return home to us soon."*
- *My sister Tana: "You've simply GOT to get her back, and I know you will. I just hope it's before you, or the folks, or Marita are hurt anymore. If only Antonio knew that it takes more of a man to let his daughter go where she can have a better life."*

Chapter Twenty-four

Saturday, February 26, 1977

MY BIG BLUE SUITCASE WAS FILLED with things I wanted Marilyn to bring to Utah in the summer. I zipped it up and left it on the brown chair in Nancy's bedroom. Next to it I stacked papers, pictures, and clothes I no longer wanted. Really, after living in the same few clothes for so long, who wouldn't want to leave them all behind? The two weeks I had originally planned on had stretched to nearly ten months. I had lost about ten pounds, too, so none of them fit well anyway.

I switched off the stereo, washed the dishes, and closed the refrigerator door on two shriveling green *limones* and two hundred grams of molding Chihuahua cheese. I took the garbage downstairs and asked the maid to open the gate. I stood there with the green cloth suitcase and the green duffle bag and glanced around the lovely yard for one last look. A joyful lift in my heart sprang from the increasing expectancy of leaving Mexico soon. Then I started off for my next meeting with Victor.

I took a *pesero* taxi cab down Reforma, for I had the two suitcases, a purse, a red jacket, my journals, and a bulky sweater. It would have been far too much on a bus.

The Metro policeman whose job was to prevent people from carrying on too many bulky boxes and packages saw me but did nothing. I watched all the familiar landmarks of the past few months pass swiftly. When I reached the law office, I put everything except Rosalyn's green suitcase and my purse into the walk-in safe.

Gloria told me to call Bishop Morrill. He'd talked to the stake president again about Church policy, but without authority or permission from Elder Fyans, he could do nothing about Antonio's membership status. It all seemed extremely complicated to me, but nothing could be changed until someone talked to Elder Fyans who was on Area Conference tours.

After Bishop Morrill verified my decision *not* to agree to Antonio's divorce terms, he asked if there were anything else he could do. I hinted at what I was considering.

Bishop Morrill was appalled and interrupted me, "Why MariVawn, you could lose everything you've gained in court so far. You put your life in jeopardy. And you could cause a real mess legally and in the Church if you get caught while you are still in Mexico. You would probably be kept from seeing Marita ever again if Antonio or his family stopped you. If anything goes wrong, you will never have another chance to try again!"

I said nothing. I had thought of these risks so often.

The silence lengthened, then slowly he said, "MariVawn, if you *do* decide to go ahead with this, will you call and let me know so I can be praying for you?"

"Bishop, *I'm telling you right now!*"

"All right," he said quietly. "I'll support you."

After the call, which I made in a small private room, I grabbed some Kleenex to wipe up the flow of tears. They weren't from sadness or fear, but from the overwhelming realization that he supported my decision without hesitation, and in those same moments, I felt a confirmation of the Spirit accepting my decision of what I had to do. A calmness spread and filled me, and I wasn't afraid to go ahead with my plans. I had no doubts about Victor's role. I left the telephone a changed person—stronger and more determined.

Down the hall I entered a small room to the left of Mr. Rivera's usual consultation room. It was furnished with only a handsome round oak table and matching chairs. I greeted Victor and Mr. Rivera who sat down with us for about an hour while we firmed up our escape plans. He covered his ears and mouth symbolically at first to indicate he knew nothing of our meeting. Somewhere we had passed an invisible point of commitment, and I knew Victor had accepted the contract to be the pickup man.

On the table lay a map of Puebla with all the possible escape exits marked in red ink. I drew rough maps of nearby streets around the Cruz's property and a floorplan of the home. I detailed the general routine of the families' comings and goings during certain hours of the day and answered questions about other details.

Victor even proposed the possibility of drugging the family with phenobarbital. But how to drug four dogs and fourteen people? And what might be the effect on Antonio's father who had suffered a recent stroke? There were four different apartment areas on the property. I didn't know how I'd get around to drug them all.

Next we discussed the timing. Victor hoped we could do something before 4:00 A.M., before people came out of their deepest sleep cycle. I reminded him that the dogs on the roof would be roused with unusual noise even if the family slept.

Victor methodically asked questions until two times in the day emerged as the times with the least risk. He insisted that the pickup had to be close—I couldn't walk more than a block with Marita. More than that would take too long, and we couldn't risk it.

Plan A would work on Sunday, only hours away, if family members visited relatives after church or rested after the meal. Victor would pass the Cruz house about 4:00 P.M. and would park and wait only five minutes on the dirt road at the end of the block to the east.

If I could, I was to open the gate and walk quickly to him carrying Marita. Only if someone ran after me was I to run.

If Plan A didn't work, we'd try Plan B: At five minutes to one he would wait there on Monday. Marita would be coming home from her preschool and very few people would be home. Victor constantly reminded me not to take any chances. If I aroused suspicion, I might end all further chances of escape. I learned that the first three minutes of an operation were the most crucial, and if those beginning moments and moves were successful, the odds were that the following ones would be too.

The time pressure of the court hearing worried me. Antonio had been pressuring me about what my terms would be for our voluntary divorce or my decision to stay with him as a family. Victor suggested, "Just tell him, 'OK, I'll give you a list just before I leave on Monday.' He won't keep bugging you, and it will put him off guard some."

I hadn't been able to formulate a list yet, and I felt relief to have a plan on that matter.

"What if we don't escape before March fourth? I can't go to court under those conditions that await me," I asked Mr. Rivera, who had been mostly silent during the hour. This was my greatest fear.

He assured me I didn't have much to worry about. Voluntary divorce proceedings would take another two-week waiting period and other meetings where both parties would have to appear to render it valid. The way he saw it, I had a two-week leeway.

I stared down at the map on the table. The way I saw it intellectually, he must be right, but in my heart, I knew I only had until Monday or Tuesday morning. No more.

We walked downstairs and looked at Victor's car so I could recognize it. It was American, long, big, expensive. Coppery brown. I'd never seen a car like it in Mexico. I wouldn't miss it.

I returned to the building for my Puebla supplies. I taped the gate key just under my left bra strap below my shoulder with a piece of adhesive tape. It would be difficult for Antonio to find it, yet I could quickly tear it loose with one hand while I was holding Marita. With the key hidden, I was ready, except for calling my father from Mr. Rivera's office. He supported my plan and told me they would be fasting and praying for me.

All the way to Puebla, I prayed that it would be my last trip. Since I had stopped to eat before I took the bus, I arrived an hour late for the art class. Antonio cordially drove me over to the art studio and I finished a painting of Christ. By the time he returned for us, I had also finished everything on another painting of some roses, except the roses themselves. I was enjoying mixing the colors and blending them on the canvas. Marita ran under the tables and hid among the sculptures and stone blocks. I knew I would never see my paintings again once we left the studio.

While I helped Mama Rosita fix supper, she mentioned that the dogs on the roof were usually noisier at night. I decided that their barking wouldn't arouse suspicion when I went out later to try out my key. I was almost ready to go to sleep when Antonio came in and asked if we could pray together.

As we stood up afterwards, he said that he suddenly felt inspired to give me a priesthood blessing. He had actually refused when I had asked him for one earlier. I accepted it happily and humbly, hoping that despite his lack of honesty with himself the Lord's will might still be given through him. I had learned not to pay much attention to blessings he was mouth to. I was never sure if the words came from a dark source, Antonio's own mind, or from the Lord.

He said that the Lord loved all three of us; that I was to be happy and cheerful instead of talking about ailments (I was suffering from an outbreak of hives right then); that I shouldn't choose the easy way to go and the Lord would bless me; and that the Lord would help me sooner than I realized.

Antonio was instantly happier and less suspicious. He obviously interpreted the words in support of his own will. His surveillance slackened to the point that I could have slipped out with Marita except that I wouldn't try it until I knew Victor was outside the gate. And I still didn't know for sure if my key to the front gate would work. I'd spent one day going through Mexico City looking for someone to file the key down. Most of the shop owners were indignant, assuming that I wanted it for illegal purposes. I finally found someone who would do it, but I still didn't know if the key would work.

Not having an alarm clock, I told my subconscious mind to wake me up a little before four to try the key. I woke up promptly at 3:45 A.M. I was a little chilly in my yellow bathrobe and yarn slippers, but nervousness was my real problem. I tiptoed across the patio and pushed the key into the padlock. I held my breath.

It turned! It opened easily! Relief flooded me and I gratefully glanced up to the stars. The extra filing on the key had done the job! Tucking the key back under the tape on my shoulder, I padded back to my room smiling with joy and slept more peacefully than I had done for days. And the dogs hadn't barked once.

Sunday, February 27, 1977

In church I sat with Antonio as usual, in the second row of the folding chairs in Ana Maria's part of the house. The scriptures in the lesson on Isaiah comforted me, especially Isaiah 12:2, *Behold, God is my salvation; I will trust, and not be afraid: for the Lord Jehovah is my strength and my song; he also is become my salvation.* I, too, was relying on the Lord's promises, power, and grace to help me go beyond what I could do on my own to save us. I had done what I could in the most honorable ways I knew to be in a better position to receive the extraordinary help I knew we would still need.

Marita and I sat on the couch at the back of the room looking at picture books through a boring Relief Society lesson on New Zealand. In between meetings when I was out on the patio with Marita and other Church members, Antonio's eyes followed us. This was the only time during the week that the gate was left unlocked for more than a few minutes at a time. But since I knew I couldn't leave then, it was easy to stand around calmly, smiling and making small talk with everyone. At last sacrament meeting started, and as usual the three of us sat together at the front. Marita sat on my lap most of the time, finally falling asleep towards the end. Holding her in my arms was a coveted pleasure, and I decided to remain there holding her until she woke up.

After the meeting, everyone drifted from the room within ten minutes for the planning meeting upstairs in Mama Rosita's dining room, Antonio included. One nephew folded all the chairs except mine and stacked them against the living room walls. A few children ran in and out, playing with balloons, plunking on the piano, and chasing each other. After a while a cousin began practicing the piano, missing the notes badly. Papa Dan wandered in, corrected the boy's notes, and sat down to play a few songs himself. Then wordlessly, he began watching me holding my sleeping daughter.

I just looked back at him and around the room. On the wall straight ahead hung a little wooden house with three hooks at the bottom. On the hooks hung Ana Maria's keys—including her keys to the front gate. I wondered if they were left there on purpose to tempt me into taking them while everyone else was in the meeting upstairs. I cradled Marita and sat patiently for more than an hour until the meeting ended.

Antonio came down to wake Marita up, and we left to buy some steak from the butcher shop a few blocks away. He knew I hated to buy things on the Sabbath and not keep it as a holy day. I said nothing but went with him to keep my eye on Marita.

Marita, as usual, hardly ate anything. I was hungry and ate quickly. We left the table sooner than the others. It was a few minutes to four. As we finished brushing our teeth, we tried leaving the house. Antonio appeared right outside the door to the patio. Arms akimbo, he growled, "Where do you think you're going?"

I answered brightly, "To push Marita in the swing."

He stepped aside. The swing was attached to the overhang produced by the apartment built over the patio-driveway. I could not see the gate because it was directly behind me. I tried to get Marita to sit facing the opposite direction so I could look for Victor's car as I pushed her, but she protested.

One by one, all of Ana Maria's children came out to the patio. Antonio began fixing the string on a bow. The oldest cousin showed the other cousins how to make human pyramids, walk in worm fashion, and do other gymnastic stunts. Antonio brought out three folding chairs and made us sit on them while we watched the children. It wasn't long before Marita wanted to join in, but she wasn't dressed for the antics.

It was exactly four, but though I rushed her to change her clothes, it still must have taken too long. I never saw Victor's convertible pass by.

With nine people out on the patio, especially with Antonio sitting there for an hour, it was obvious that there would be no escape on Sunday. By five o'clock everyone had left the property to visit relatives except Antonio, Marita, and me. That planning meeting I hadn't known about had thrown off my plans by one crucial hour. Left alone in the house with him, I maneuvered our time so as to avoid talking about my decision for court.

About dark we all went downstairs to watch TV. When his parents returned, I cheerfully helped Mama Rosita fix supper and a plate of enchiladas for Antonio. Pleased, he gave me fifty pesos to buy some material to make Marita another pair of pajamas. I was delighted! It gave me a good reason to stay there longer the next morning while Marita was in school and until 1:00 P.M. so I could try Plan B.

I truly felt the faith of others being exercised on my behalf. The pajama project seemed to have happened naturally, without making my presence there on Monday contrived. In Montana, my parents, my aunts, and many members of our ward were fasting and praying. My mother later told me even young children were praying so "that little girl could be with her mommy." My name had been kept on the prayer roll in Utah and Idaho temples, and friends and relatives were praying for us there also. Although I was three thousand miles away from home, I felt a peace, and I knew I wasn't alone.

Marita: Missing in Mexico

Monday, February 28, 1977

When Marita awakened about 8:20, I carried her downstairs to the bathroom as I usually did. It would have been an excellent time to escape, if Victor had been there. I helped her get ready for school, dressing her in clothes that would be nice to travel in later on that day. She ate breakfast, and Papa Dan took her to school about 9:30.

Ana Maria was going to the market, and Mama Rosita wanted me to buy some eggs as long as I was going downtown to buy flannel. They both said that one pair of pajamas was enough and were surprised that Antonio had given me money for more. Just as we were leaving, Mama Rosita decided to go with us. We were all in a good mood, and I was still acting as relaxed and cheerful as I could.

Puebla's central market had several stalls of colorful material, and I bought one and three-quarters meters of thick flannel with pink roses. Back at the house, I had already cut out the pieces and had begun sewing when I realized Ana Maria had to leave again, that Marita would come back in an hour or so, and only my in-laws were there. It would be easy to escape after all.

The phone rang. Mama Rosita answered it, then held the receiver to me. I jumped up from the sewing machine saying it must be Mireya, my girlfriend from Saltillo, but Gloria's voice told me in steady professional English, "Your dentist's appointment for today has been cancelled. The doctor won't be able to make it. Can you give me an acceptable time for tomorrow?"

Stunned with disappointment that Victor couldn't come, I recovered when I realized no one else in the house spoke English, so I was safe. I answered in English, "Today would have been such a perfect day!"

Gloria's receptionist voice continued, "I'm sorry. What about this time tomorrow?"

Marita would be in school this time tomorrow. I said, "How about between 8:15 and a 8:45. Will that be OK?" I knew that masonry workers would be showing up to work outside in the patio on Tuesday. I couldn't risk having them here watching us after Marita returned from school. It simply had to be before she left for school at 9:30. I knew Victor only had wanted to wait for five minutes the day before, but this was the best I could think of on such short notice. So, I asked for fifteen minutes on either side of 8:30.

The voice on the line confirmed, "Yes, that will be fine. Your appointment will be between 8:15 and 8:45 tomorrow then."

So, just like that, I had to wait another day. Immediately I began praying that I would find a good reason to stay one more night. Never before had I stayed till a Tuesday. I found out later that Victor had been afraid I'd be so upset over the change in plans that I would be paralyzed. Instead my calmness and new suggestion of a pickup time told him I was ready. He even deduced that I had tried the key.

I kept sewing, visiting with Rosita about my girlfriend Mireya. I explained she had been one of my best students in the American School, that she always called me two or three times a week and always talked to me in English. I didn't say that it had been Mireya who had called, but I hoped she would assume that it was. Because I knew that she had probably detected my disappointment, I mentioned how sad I was that Mireya couldn't come to Mexico City the end of this month to pick up the painting I had finished for her. Rosita had seen the painting. I felt assured that she didn't suspect anything. Marita returned from school, and I watched the clock.

At five minutes to one, I heard a commotion by the patio gate, the voices of strangers and family members who had just arrived, and the rumble of a large engine. Mama Rosita ran down to unlock the gate. By the time Marita and I went downstairs, I could hardly believe what I saw!

A big dump truck was emptying its entire load of sand and gravel into the driveway, a pile several feel high that blocked the driveway. We couldn't possibly have left at one as planned.

I remembered the words from the blessing given in Cuernavaca: *At times it may seem you will lose and there cannot be much hope. You must try even just one more time.* I was glad Victor didn't make a wasted trip that day after all.

That afternoon I played with Marita and her cousins, finished the handwork on the pajamas, and spent some time alone thinking. About dark, Antonio returned.

Somehow he had made five hundred pesos that day and was pleased with himself. He showed it to me and sat down for a chat. "You know, Mari Vawn, our hearing is only three days away. You still haven't said anything about your decision. You've had all month to think about it. Can you tell me anything yet?"

I said, "I've been thinking about the priesthood blessing you gave me, and I feel a lot better about things lately."

That nonanswer satisfied him. He smiled and jubilantly said, "Well, I've got a lot of money right now. How about going to that Italian movie downtown before you go back to Mexico?"

"I haven't been to a show in a long time!" I replied enthusiastically.

I felt the inner knots unwind. A movie would take up the evening and give me an excuse to stay overnight. Marita went to bed, and Antonio got ready. I managed to shower and wash my hair before we left, being careful not to dislodge the key and tape. How it was itching by then!

Italian comedies are more farfetched than French or American ones, and I always enjoyed them. We both laughed and relaxed watching *El Ultimo en Saberlo*. Antonio was pleasant all evening, and it was easy to be pleasant in return.

As he said good-bye until the morning, I secretly told myself, *This is good-bye—forever!* But my last words to him were, "I'll be leaving in the morning after Marita leaves for school." My sleep was fitful because I woke up often to plan alternative courses of action if something unexpected came up.

Chapter Twenty-five

Tuesday, March 1, 1977

IT WAS BARELY SEVEN when I was awakened by Antonio banging around the kitchen fixing breakfast and singing the *Saturday's Warrior* theme song enthusiastically. Before he left for school around 7:15, he rushed in to give me a quick kiss and was gone.

Carlos didn't leave as early as usual. I heard him clang up the metal stairs to the roof and shout something down to Ana Maria who had shuffled outside my bedroom window to light the water heater that stood on the second-story patio area. With Antonio and Carlos gone, I relaxed a little. Carlos's car was the fastest and the newest. It wouldn't be safe to leave if he were still in the house.

Ana Maria returned every few minutes to fuss with her water heater, meanwhile shouting instructions to her children about getting ready for school. I had hoped to go into Marita's bedroom and leave quietly with her before Antonio's parents got up, but I knew Ana Maria's shouting would soon wake up everyone in the complex.

By **7:20**, I was dressed, but I sat on the bed waiting for time to pass. I prayed a lot. I knew the time for escape had to be within the next hour.

At **7:55**, I heard the chain clink on the patio gate. Peeking out the dining room window, I watched the older cousins leave for school. So far so good. That only left a few people in the house. Putting on orange knit slippers to muffle my footsteps, I walked downstairs, lifted a folding chair closer to the door that opened out into the patio, and painstakingly inched the door open, stopping to lift the wind chimes over its edge. With the door standing open to the patio, I would be able to walk through it quickly without the chimes announcing our departure.

Still in the slippers, I sneaked into Marita's bedroom. She wasn't there. I guessed that Antonio's parents had taken her into their room when Antonio had left. Disappointed, I removed the slippers, put my brown loafers back on, and tried to think what to do. My thoughts were interrupted by the sound of feet moving up the stairs. Who could it be? I peeked through a crack in the bedroom door.

Soon I saw a lady missionary come up to light her water heater! I'd completely forgotten about their living in the apartment directly over the patio gate. I prayed fervently, "She's just got to leave the door open when she goes back to her apartment! I don't have time to go open it again! Don't let her shut it!"

She left it open.

8:10 I was kneeling in the bedroom to see down the stairs. I glanced up and around to my left in the bedroom before I stood up. Level with my head, I noticed a folded MIA theme card in English stuck on part of the vanity. On the card stood Nephi in full color on one side with this familiar scripture printed on the other, "I will go and do the things which the Lord hath commanded, for I know that the Lord giveth no commandments unto the children of men, save he shall prepare a way for them that they may accomplish the thing which he commandeth them" (1 Nephi 3:7).

I read it over and over, wondering who had put it there, an angel or a Cruz or what. It had not been there before, I was sure of it. It did not seem to be a coincidence that this particular card had found its way into my hands in those precise moments . . . in English—a card that had been distributed when I was a teenager—to give me the strength to go and to do and to succeed. I stuffed the card into my jeans pocket.

8:12 Mama Rosita began stirring around in the kitchen on the other side of the wall from my bedroom, cleaning up from the night before and clattering dirty dishes into the sink.

8:15 I was sure that Victor was outside waiting. But before I left the bedroom to wake up Marita, I messed up the bed I had so carefully made an hour earlier, so it would look normally messed up for that hour of the day. Mama Rosita was standing at the stove when I stepped into the kitchen.

"*¿Cómo amaneciste?*" we both said. I brushed my teeth at the kitchen sink and chatted with her about the comical tangle in the last night's movie, laughing at her jokes, too. Then, mentioning that I hadn't seen Marita in her new pajamas, I moved toward the hallway. I paused at the second bedroom door. "*¿Se puede?*" I asked.

Papasito answered, "*Sí, pasa.*"

As I opened the door, I saw that he had just crawled out of the bed where Marita was stretching and opening her eyes to a new day. Papasito ambled over to the window, pulled back the thin curtains, and opened the window as far as it would go. I picked up Marita and we looked out on clear bright blue skies and sunshine. He left.

Victor had advised me not to take anything of mine or Marita's when we left so the family wouldn't notice things missing right away. But I put her red patent leather shoes on her feet before we went downstairs to the bathroom. She was wearing the new pajamas I had made her.

Passing by Mama Rosita with an offhand comment, I headed for the stairs with Marita riding on my hips. This is what I always did every morning to help Marita get ready for school. Down on the first floor, Papa Dan was in the bathroom with the door shut so we waited in the living room, talking quietly.

8:30 Between comments, I looked into the patio. Ana Maria was sitting in her kitchen with her back to the window only two feet away, talking to her youngest daughter who was facing the window. Ana Maria usually took Estela to school at 8:30. Yet, there she sat with Estela nowhere in sight.

Marita was sitting on my hips with her legs wrapped around me but had started coaxing me to go play in the dirt pile left outside by the dump truck. She weighed only thirty pounds so it was easy to carry her comfortably on my hip. We could easily walk outside to the patio, but I hesitated.

Papasito stayed in the bathroom with the water running. I could hear Mama Rosita operating the blender in the kitchen.

Could I pass Ana Maria? What if she heard my footsteps in the patio as I walked by her window? What if Papa Dan opened the bathroom door? What if Antonio's mother called us to breakfast just as I reached the gate?

I stood mired in indecision.

Everything seemed to be holding its breath and we were trapped in time while the clock had stopped... waiting... waiting. Suddenly, I felt an urging inside, *"Go! Now!"*

8:35 It was my window of opportunity. I felt free to move, to take Marita right then, risking everything. I glanced at my watch. I couldn't wait any longer.

I noticed a sucker, one that I had bought for Marita a week before, stuck between two books at my eye level on the shelf before me. I gave it to Marita and whispered, "Don't say anything at all. We're going out very quietly to look at the gate."

I wrapped my arms around her, tucked her legs around my waist a little tighter, and moved to the doorway.

Leaning over, I scrambled under Ana Maria's window, stood up and walked quickly past her living room door to the gate about thirty feet beyond that, and ripped the key free from the tape on my shoulder.

Before I inserted the key, I glanced around to see if anyone were looking yet. No one was. Marita hadn't made any noise, and apparently my footsteps had blended in with the other everyday background noises. The key turned easily in the lock.

The round metal bar slipped up and out of the padlock. The tattletale clinking of the chain and the audible squeak of the hinges made me cringe as I opened the large panels wide enough for us to slip through to the sidewalk.

As I closed the gate, I still saw no one. Amazed that they hadn't heard us, I marveled at the miracle of standing there free to walk away with my daughter. The padlock slipped around in my shaking fingers as I fumbled to close it. The last click, our signal to freedom, seemed to fill the air, loud and decisive enough to reach everyone inside the compound.

Then I turned to walk swiftly down the sidewalk towards the little dirt road at the end of the block. I had only taken a few steps when Marita questioned me, *"¿A dónde vamos, Mamá?"*

I answered her in a normal-as-possible voice, "Down the street a ways." To focus her mind on something else, I unwrapped the sucker she had held and put it into her mouth, then kept walking quickly along with students, maids, workers, and other mothers with children. Everyone was in a hurry to get somewhere.

I knew Victor wouldn't wait a minute past 8:45. As I approached the end of the block, I began searching for Victor's car. If he weren't there,

I would find a taxi to take us to Mexico City. I had 1,150 pesos sewn in my bra under my left arm, and the boulevard was only a block away.

Where was he? A panicky feeling soured my stomach. My body tingled with adrenaline. No car waited for us on the dirt road.

Then suddenly, as I turned my head to the right, I noticed that a strange car had pulled up silently beside us. I jumped but recognized Victor in spite of his dark glasses, the bulky Chiconcuah sweater, and the rented car.

I stood frozen in half shock, staring at him.

His right arm reached over to open the door on the passenger's side, and he motioned for me to get in.

In seconds, I had my hand on the door and collapsed across the seat, exclaiming, "I think I'm going to faint."

"Get your head down!" Victor snapped. I ducked. He turned quickly onto the main boulevard and headed the car toward the freeway. Once we had crossed the last major intersection, he told me it was all right to sit up and put our seatbelts on. Next he asked which cars might follow us. I told him to watch for the old white VW and Carlos's Chevy. We looked behind us often, but no one was following.

Ten minutes from pickup time we were pulling into the first tollbooth on the freeway to Mexico City. Victor was elated! He had planned twelve minutes to drive that far instead of the actual ten, and he was driving a slower car than his own. From then on, we both relaxed. It was a perfect operation and the worst was over.

For miles through the mountains I savored the reality of holding Marita safely in my arms outside that jail, of feeling that we were free to live our lives again as we chose.

I gazed at her. I touched her. I held her close. I talked to her. She quietly licked her sucker until we made a rest stop at Rio Frio. She was calm and happy—happy to be going to Mexico to see where I lived. She had asked so many times to go with me.

But this blessed day of days, a few minutes after we had left Puebla, I told her we were going to see Grandma and Grandpa in Montana and she could ride on the airplane with me.

Avión was a magic word. For five months, she had been waiting to go with me on the airplane. It was all she thought of for the next three days until she actually boarded one.

As Victor drove, I filled him in on all the details, and he did the same. Victor had arrived in Puebla a little after 8:00 A.M. and parked the Ford one block west of the Cruz home. He then killed half an hour in a little *tienda* eating Twinky Wonders and cupcakes, drinking Orange Crush, and telling his stomach that the sacrifice would be worth it. A strange car with an American sitting in it that long (not knowing which minute I would appear) would have called attention to itself. At that time of the morning, Victor blended in with other Mexicans there eating breakfast.

I asked him if he would have waited past 8:45 if I hadn't come out. "Yes," he said. "I knew from your response during the emergency phone call that you were ready. I also felt it was the right day."

When he saw me stepping through the gate a block away, he set down the pop bottle, rushed to the car, and drove down the street right behind me. Not what we had planned, but it worked.

Before we reached Rio Frio he chuckled, "I'd like to see the scene going on at the Cruz home right now. They are probably searching frantically for you and Marita. And they must know you've outfoxed them!"

An hour from pickup time we were at the second tollbooth nearer Mexico City. Soon afterward, we pulled into the driveway of Victor's home in Churubusco, around 10:00 A.M.

His wife, Inez, came out to greet us, and we walked into the kitchen. Victor prepared some eggs and toast for us, and we drank all their milk. Since I had worn the same set of clothes too many days, I wanted to wash out what I had on. Inez took us to our bedroom and brought me some of Victor's clothes to change into.

I made a little pile on the dresser of my belongings: my contacts, my nail clipper, the MIA theme card and $1,150 pesos. Marita had only her new pajamas and her red shoes. Inez showed me where to wash my clothes, introduced us to their blue and red talking macaw parrots, Biki and Coco, and let me call Mr. Rivera. He and Gloria were elated, and Mr. Rivera told me he'd try to come see us before we left.

Victor went out for the day to prepare for our departure the following day. Inez brought in some groceries and a surprise for Marita—a coloring book and some crayons. Then she left for the remainder of the day.

Victor gave me a parting lecture: I was not to answer the phone, not to leave the house, not to stand on the balcony where I might be seen from the street, and not to answer the doorbell.

I assured him, "Don't worry. After all I've been through, I'm not going to blow it now."

We were alone, but safe in a place no one would ever think to look for us. Marita and I went out onto the patio and stood side by side under the shade of tropical trees at the cement scrubbing sink, washing our clothes by hand, playing with the soap suds, and sailing empty tuna fish cans.

I found tears pouring down my face into the water—tears of gratitude, relief, joy—the release of a flood of emotions, pressures, and worries long locked inside. I had passed through the refiner's fire and I stood with my daughter on the other side of it!

We splashed in the water until one of the parrots got loose. Afraid it would bite us, we retreated to the house and washed the dishes. Marita raised a lather that covered the sink entirely as she washed one cup for twenty minutes at least. By then, exhaustion overtook me.

I fought off dizziness and walked upstairs with Marita. We knelt together on the multicolored braided rug. I offered a prayer of thanks.

I desperately needed to rest but I couldn't turn my mind off. The previous days' miracles, memories, close calls, and decisions swirled through my thoughts. I understood better why the American consul had told me to give up and go home, and I felt awed and humbled with the reality of the Lord's power, grace, and love. Tears wet my pillow.

"After all we can do . . ." My lawyer said that we can do anything we want if we work hard enough and wait long enough. But I learned that too many things were beyond my control no matter how hard I worked and I had to let the Lord and the right people help me along the way. Their words, prayers, money, food, smiles, advice, and efforts had all contributed to the success of our rescue.

And it was done. Over. Some marriages are missions and I was finally released and on my way home. I felt burned out, yet I'd not only survived the 1977 Battle of Puebla—I'd won. I didn't know if I ever wanted to see Puebla again, but I would join in marveling at the story of the angels, for I believed the angels of Puebla came down again to build bridges and open gates and stop cars for me.

I had Marita safe in my arms. I had gained more than I could express from doing all I could to get her back. When more was needed beyond what I could give or do or say, unseen helpers had opened the way for me. I knew that when I had been told "someone will be there to help you," it was not only Victor—I now knew the Lord on levels I never could have imagined a year before. It seemed that he and his angels stood near my side at so many of the turning points, such as letting me know the exact moment I should leave the house in Puebla and slip through the gate. Now I understood from my own experience what a survivor of the Martin Handcart Company meant when he said that everyone in that company came through with the absolute knowledge that God lives because they became acquainted with him in their extremities.

I didn't know yet why it all went the way it did. But I understood something about learning to be faithful in the dark and when it seemed I was all alone. All along, all through those many months, the Lord wasn't far from me. He was there, waiting. Listening, watching, helping. I had to find out for myself if he could trust me when put to the test. I learned that the support systems women expect to help them—family, friends, church, government—all have their limits. Only One had the power to turn small details to my advantage when others felt that I had surely lost. Somehow this time of testing wasn't just for me, but it extended to everyone in my family, Antonio's family, and those in our wards and stakes. How each of us responded is recorded in our souls, to our growth and eternal perfection or to our detriment. Once we have acted, there is less doubt as to what to tilt of our soul is.

My restless brain reeled with more thoughts. Unable to unwind, I got up and read some magazines. Later in the afternoon we both fell asleep at last and did not wake until it was dark.

As I ran bath water, I heard Victor calling from the stairwell: "I'm home! And Albert's here too!" Victor and Lic. Rivera had arrived just in time with our clothes I had left in the office safe. Marita was pleased to put on some new clothes, and we went downstairs where I introduced her to Mr. Rivera.

Smiling faces. Happy eyes. Relieved voices. Good food. Laughing. Rejoicing. All reassuring to a little girl who spoke no English.

We all sat around a small table in the kitchen and enjoyed hearing how Mr. Rivera had avoided a tail. Earlier in the afternoon, a former roommate had called Gloria with the news that Antonio had been in Polanco with a detective trying to find me. Mr. Rivera and Victor had kept in touch with each other through CB radios. Victor watched Insurgentes to see if anyone were following Mr. Rivera. They went through several evasive maneuvers, then Mr. Rivera left his car in an underground parking area and walked through an overhead building to the street where Victor was waiting for him.

When Inez returned from rehearsal, we discussed details of the operation, the law, and the past and future. I agreed to send Mr. Rivera a copy of my divorce decree from Utah once it was final, to register in Mexico and use in the courts to finish tying up all the loose ends I was leaving behind. I also signed an agreement to pay the balance of the bill. The total was alarmingly above the estimate, but at least I knew it would end there. He had done his work well. Victor would receive his pay when we arrived in the States. It had all cost more than I had thought, but what price for the soul of a child?

Mr. Rivera had Gloria call my folks and give them Victor's number so their call to me could not be traced. My mother cried for joy at the reality of having Marita so much closer. I promised to call as soon as we reached Texas in safety the next day. I put Marita to bed, then the four of us adults spent a few more hours talking, laughing, and looking at American catalogs and magazines. The clock on the kitchen wall had stopped so no one knew what time it was. Our victory celebration ended when we realized it was 1:00 A.M.

I felt extremely saddened to say good-bye to Mr. Rivera, knowing I would not see him anymore. He would always be more than an international lawyer to me. I was certain he had stood on heaven's shore with me as I contemplated the learning curve in my customized curriculum in earth's schooling. I had long felt he was one of my eternal friends who promised to be there for me at crucial moments on earth. He kept his promises and saved our lives. He had the skills, insights, power, and contacts to do what no one else could do, with the help of the Lord. Although I stood in awe and deepest gratitude before him, when we shook hands, all I could manage to say was a "Thank you for all you have done to help."

He was solemn, too, as he responded, "I'm happy everything has worked out well for you. I wish the best for you in the future, and please have a nice trip." After a few minutes I heard the rumble of a car's motor, and he was gone.

Chapter Twenty-six

Wednesday, March 2, 1977
Our last day in Mexico!

EVEN BEFORE VICTOR KNOCKED on our door at 8:00, I had been awake to what I knew would be a beautiful day. We loaded an ice chest with drinks and snacks and set off. Our route took us past the Churubusco Stake Center and the Deseret Offices, down Cerro de Jesus, down Tlalpan, across to Periferico to the western ring of the city. As we passed Insurgentes and Chapultepec, I mentally said good-bye to every passing landmark and to the hundreds of memories they shouted back to me.

Soon we passed Satelite and its gigantic cement towers, then the slums of Tlanepantla. We pulled into the tollbooth on the highway going north through Queretero. We drove most of the day, and the kilometers slipped by until I saw signs reading Saltillo and Tula, and finally, Matamoros, near the Gulf of Mexico. Victor turned onto a barely paved road, so bumpy that few cargo trucks used it and it had no checkpoints with officials asking for FM forms. About dusk we neared the border, and the closer we were, the quieter I became. What a difference in freedom and protection just a few miles could mean.

As we rode through the streets of Matamoros, we both noticed a clock high in a lighted tower. I looked down at my watch. It said nine o'clock too! We both laughed. A city tower clock that worked! We passed plazas with brightly lit, whitewashed stands selling fried pork skins, tacos, tortas, fruit drinks, and ice cream delights. People were out for evening strolls. It was my last glimpse of Mexico. A few minutes later we approached a little-used bridge to Brownsville, Texas.

Standing in his greenish khaki-colored uniform, a bored Mexican immigration official watched with his arms folded as we drove right by him. I was breathless. At Ciudad Juarez they would have stopped us thirty kilometers out and at other check points besides, asking for my papers. We soon stopped at the American checkpoint on the other side of the bridge.

The official stooped over and looked into the car. "Are you all American citizens?"

Victor took a red lollipop out of his mouth. "Yes, we are."

I nodded my head and said, "Yes." Marita said nothing.

The official recognized Victor. "How are you? How's the movie business?" he asked. "Who've you got here with you this time?"

"A friend and her daughter."

"Where's her husband?" the official demanded.

"Oh, he's down in Mexico visiting his family."

Satisfied, the official went back to the subject of movies and they swapped gossip about various actors in Mexico. After a few minutes, he waved us on to the next checkpoint where three more of Victor's acquaintances were waiting to check our baggage. No one asked to see our passports or asked any questions at all, even if Marita didn't look like an American citizen.

Victor was as astonished as I was. "I've passed through this same check station so many times in the past few years, and I've made friends with these men. But is it more than a coincidence that at this specific night and time all the men on duty were men I knew? It's never happened like this before!"

The broad, well-lighted Texas streets ran clean and smooth before us into Brownsville. We next stopped at a self-serve gas station. When Victor stepped back into the car, he handed a cellophane-wrapped package across the seat to Marita. Inside were three brown stuffed bears dressed in denim.

We drove on, not saying much. I kept looking out the windows at the American homes, stores, streets, businesses, and billboards. I had almost forgotten how clean, how well-built, how well-spaced and organized, and how beautiful most places in the United States were. And all the signs were in *English*! My senses were bombarded with the feelings of home, of belonging, of relief, of safety, of the final pressure and worry being lifted from me.

I did not try to restrain my tears and cried and cried with joy and with thanksgiving. I leaned over Marita with my arms around her and my tears splashed down upon her. We heard few other sounds the next few minutes except for those of the engine's quiet hum and those of Victor clearing his throat. He was crying too. Marita reached up, held my face in her little hands, and tried to comfort me. When I could find my voice, I explained to her, "I'm not crying because I'm sad. I'm crying because I am happier than you can ever imagine."

I relaxed and dozed off while Victor talked on his CB. About 11:00 P.M., we stopped in Kingsville, Texas, for the night. He paid for two rooms, and we ate dinner at a pancake house—real hamburgers and French fries. It was after midnight when I made phone calls to my relieved parents and to Joann Embry in Orem. She would start the remaining procedures on my divorce the next day and tell Bishop Morrill and Linda my good news. Then Marita and I settled in for a relaxing night in a spotless, comfortable Rodeway Inn.

Thursday, March 3, 1977
Home for my father's birthday!

We all slept in. Marita didn't want to leave the warm bathtub after more than a year of showers in a cold, tiled bathroom. After I coaxed her away from the tub, we ate delicious blueberry pancakes, sausages, and juice. She ate more than I had seen her eat all year. We left Kingston in the rain for the airport in Houston. A truck passed us with a bumper sticker instructing: *Do Unto Others—Then Split!* We laughed.

Marita kept asking when we would get to where the airplanes lived. We stopped to buy her a pink, hooded nylon jacket appropriate for Montana weather, and at last she saw the towers and the planes.

Inside the airport we inquired about connections to Glasgow, Montana. The harried ticket agent stopped her rushing around and stared at me in amazement. She snapped, "What on earth do you want to go to Glasgow, Montana, for?"

"Please check to see if someone made reservations for us," I said.

She muttered, "I dearly hope so," and soon her face popped up out of her books, beaming. "Cruz? Yes. You have reservations."

We were all relieved. After I paid for the tickets, she said, "The flight destination is Williston, North Dakota. Don't forget to get off the plane at Glasgow."

Tears sprang to my eyes. "Don't worry," I told her. "I won't forget."

We didn't check any luggage. All we brought from Mexico was a bag of books and a duffle bag. Marita carried her bears. Before we left the ticket counter, Victor looked at me in a solemn way and remarked, "I can't help but feel the influence of divine guidance and intervention in this entire operation. Do you think it was any accident you found Mr. Rivera to handle your case?"

Emphatically I assured him it was no accident and explained how I had found him. Then he commented, "You were very lucky. He's a good man, and he helped you more than most lawyers in Mexico would have."

Puzzled, I looked back at him and he revealed, "When you came back from Cuernavaca, Mr. Rivera told me he had decided to help you escape himself! I wouldn't hear of such a risk! He is an amateur as far as that kind of operation goes, but I had to talk him into letting me be so directly involved. You only had one chance, and I was afraid he would bungle it."

My knees weakened. I had no idea. We went to the cafeteria area where Victor ordered large dishes of chocolate ice cream, and we reminisced as we ate. Marita was so busy taking in all the new sights and sounds, delight shone from her face. She couldn't concentrate on eating, and her ice cream melted into a light brown puddle.

Between spoonfuls of ice cream, Victor admitted, "I'm an agnostic although I come from a Jewish family. I never thought the power of God had so much to do in our lives, but I can't explain any other way how perfectly and smoothly this operation went. It's amazing!"

Earnestly I assured him, "I hope you will believe that the Lord told me there would be someone there to help me. I didn't know who, or how I'd find him, but I knew he would be there. We both know that you are the one and I want to thank you again."

He put down his spoon and looked me in the eyes. "I can't argue with what you're saying. I know that something extraordinary has happened. I guess God uses who's available. I'm pleased I was able to do the job. I know it was more than just luck. Even my schedule this week worked out perfectly and gave me more free time—more than

I'd had the past month or would have after this." We retreated into our own thoughts and finished our ice cream.

How comforting to know at last the specifics of what the Lord knew beforehand about our rescue. Now I had them on record and could join with those other Sarahs to tell the hour of deliverance and rejoicing. I could tell my children how the Lord kept his promises—at the last possible moment—but he kept them.

As Victor prepared to leave, I said, "Good-bye. I probably won't be seeing you again."

He smiled and said, "Of course you will! . . . At least in the movies, someday, maybe." He leaned over and gave me a light kiss on the cheek. Then he walked away and was gone.

Marita and I entered the boarding area. Storms delayed our plane for almost three hours, but the waiting didn't seem long. Lakes formed on the runway, and we watched planes come and go. With each one that passed near our window, Marita asked if it were our plane. She ran back and forth, back and forth in front of the large windows. When the waiting was over, she was thrilled to board the plane.

The flight to Denver was uneventful and we both napped on the leg to Billings, Montana. We arrived barely in time to board the flight to Glasgow and took the last two seats. Marita slept, but I couldn't. I was too close to home—and my parents! It was my dad's birthday. I looked down at the winter Montana landscape lit by the moon and lightened by patches of snow here and there. How different it was from the smoggy haze of Mexico City; yet they both had formed me—the snow and the smog.

They both triggered feelings of home. The snow had its place in my life. How many below-zero days had I trudged the mile to school and back, learning to endure the cold and the distance, making my feet lift one step after another until I had reached the warmth of our floor furnace? Sometimes I stood immobilized, unable to make myself go one more foot. I used to glare at the lane from the top of the dike surrounding our town and wish that our house wasn't the full thousand feet beyond that.

It had often seemed like more than a thousand feet. More like a second mile after I had already walked so far. But my dad always said that a person had to be strong to live in Montana. And we persevered, no matter what the weather or circumstances brought us. I realized that one reason I could keep going in Mexico was a direct result of the conditioning I had received as a child. Yes, even the snow had played a part in regaining Marita. I loved both worlds, and I hoped Marita would, too, someday.

I looked down through the tiny window at the ice floes on the Fort Peck Lake and fingers of land stretching into it, forming a thousand miles of shoreline. Soon, the lights of Glasgow appeared, and we touched down and taxied down to the terminal. Two people left the building and walked toward the landing gate where they stood alone on the tarmac—my mother and father!

Marita and I were first to leave the plane. Seconds later, I felt my parents' arms around us, and we clung together tightly. I had never heard my father cry before, but he cried then. My mother cried with the same relief, joy, and thankfulness, I'm sure, that I had felt two days before at Victor's house. We both had our daughters back.

We drove past the seven sets of railroad tracks, past the Markle gas station and the Civic Center. Glasgow had never looked so good!

As we reached the top of the dike, Daddy slowed down so I could appreciate my first glimpse of home since the fall of 1974. A thousand feet away, I saw the house in the shadows of light from the barnyard and the Christmas tree lights left shining on the trees near the living room. That was our first welcome home—Christmas lights in March—such a symbol of love. The LTD stopped under the carport, and we took our things into the house.

The rooms had never looked more beautiful! My mother had added some lovely new touches in my absence, but basically, it was the same as always. I felt lucky I could return to my childhood home and share the familiar textures and rooms with Marita. On the living room table was a large pink rose for me and a white carnation for Marita. The mayor of Glasgow had sent us a welcome home card. Covering the coffee table were presents for Marita from people in Glasgow, and we gathered around her as she opened them.

I told my parents most of the details of the last week. The freshness of the miracles had not faded, and we sat together on the couch, humbly pondering our refiner's fire. By 1:30 A.M. I took Marita down the hall to my old bedroom with me. It was March 4 by then, and we wouldn't have to go to court in Puebla on that day after all. I slept more soundly than I had for months.

Marita enjoying Christmas 1975, only a week before she was abducted.

Marita in Orem a few months before she was taken.

Marita and Mari Vawn in Puebla together again for the first time in seven months! July 30th.

Marilyn Moreno, Mari Vawn, and Elder Fyans in front of Mari Vawn's displays at the Churubusco stake center.

Marita and Mari Vawn on patio in Puebla, early August 1976. Marita is in the dress Mari Vawn made for her.

Mari Vawn with Marita sitting on Victor's car at their last fueling before crossing the border to the United States.

Marita on the plane on the way back to Montana, March 3, 1977.

Celebrating Grandpa Bailey's birthday at home, March 1977.

At the time of Marita's baptism in 1981.

Marita "Sweet sixteen" in their Gaithersburg home.

August 12, 1993 outside the Logan Temple after Marita took out her endowments.

Brian and Marita's engagement picture.

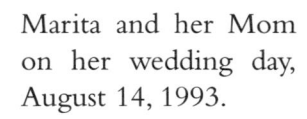

Marita and her Mom on her wedding day, August 14, 1993.

Epilogue

NOW, MORE THAN EIGHTEEN YEARS after it all happened, I still wonder why we had to go through that experience. Yes, of course I learned things about life and people and myself that I hardly wanted to learn or thought were necessary to learn. I hope that most people can learn those truths in ways other than suffering from a missing child and divorce.

Perhaps it was not only those two ordeals that brought the pain but also the faulty assumptions and inexperience that lay unrecognized within me until I faced dealing with a missing child. The experiences of the past twenty years have demanded that I examine my life, the assumptions, the institutions I took for granted in 1969 when I received my B.A. and started out on the passage to adulthood. As life's harder experiences came to me and I suffered a loss of innocence when faced with limitations of human nature, government, church, and health, I eventually toughened up. Some pain returned in varying degrees, however, each year when I pondered the journals or the manuscript describing my separation from Marita. The words written in 1976-77 still had a gripping power over me. Not until fifteen years later could I read them without feeling the pain.

I had suffered wife abuse, but in 1972 I did not realize that such a concept and situation had even been verbalized by others and given a name. I had lived my early adult life in Mexico, isolated from the knowledge that Americans were beginning to create safe houses and shelters for abused women and children. So I was naive enough about our dysfunctional relationship to keep hoping Antonio would stop the abuse as he got older and we had more time together to build a stronger marriage.

I had never witnessed open conflict between my parents as I grew up, so I was extremely ill prepared to deal with an abusive husband. My parents did not allow us to quarrel much at home either, and as an adult I still lacked experience in standing up for myself effectively in any situation. It was my nature to want to think well of others, give them a chance, and be patient with human weaknesses. My soft-spoken voice made it difficult for me to be heard although I learned in time to scream at Antonio to leave me alone. I did not feel comfortable showing anger to anyone and would keep it inside while I felt helpless to find my way out of the abuse.

In the early '70s I tolerated the abuse because I did not know any better and I did not know how to get help. Few people in the Church then acknowledged wife abuse as an issue, and my bishop in 1975 did not receive training in how to help Church members deal with it as bishops do now. The evils of wife abuse were never discussed in general conference then as it has been in the '90s. In 1976 most Church members thought that only adultery was horrific enough to justify getting a divorce or sealing cancellation.

During the years I was writing this book, sometimes my arms shook after reading the pages for only a short while. I felt totally drained after I wrote a longer version of the story for Marita. But by the time I completed later versions of the story, I no longer became physically ill or angry as I did during the months and years it took to write the first version of the manuscript. The act of forcing myself to sit there and relive the experiences as I searched for words to make the situations clearer to readers was the process of catharsis. This opening the door to the past brought surprising new healing, insights, cleansing, and strength I had not expected. I was a stronger, wiser woman after the ordeal in Mexico in 1977, but the struggle in pulling my words from the journals during the 1980s to form a message to others also brought me new life, energy, and truths heretofore unknown to me.

The end of this book is not the end of the story. Although I got home to Montana safely with my daughter, the trials didn't cease. After six weeks of blessed healing in Montana, Marita and I returned to Utah for the divorce proceedings, a new job, and single motherhood. I had hoped the Mexico ordeal of '76-77 would be the major trial of my life, but each year since I have had to use what I learned then to endure and survive exceedingly difficult situations.

I will give a perspective gained from twenty more years of adversity (1972-1992) in my next book, *Home from the Trenches: Spiritual Survival Keys for the Last Days*. During those years I survived and overcame close calls with death, seven years of poor health, frequent moves, unemployment, a second divorce and more custody battles over my son Wesley Owen from my second marriage. The second marriage was more difficult in so many aspects than my marriage to Antonio that I could not have survived it alive without the insights gained from my life in Mexico and with Antonio. Yet, I know both marriages were necessary to fulfill many purposes. Of the treasures I received from those twenty years, my two children are the best. I needed to bring them to earth when I did, and I could not have waited until my third temple sealing, when I was too old to start my family. From crisis after crisis and longer-lasting ordeals, I learned still more about human nature, the Lord's love for me, and of his power in the priesthood.

At least the later trials didn't involve Antonio. He called from the border two weeks after Marita and I arrived in Glasgow, asking to see us if he flew up to Montana. I refused to consider it and warned him that I would use the considerable legal weapons at my disposal to protect myself if he came into the United States. I expressed the hope that he would remarry and be happy. He asked for permission to see Marita at regular six month visits, but I specified that he would have to first pay his American debts. He never did.

Until the summer of 1984, he wrote to us via Glasgow, and my parents forwarded his mail to us. We returned photographs and cards by the same route. In each letter he said that he loved Marita, missed her, and thought of her constantly. Relatives in Puebla sent cards for Marita's birthday and Christmas. She responded rarely and stopped speaking Spanish within six months after we left Mexico. Although I had tried to maintain it by talking to her only in Spanish and asking her to repeat her bedtime prayers after me in Spanish as well, she preferred English. She didn't see Antonio again until she was a teenager.

The divorce came through easily once I had possession of Marita in the United States. I signed an affidavit, and a summons was mailed to Puebla while a notice was published in the Utah papers for a month. I drove back to my Orem house on April 20, 1977. My gratitude to Rosalyn, my faithful roommate who had taken such good care of my property, and Linda, who had been a spiritual lifeline for me, was unbounded, and we all enjoyed a happy reunion.

Antonio didn't respond to either the affidavits or the publication notices by the deadline, April 25, which also happened to be Marita's fourth birthday. On April 26, Marita, Rosalyn, and I walked over to the Utah County Courthouse with my lawyer, Konrad Becker. The courtroom was elegant and quiet, a noticeable difference from the Mexican courts. By 3:00 P.M. I was divorced with permanent custody of Marita, which included a permanent restraining order that prohibited Antonio's taking Marita out of the court's jurisdiction. I was granted possession of the lot, the car, our house, and things therein. Antonio was restricted to visiting Marita only in my presence and that of other people I might choose.

I was given back my maiden name and Marita's name was ordered to correspond to her Mexican birth certificate, as I had requested. (In Mexico the mother's maiden name is listed as a second last name: i.e., Andrea Marita Cruz Bailey. Consequently Marita was able to legally go by Bailey in the United States.) Antonio was ordered to pay child support and alimony—modest but still impossible for him to pay in pesos at the time. Throughout all the years since then he has paid no child support or alimony.

After the hearing was over, we returned to the law office across the street to give the details to Joann Embry. She had gone the second mile in doing extra work, much of it on her own time, trying to get things to help me in Mexico. She told me later that when she took the divorce decree over for the judge to sign, he said, "Cruz VS. Cruz! Hmmnn. Is that the bastard that took that little girl and ran away to Mexico? Well, I'm going to sock it to him!" And he signed the decree with a flourish.

Soon afterwards a welcome letter from our prophet, President Kimball, cancelled our temple sealing, severing the last remaining tie to Antonio.

In talking to Arturo Martinez I learned that there was a valid reason none of the Church leaders in Mexico could get involved in our situation and help either one of us much during the ordeal. He had visited with many Mexican leaders of the Church who were in Salt Lake for April general conference. They told him that they were very concerned about me while I was in Mexico, but they did not know how to get around the traditions and laws that existed there.

Because our situation was so complicated, involving international and political issues and sensitivities as well as our own personal issues, it could have escalated to the point of endangering the Church's approval from the Mexican government to have a temple built in Mexico. Since Church leaders had been carefully nurturing the process along for years and were so close to making the arrangements for a new temple, they could not risk taking a stand in declaring what either Antonio or I should do. They left it to the Lord to work it out with us, and he did.

Because I wanted to stay as far from the border as I could with Marita to allow a cooling down period, I found work at the Family Training Center near the Canadian border north of Glasgow and stayed there for a year before I returned to BYU to complete my master's degree. I felt safer that year with two thousand miles separating Antonio and Marita in case he considered coming after her. But all went well enough that in August 1978 Marita and I returned to live in the Orem house while I studied for a year, receiving my master's degree in Linguistics (TESL Materials Development) and Instructional Science in August of 1979.

Antonio remarried and has other children now. In the summer of 1985 for the first time in eight years, I decided to tell him where we were living. On February 28, 1986, he paid our fare and Marita and I flew down to visit him and his family. This was almost nine years later to the day that we escaped from Puebla. Our trip wasn't planned to coincide with that anniversary of sorts; I realized it after I got the tickets. And we returned on March 3, just as we did that other time. However, many things had changed in nine years.

Antonio had matured and had graduated from college. He tried in every way to make our visit a positive, memorable one, for Marita's sake especially. There were many good times to help develop a new relationship. The trip helped put the past behind, and by the time we left, I felt a total forgiveness toward him. (I had finished writing an early draft of this book by then, and much healing had transpired already. I had spent many difficult, painful months doing what I call "The 490s," a process of writing down specific instances I had to forgive Antonio of. I numbered the grievances from 1 to 490 [70 x 7] and burned all the pages at one time. I felt totally released from the pain of the memories.)

During our visit, I had long chats with his wife while Antonio entertained his daughters nearby. I received flashes of insights and relief as she talked. Herein lies the difference between us: if Antonio ruins or misplaces a cassette tape or something of hers, she does the same thing or worse to one of his tapes. He remembers for a while and watches his step. She holds her ground. I told her I had been raised differently and I hadn't learned to retaliate. I realized I had not stood up for myself enough early on in our marriage, and it might have made a difference if I had.

But I wondered what would have happened had I responded that way—an eye for an eye, as many generations of Mexican women had learned to, just to survive in a macho-led society. This way of living isn't in my nature. I wondered if I had responded as others usually learn to, would I still be married to Antonio, trying to hold my own in an intense power struggle of wounded egos? What would our children's lives be like? What tactics would they pass on to another generation? The suffering needs to stop in this generation. Just as these thoughts flashed through me, a confirmation also surged through me with the peace of knowing I had done my best, chosen the better way, and although my marriage was over, *everything was okay.*

Perhaps a long-suffering person is less sensitive to pain than a person who knows little of adversity. I have compassion for the many women who endure difficult marriages, but I understand more about when choices should be made, when to say "Stop" to a negative cycle and walk away. I realize now that there are two versions of the *mujer abnegada*, and one of them is a sad counterfeit of the Lord's sacred role model of blessed women known in the scriptures. I was trying to be the scriptural kind of *la mujer abnegada* and rebelled against being forced to become the other kind.

Although I never knew the term "codependence" until the late 1980s, I recognize now that this term describes my marriage to Antonio and I know that codependent relationships destroy lives. I have taken care to teach my daughter to set boundaries of what she will tolerate in the actions of others around her. Marita is sensitive to unspoken dynamics of relationships and is much wiser as a young adult than I was at her age.

Marita: Missing in Mexico

She has learned much from my suffering, and she stands up for herself and maintains her integrity. Many people have told me that she is a "bright light," a "good girl," "such a good example." People who knew her when she was in grade school are pleased when they see her now. They all tell me what a beautiful young woman she has become, and I am proud of her.

When Marita graduated from high school in the DAR Constitution Hall in Washington, D.C., I watched her receive her diploma and walk down the steps in her new status of being on her own for her future. I bought some space in her senior yearbook, as other parents did, to write graduation wishes. My wish went like this:

> *Andrea Marita, May you always walk in Beauty although our paths may separate for a while now as in 1976. Trust in your dreams, in love, in the trials that come to you, for in them is hidden the gate to eternity and Home. Whatever form tests in life take, be willing to pay the price and pass them so you'll be proud of the woman you will become. Look well to This Day and living each day your best, for it is Life, the very life of life. The love and respect I feel for you and who you are already is beyond mere words. Thank you for sharing life with me. Suerte!*
>
>

With a Forever Love,
Your Mom,
Mari Vawn Bailey

What a long ways we had come since 1976, and it was worth it all to give her the opportunities in life that she enjoys. She gave me only a few of the anxious moments that cause concern for the parents of many teenagers. As she grew, I tried to enjoy every day that she lived with me, not wanting time to pass until she would leave home as an adult. Maybe I will never get over it: having her kidnapped and losing those months and years from her life made it harder to let her go again.

Antonio has rarely seen Marita since we left Mexico, but she did visit him every year while she was in high school and he is paying for her college education. From the forces that have shaped her life, I feel confident that she will make an important contribution as part of the rising generation and join the women who will be bridge builders in the 21st century.

Many women suffer because, while they have been enlightened to catch a better vision of their role as a woman, they still live the counterfeit reality of all the generations before them, in the "traditions of their fathers." Today's generation is pivotal. What role models of womanhood will be passed on to the next generation? Where will the change begin? It doesn't all fall on the women, for many of them would more easily be able to respond in a truly charitable, long-suffering, noble way if they would be allowed to do it without guile, revenge, or survival fears created by unreasonable demands or demeaning treatment by macho-blinded husbands.

Not one of the marriages I know of where the American woman had married the Mexican man has survived, even those who had hung in there for more than thirty years. In the LDS church I expect better of the men because they have been given the priesthood, high church callings, and many words of inspiration intended to bring about mighty changes in their minds and hearts in order to bless the lives of their wives and families. Many men are improving in their stewardships, but still far too many men and women have much to learn.

Whether in or outside the Church, people are basically the same as they struggle to overcome the lower instincts of human nature. By now I have learned how much we all need more forgiveness, acceptance, and love in our lives. These are the bases of true freedom, power, and happiness in the long run. I remarried in 1992, and Bill Tinney and I live more happily than I ever knew was possible.

I do not know what the future holds, but I face it calmly and with increasing joy. I have proved in my life the truthfulness of the scripture, *As thou goest, step by step, I will open up the way before thee (Proverbs 4:12).*

Promises Fulfilled

Sunday, August 22, 1993
Gaithersburg, Maryland

TODAY I WILL WRITE about my daughter's marriage while it is still fresh in my mind. On Saturday, August 14, 1993, Andrea Marita Cruz Bailey was sealed to Brian Butler Mecham in the Idaho Falls Temple with about seventy-five well-wishers as witnesses.

I first met Brian August 12 at the recommend desk in the Logan Temple as he brought Marita to take out her endowments. *I really like him!* He has a vivacious, friendly wholesome spirit and personality. He is the kind of person I had hoped she would marry. I feel completely content and at peace whenever I think of how they are at their new beginnings. Seeing them together is a delight, and they do make a cute couple.

The day she took our her endowments, Marita and I enjoyed the beauty of the bride's room while we listened to instructions for her new life. Then we joined the others who were waiting to go through an endowment session with us and experience with Marita sacred covenants of obedience to the Lord's ways. This was the day I had waited so long for—to be able to attend the temple with my daughter!

We took pictures afterwards with the bright flowers surrounding the fountain near the Logan Temple. We stood in front of the temple that my great-grandfather Wray helped build as a stone mason more than a hundred years ago. He brought his family from England to Cache Valley where they lived in a sod hut through chilly, snowy winters. Then they moved on to Idaho for the rest of their lives, not too far from where Brian's family settled and lived all these generations. I thought about our roots as we all stood there together, posing in one sacred spot where so many paths met in eternity for rare moments in our lives. Now we were ready for the wedding scheduled two days later in the Idaho Falls Temple.

Brian picked Marita and me up the morning of the sealing at 6:15 A.M. He was precisely on time. As he opened the door for Marita to get into the car, she looked down at a surprise in the front seat—a single long-stemmed red rose! I don't know if he knew of the symbolism that the red rose has for Marita and me ever since 1974 when Antonio had his Vision of the Rose.

She was happy to receive it, and it was a perfect lead-in for the gifts I had in the car to give both of them on the way to the temple. First, a newly printed and revised version of the manuscript of Marita's book. I wanted Brian to read about the fragile circumstances so long ago that shaped her life and made it possible to get her back to this country, to know that it was because of the Lord's divine intervention that he has a wife who received an excellent education, is sensitive to people, and can speak English. Along with the manuscript, I gave them a copy of the same picture Marita gave to Bill and me last Christmas.

I remembered my tears when I saw the painting that first time because it also reminded me of the Vision of the Rose. The hand of the Lord is reaching through the clouds extending a red rose to the hand of a man. This symbolized to us a new husband accepting a stewardship to watch over and care for, to love and cherish, and honor the best interests of his wife. When Brian and Marita had the painting unwrapped, I said, "Brian, I'm giving you my daughter. Please take good care of her!"

I also remembered the phone call when they let us know Brian had proposed. On June 5 while we were watching *Fried Green Tomatoes,* Marita called with so much excitement in her voice that I knew she was engaged even before she told me. It had been only a few minutes since Brian had given her the ring and had really surprised her! Brian got on the phone and told me that he would take good care of her. I had started crying and said, "Yes, you have to take good care of her!" After a few minutes I talked to Marita again. Before she said good-bye, she said, "Mom, it was Brian after all."

She was referring to a dream she had when she was four years old and saw how it would be on her wedding day. She had described her dress to me then and the car they drove off in after the temple wedding. I wrote down what she told me of her dream and saved it all these years. The last sentence, "Mom, it was Brian." She knew from the dream that his name would be Brian, and in 1977 the only Brian she knew was the son of a seminary teacher stationed in Glasgow. Now, in 1993 the Brian she was marrying was Brian Mecham, the son of a middle school teacher in Idaho.

After we entered the temple on her wedding day, the temple matron took us to the bride's room where she told me, "Wait here a minute and you can dress your daughter." Immediately I thought of the first time ever I had dressed Marita. The nurses in La Raza Hospital had led me to a room filled with fifty other mothers and their babies on the morning we were all discharged. We were supposed to find our own baby, dress it, and walk out of there to a new life. When I finally recognized my daughter out of the long line of squalling babies in their beds lined up against the far wall, I was afraid to dress her, afraid I would not get her tiny arms bent into the little pink jacket successfully. She was so fragile at only five pounds.

I looked at her enter the bride's room twenty years later, still small and thin but oh, so beautiful! She stood in front of a long mirror in her dream dress with pearls, lace, frills, puffy sleeves, gorgeous satin and roses in appliques all over. This was the one day Marita could wear the dress she wanted, be the star, and be stunningly gorgeous all day. It was a dream dress for the day of her dreams. I kept looking at her then, trying to drink in all the details to remember forever.

As I added layer after layer of special clothing on her wedding day, memories of all the years of her life flashed through my mind. August 14, 1993, was payday with so many prayers answered and promises fulfilled that had been given in priesthood blessings. Since Marita was a tiny girl, I had been promised over and over that she would marry in the temple. We both had so much to be grateful for!

In addition to all my blessings in regard to Marita and her marriage, I felt so grateful that I had been sealed this year and that my new eternal companion was at my side for this occasion. Bill stood by me every moment as a buffer between me and Antonio, who was attending the wedding with his new wife. Over and over, I realized just how glad I was to be happily married and not alone. So many friends and family said that I was *glowing* and that I was like the Mari Vawn they used to know before I married Antonio, the MVB from twenty-one years ago. YES!

When Bill and I were sealed in February I had made two large satin hearts with rolled satin roses and pearls to decorate for our reception. Those hearts also decorated Marita's reception, and I gave her one so we would have matching hearts that would always remind us of this special time in our lives when we both were sealed the same year, 1993!

Brian had requested the largest sealing room in the temple, and it was soon filled with family and friends. I was so grateful to have my new husband by my side when Antonio and his wife came into the room. The officiator hadn't been told the Maria's parents were divorced, and he mostly looked at the new couple as he spoke. But suddenly he turned and looked at Antonio and said, "You've never had any trouble in your marriage, now, have you?"

Antonio, taken by surprise, rolled his eyes in an "If-you-only-knew" upward stare while the rest of us laughed spontaneously. Enough trouble that his ex-wife was writing a book about it!

I could see Marita's face perfectly as she knelt at the altar. She looked happily into Brian's eyes as the officiator pronounced the words to the sealing ordinance. Then they kissed over the altar, a long yummy kiss.

After they exchanged rings, they stood outside the door of the sealing room so we could file by and congratulate them. I hardly wanted to leave the temple. Everything was over so quickly. But then it was time for a few photographs out in front of the temple and near an old gnarled tree in a garden behind the temple. It was a fine morning, just the way Marita always hoped it would be for her wedding day.

It was the first time all of us had met from both families, and we were sizing each other up and sighing inward sighs of relief. I was thrilled for my daughter to have the blessing of enjoying this extended family who all live nearby. She had lived most of her life so far away from her family. In Brian's home town of Firth, Idaho, the "homestead" land has one street particularly thick with Mechams. Brothers, grandfather, uncles, fathers, all live next door to each other and down the street and around the corner, as they do in many small towns in Utah and Idaho.

Such places are fast disappearing, but for the summer of 1993, we hold dear memories of sitting down in a field full of family and friends at a wedding celebration luncheon. Brian's family have a good sense of humor, they are energetic, decent, kind, and used to serving the Lord. Brian's dad described the group of boys that Brian grew up with as the "Sons of Helaman"—so good, spiritual, and helpful. I am so thankful Marita's children will have good examples and righteous people around them to help mold their characters to be strong in the Lord, too.

The reception was held at a stake center in the middle of farmland in the little town of Basalt, Idaho. When Antonio sang "Sunrise, Sunset" at the reception we all cried! I felt the years of life melt behind us. We blink and another generation begins. Our moments on earth with our children are so precious, and suddenly our circle of influence and love gives way to someone else in their lives. My mother understood more than I can now as she enjoyed treasured moments at the reception with her husband, daughters, and grandchildren all in the same room for a few hours. I hope the years ahead will be kind to us and I can stand with joy to see my daughter as the mother of the bride as she glows with pride as another generation makes major milestones along the path toward Home.

Maybe someday Marita and Brian will understand more deeply why I chose the song "The Impossible Dream" for their reception. I sang that song often to myself while walking the streets of Mexico City alone in 1977. It gave me strength to keep going one more day, one more trip to Puebla, one more court battle, as I visualized a young woman who would grow up with me in the United States, loving the gospel of Jesus Christ and being a force for good. I yearned for the time that the line in my patriarchal blessing would become a reality—that I would *see* my children grow. The promises and impossible dreams are a reality now.

I am so proud of my daughter. Marita had a lot of pressure in regard to her decision to marry after having suffered with me through life after divorce. She didn't want to be surprised as I was to marry in good faith and then discover the nightmares. It took courage for her to decide to marry and to go forward in faith.

A few days after her wedding I received a long letter from Marita. In part she said—

I mostly want to express my gratitude for all you did to make August 14 and the days and months before it possible. Thank you SO much! We really have had a good start! And we mostly have our families to thank for that! We were both raised really well! And that was the best gift either of us could have received. Thank you! Thank you for everything else as well (the material things). Thank you again for everything, from the bottom of my heart, I love you,
    Andrea Marita.

What a joy to receive her words and find out that she has some realization of the prices paid and the eternal gifts that were given each year of their lives so that now she and Brian stand together, giving each other the gift of a good life lived so far. They have enough of what really matters to make an excellent new beginning.

Oh, how would I have felt in 1993 at her wedding if I had not kept my rendezvous with destiny and if the Lord had not provided some miracles along the way at so many junctures on our path? We owe our heartfelt thanks and gratitude to the Lord and to hundreds of people who were there for us these past twenty years, to make our joy in the temples possible on August 12 and August 14, 1993. I am at peace.

Hugh Nibley said that children and family are all that endure. I feel it forcibly now. He wrote that worlds pass away and become parts of other earths, but our children belong with us, and we continue together throughout eternity, when very little else from this earth can go with us. Perhaps I have done what I came to do: to give Marita a better chance in life, raise her, and find my own True Companion. Life is at its best now!